DEDICATION

This book is dedicated to American farmers who, by their life's work, stamp out hunger for the American people.

It is also dedicated to my colleagues in the profession of Veterinary Medicine who, by their life's work, stamp out pestilence and disease for the American farmer

TABLE OF CONTENTS

Copyright © 2018
Published by the Daily American

INTRODUCTION

In the fall on 2008, an article appeared in Time magazine about the state of agriculture in the United States. The premise of the article wasn't about the fortitude of the American farmer, nor was it about the incredible abundance of wholesome food that the American farmer produces. Neither did it address the magnificent improvements that have been made in livestock and crops over the last century. Instead, the article painted a picture of greed, impropriety and recklessness in the way farmers and ranchers operate. Knowing first hand that this isn't true, the article greatly disturbed me. It was the first motivation for me to approach the Daily American to publish a weekly article.

I was under no illusion that a local daily newspaper would rival the audience of Time magazine. But we have to start somewhere, I thought. Farmers are a funny lot, sometimes. Most of them go quietly about their work. Many of the individual interests, like the beef, dairy swine, corn, and soybean growers have a lobbying presence in Washington, DC. And there are some lobbying groups for farmers in general. But farmers have very little voice in the media. Public relations are handled locally by some individual farmers sensitive to this fact, but there is very little organized self-promotion at a national level.

Many of us do our part, and I felt a sense of duty to be a part of that. I didn't know if my column would last a month or a year. I had no idea that it would become what it has become, and words cannot express my gratitude for the positive feedback I've received. You see, it was never about me or veterinarians or cows or green grass or barn swallows. It is about the farmer.

The second motivation was a conversation I had with an anonymous lady on a plane to Chicago. During the course of our conversation, I mentioned that I was a veterinarian. Like so many people whom I don't know upon learning of my profession, she began to talk about her pet; and maybe asked some medical advice. I can't remember specifically; it was a long time ago. But when I told her that my professional activities are focused on cattle and other food animals, she was surprised. As a suburbanite, she had no direct interaction with farmers, cows, or large animal veterinarians. And she was curious.

It wasn't the first such conversation I've had with a person. In fact, I was well prepared for it since I've had those conversations many times before. But for some reason, her curiosity made the bulb light up over my head that a newspaper column would be a nice way to tell the real story. That story is one of the American farmer and the reality they face from day to day that is largely untold.

This book is about the American farmer whom I know; it's not about me. But I feel it's appropriate to provide a little background into why I've taken the path I have.

I've always had an affinity for the farmer. As a youth deciding on career options, I wanted to work in the field of agriculture in some capacity. I spent many summer days as a young child helping my father, or so I thought I was helping, bale hay for his brother to be sold or fed to his beef cattle. As I grew older, my uncle gave me a part time job as a hired man, of sorts. There were days that I was certainly more trouble than what I was worth, but I loved the work. I did the tasks one could entrust to a 14 year old boy like forking out the calf pens, feeding the cows and calves when my aunt and uncle were away, mowing hay, helping bale hay, picking rocks from the field and so on.

I remarked to my father one day that I could see myself doing this for a living after spending a clear, crisp June morning on a tractor raking the hayfield to prepare it for baling. My father confided in me that it can be enjoyable work, but the hours are long and the pay isn't. This was in the shadow of the turmoil caused by the decentralization of the steel industry in Pittsburgh. Job security, suddenly, became a priority for this child preparing to make a career decision and agriculture just didn't feel very secure. I eventually decided to attend pharmacy school.

But my love for the rural life and things that grow never really left my system. As a third-year pharmacy student, I took an internship at a large retail pharmacy on the south side of Pittsburgh. Within two weeks, I realized that I hadn't chosen wisely my profession. I was looking for a way out.

One of my biology professors as a freshman was a veterinarian who also changed careers. He had devoted his professional life to academia instead of practicing veterinary medicine. The morning after I had my epiphany about my career choice, I was in his office looking for guidance. I wanted to know what I had to do to go to veterinary school. I'm sure I wasn't the first student to have asked him that question, and he was also prepared. He suggested that before I make the same mistake again, I had better know what I was getting myself into. He arranged for me to spend one day a week with a veterinarian within a 45-minute drive of school.

As time went on and I learned more about the profession, I knew it was suited for me. I had spent time with a half-dozen or so practicing veterinarians observing, and I had definitively decided to pursue veterinary medicine as my profession. This was not without some hesitation, though. I was strongly cautioned by family and elders that the profession was a difficult one. The hours were long and the pay was not, but I think I had heard that before. Veterinary school admission was extremely competitive, and I wasn't the smartest of students. Tuition was expensive. It sounded like a tough row to hoe.

One summer night after making the decision to pursue veterinary medicine, our family dog, Amos, took ill. It was nearly midnight; he was suffering and couldn't walk. We knew that he needed to be put down, so we called our local vet. We packed Amos up in the car and made the trip to the veterinary clinic that night. The veterinarian who saw us was a true professional. He didn't complain that it was midnight on a Saturday night. He didn't complain that the he had to get out of bed to end our dog's suffering. He greeted us with a smile and took care of things. Before we departed his office, my mother had let the veterinarian know that I was planning on joining him in the ranks of Doctor of Veterinary Medicine someday. And with tears in her eyes, my mother asked me, "Are you sure you want to do this for a living?"

And I replied, "I'm sure. Look at what this man did for us tonight. I want to serve like that."

Now, that surely sounds sanctimonious. And, I promise you, I have met many clients at midnight in a foul mood because I was called out of bed. That never gets easy. But to be able to deliver a calf, or replace a cow's uterus, or euthanize an ailing best friend when it needs to be done is truly service. I don't like getting called out in the middle night; I never have. But if you take the bad with the good, there always ends up being more good than bad.

One adviser asked me what my back up plan was in case I didn't get accepted into a veterinary school. I told him I didn't need a back up plan because I was going to get accepted. But he persisted and maintained that if I didn't come up with a back up plan, he wouldn't write me a letter of recommendation. I don't recall what I told him, probably because I didn't mean it. I had made up my mind.

I never quit pharmacy school and graduated with a bachelor's degree in pharmacy. Maybe that was my back up plan, although I am fortunate to have not used it. I packed up my belongings and moved to Blacksburg, Virginia, two months after graduation and started my temporary career as a pharmacist. Blacksburg is home to the Virginia-Maryland Regional College of Veterinary Medicine at Virginia Tech, my veterinary school alma-mater. After working for a year as a registered pharmacist, I was accepted into the class of 1997 and embarked on a new journey. What follows is the result of that journey.

This book is a compilation of articles published over the last 9 years. I've made a conscious effort to leave the individual articles intact as they were submitted to the Daily American, with very few exceptions. One exception is corrections of poor grammar, which I can display sometimes too frequently. Also, where articles may have been in series, I've altered them to flow better for the reader. I did not alter any of the original intent.

Many of the articles have dealt with the economic conditions as they relate to farmers at the time the article was published. Commodity prices fluctuate depending on the state of the market and the prices farmers get paid for their products fluctuate along with them. Some articles reflect the good times, and others not so good. That reality is a never-ending struggle for the farmer and always a topic of discussion, like the weather. I made no modifications to any article based on the conditions when the article was written in order to accurately reflect the mood at the time.

ACKNOWLEDGEMENTS

This book would not have been possible without the quiet support of my wife Sheila and our children Nolan and Bena. Their patience has been vast and undeserved, even when I come home smelling like the rear end of a cow.

My first partner in White Oak Veterinary Clinic, Dr. David Welch, went out on a limb to give me an opportunity as an employee nearly two decades ago. Without his mentorship and guidance, I would have never had the opportunity to enjoy the experiences necessary for this book to become a reality.

My current partner in the practice, Dr. Dan Zawisza, quietly goes about his work, taking the heat off of me to pursue various endeavors and harebrained ideas like this book.

My associates at White Oak Veterinary clinic do the hard, time consuming, thankless work that have enabled me to steal a few hours here and there to compile this book. I am humbled by and grateful for their dedication.

My first employer, Camboro Veterinary Hospital in Edinboro, Pennsylvania, gave me my first exposure to rural veterinary practice. I was young and green and I made my share of mistakes, but they never lost confidence in me.

My professors and instructors in veterinary school taught me more than veterinary medicine. They taught me critical thinking, work ethic and how to solve problems. I still lean on them for advice and I'm happy they remember me.

My parents, Bill and Liz Croushore, have had more patience with me than I deserve. As a rebellious and sometimes misguided teenager, they kept me out of trouble (most of the time) and pushed me to live up to my potential.

The readers of my column, "The View from the Back 40" in the Daily American, have showered me with positive comments and compared me to writers with whom I have no business being compared. These comments sustain my desire to continue to write the column, even though the demands of my schedule make it a challenge sometimes.

And finally, the American Farmer with their diversity of personalities taught me that farmers are not straw hat wearing, tobacco chewing, hayseeds. They are smart, successful, innovative and underestimated. Their dedication to a way of life in a changing world is steadfast and remarkable. While they endure some hardships from time to time, as long as there are people there will be farmers to grow the food that feeds them. They deserve our gratitude.

CHAPTER 1
Where it all began

The View from the Back 40
10-13-09

I am a cow doctor. Occasionally, I am a doctor to sheep, alpacas and llamas, goats and sometimes even pigs; but mainly, I am a cow doctor. As my 4 year old daughter, Bena says, "My daddy fixes broken cows." Since only about 2 percent of the population in this country is involved in agriculture, I get to field a lot of interesting questions from people who don't really know what it takes to produce meat or milk. I don't mean you folks reading this column, but mainly all of those other people out there.

For instance, somebody asked me once if a cow has to have a calf to be milked. Yes, of course she does. Now if you didn't know that, don't be embarrassed; you aren't the first person to not know that. A dairy cow has to deliver a calf to be able to make milk. I have seen cows milk for as long as 3 years after having a calf, but usually they only produce milk for a little over a year. She will have to get pregnant again and deliver another calf to continue making milk.

A client once told me about a car that stopped at his house to let him know that his bulls are out of the fence. Confused, the farmer told the well-meaning people that he does not own a bull. The folks in the car replied, "Yes you do; the ones with the big horns." Well, the ones with the big horns were actually cows. Since the good travelers didn't know that both male and female cattle grow horns, they assumed they were, of course, bulls. In fact, both the male and the female bovine grow horns, but, again, if you're reading this column, you already knew that... right?

So "Why," you ask, "do all of these black and white cows that dot the landscape of our county have no horns on their heads?" That's a good question and it deserves a good answer. The cows, when they were calves, had their horns removed surgically. We do this to first prevent the cows from hurting each other and second to prevent them from hurting the people handling them. Cows, if you've ever spent time with them, can be pretty nasty to each other. The horns become a formidable weapon attached to their 100-pound head. I have seen some pretty dramatic injuries to other cows as a result of a cow with horns.

It is important to note how specialized our society has become. I was on a flight to Chicago a few weeks ago and I struck up a conversation with the lady sitting beside me. She works for a company that makes products for power delivery in homes and factories. I had no clue what products her company makes, but as she explained them to me, I realized that if I had to do her job, we would all be reading by candlelight. Likewise, she had no clue what types of things I do every day.

And as I was talking to her, the light bulb over my head lit up. Why not write a column about being a cow vet? Every week I'll include some tidbits of information about animal agriculture and some anecdotes of what the life of a cow vet is all about. So, if you have any burning questions about livestock or an idea for a topic, write it down and send it to me.

CHAPTER 2
Veterinary Medicine

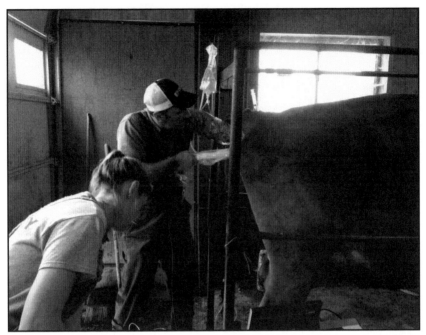

Photo by Liz Croushore

Cows, from time to time, get broken. And when they do, the veterinarian often gets the call to fix the broken cow. This has been the staple for the large animal veterinarian and, in fact, it was the first purpose of the profession. So, I would be neglecting the obvious of I didn't include some tales of my experiences fixing broken cows.

The practice of veterinary medicine has made great strides in the last decades, but large animal practice is undergoing a transition. It is transitioning from a profession that primarily fixes broken cows to one that prevents broken cows. That is a laudable endeavor, however, as long as there are cows, some of them will break.

A lot has changed in our understanding of why cows get sick. The answer is, to use one of my favorite doctor words, multifactorial. Combine stress and exposure to a pathogen and you have a broken cow. Once they are sick, fixing them can be difficult and expensive. Finding a way to lessen the stress on the animals and reduce their exposure to pathogens can prevent a lot of broken cows. Indeed, the adage that "an ounce of prevention is worth a pound of cure" is true.

But it's been my belief that the practice of veterinarians doctoring cows will never completely fade away. Cows are simply too valuable, farmers have a lot invested in them and there are some things that are just too dangerous without the proper training. A scalpel in the hands of an untrained layperson is simply dangerous for the cow. Improper use of antibiotics and other medicines by those lacking the proper background can make the animal's condition worse and possibly. adulterate food. Veterinarians will always have a place fixing broken cows. Yet, the profession looks different than it did when I graduated in 1997.

Surgery on cattle is an amazing thing, especially when it's performed in a barn. Dairy cows, especially, are prone to some pretty interesting conditions that can only be treated surgically. The most well known is the twisted stomach. Successful correction of a cow's twisted stomach is best done through surgery, although there is medical treatment described that is effective on occasion. And surgical correction is no simple deal either. It's full blown abdominal surgery.

Open the cow up from the side or on the bottom of the belly, rearrange her guts, place a stitch so the stomach doesn't wander again and close her up. It sounds simple, but it's not. It's one of the most difficult surgeries veterinarians have to learn. And often, there are complicating factors in the abdomen. In my career, I've performed thousands of surgeries to fix the twisted stomach and I feel a sense of awe every time that this can be done on a standing cow, with local anesthetic, and she gets better. There are surgeries like the caesarean section and others that are not done as often but are even more thrilling.

So, the following are some of my thoughts on the day to day, hands on repair of the broken cow. Don't worry, they aren't technical descriptions. I know better than to geek out since my interest in the technical aspect of fixing broken cows isn't shared by anyone outside the veterinary community. They are stories that have veterinary medicine sometimes in the background and sometimes in the foreground. But they all deal with broken cows in one way or another.

Catch Phrases
6-27-17

Surgery is never easy and it's especially challenging in farm animals. First of all, barns are not the epitome of sterility, but that's where most of the farm animals who need surgery live. Second, a surgical assistant is usually not available since most farm vets work alone. Third, the patients are typically awake for the procedure because general anesthesia is really not an option most of the time. Don't worry, though, a generous local anesthetic is used so pain to the patient in kept to a minimum.

We play the cards we've been dealt and do what we can for the farmer and the patient. But a stressful situation for all parties involved can be lightened with some popular figures of speech.

I didn't coin these phrases; they're ones I've learned from colleagues. I really don't have an original bone in my body. Don't take that literally; my bones are all original. It's just a figure of speech.

But if you want to get a client's attention, stare curiously into the dark abyss of an abdominal incision in a cow. Pause for dramatic effect and say, "Huh, I wonder what that thing does?" That usually lightens the mood. If that doesn't work, wait a few more seconds and say, "Wow, I've never seen one of these before."

But farmers know that a chance to cut is a chance to cure. At least that's what I've been telling them over the years. And no farmer should be afraid to let their animal go under the knife, or beside the knife in the case of a cow still on her feet.

And occasionally, surgery has not only therapeutic benefits, it also has diagnostic value as well. Many times, we explore the abdomen of a sick cow to see if we can find what's ailing her. When we don't find anything, we just hope we've let the evil spirits out.

Many farmers are unnerved at the amount of blood a cow can lose during surgery. Indeed, they can be bloody. While making an incision through the flank of a heavy cow, there is usually some well-developed vasculature we must cut through to breech the abdomen. Consequently, blood can spray over the surgeon, the farmer, the floor and anything else within a 10-foot radius. I like to remark that the artery I just cut must have had a name.

The accumulated blood on the floor, coveralls and everywhere else can add up. But cows are blessed with a huge blood supply. A 1,500 pound cow will contain within her veins nearly 17 gallons of blood. The pint or two on the ground is insignificant to the cow. But I still reassure the farmer that, eventually, all bleeding stops.

Once in the abdomen and bleeding is under control, the hard part begins. This is where manual dexterity and tissue handling skills separate the surgeon from the lay person. Carefully, the surgeon finds the pathology and tries to fix it. Recognize that tissue inside of a cow is both slippery and fragile. And to attach a fragile, slippery thing to another fragile slippery thing inside a moving cow with a big needle and suture material can be a daunting task. So, when things don't go as planned and I drop something, I reflexively say, "Oops." That's a word you never want to hear your surgeon say.

Surgeons are often the perfectionist type. And once the final stitch is placed in the abdominal organ involved, the perfectionist has to check and double check the end result. I find myself not being totally satisfied that perfection has been achieved, probably more often that I'd like to admit.

To remedy the situation, a sleeper stitch is used and I'll call it by that name when explaining my actions to the farmer. I always get the question, "What's a sleeper stitch?" It's the stitch I place that I hope lets me get some sleep tonight.

Once the inside is patched up, we have to patch up the outside. A pretty incision is, to some, the most important part of the whole procedure. Even the most accomplished surgeon in the world is judged by one criterion- the skin closure. If it isn't pretty, it makes you look like an incompetent surgeon.

I'm not saying that the skin closure is the easiest part. On the contrary, it can be very difficult. By now, the cow has had about enough of the ordeal and she tends to get a little feisty. She may have a bit of sensation returning to her skin and every time the needle contacts her, she jumps. It's hard to suture a moving target.

Surgery is serious business, but it's made enjoyable with catch phrases. If you have one you'd like to share, feel free to email me. It might make my next surgery more fun.

Pain
3-7-17

"Ouch! That hurts." How many times have I barked those words after smashing a finger or stubbing a toe.

I have a low tolerance for pain. People, in general, have a low tolerance for pain. Some people tolerate pain better than others, of course, but compared to the cow, people are wimps.

Now, I know that statement might be provocative; I like to provoke thought. I've seen cows tolerate things that would make a mixed martial arts champ fold like a clean towel.

Cattle are domesticated animals. Generations ago, they were wandering the grasslands trying to forage and elude predators. Predators know when something is bothering their prey. When they see a sick or lame animal, they make their attack. So, it's in the interest of the prey species to not display pain, lest they be singled out by the hungry lion.

This instinct remains in domesticated cattle to a degree. It is most pronounced in beef cattle. But even dairy cattle, though they can be considered high maintenance, have a tough streak in them. The instinct for toughness has been completely lost in sheep, by the way. Sick sheep seldom survive.

We routinely perform management procedures and surgeries on cattle and their calves. Some of these, admittedly, should be considered quite painful. We surgically remove the horns of dairy calves to prevent them from growing weapons on their heads capable of injuring an adult cow or person. We surgically castrate calves to improve carcass quality and prevent fighting injuries before they reach sexual maturity. We don't do these things to create pain, but it is does result in pain.

But what's remarkable about these calves is that once they have been dehorned or castrated surgically, they don't display many signs of pain. Once a beef calf is castrated, it runs to find mama and begins to nurse. Once a dairy calf is dehorned, she licks her lips looking for a bucket of milk. Cattle perceive pain different than people.

You might be tempted to think that the same stoic instinct preventing attraction of a predator overrides any outward response to pain. That probably is true to a degree. But they do have a high tolerance for pain as evidenced by the following.

I've watched cows scratch their head on a gate. There's nothing gentle about a cow scratching on a gate. I've been known to scratch my back on a post. It feels really good. But a cow scratching her head on a gate will destroy the gate.

She does this with her head, without a helmet; while scratching. Try to break a steel gate with your head. Forget steel, try to break an aluminum gate with your head. I'll bet after trying, you fail a concussion test and the gate remains unscathed. Cattle perceive pain differently. And I'm convinced it's more than just being stoic.

Pain perception in people has a distinct psychological component to it. The anticipation of the painful stimulus makes the pain much worse. Remember the last time you got a flu shot? Before it was even out of the sheath, your heart rate went up as you were anticipating the little needle plunging into your arm.

But remember the time you found blood dripping off your hand and wondered where it came from? Once you found the laceration, you could barely remember the injury. There was no anticipation and there was very little pain, until you found the blood. Then the injury became painfully evident. So it is with cattle. They do not anticipate the pain of procedures like dehorning, castration or other surgery. And as such, they perceive the pain differently.

I've seen cattle suffer devastating injuries and they shrug it off like the Black Knight in Monty Python's "Holy Grail." A cow may have a broken leg that's dangling and you can almost hear her say, "Come on, now, I have three more to kick you with!" Or a cow may run through barbed wire nearly amputating a front leg at the shoulder. "It's merely a flesh wound!"

They do anticipate pain under some circumstances. Take for example a cow who is an embryo donor. She must get shots twice a day for sometimes as many as six days in a row to stimulate her egg production. These cows know that when the farmer gets her up in the chute, she is going to get stuck with a needle. Consequently, she will balk after the second or third time through the chute. For these cows, a needle stick is worse than a broken leg since the pain is anticipated.

I don't mean to minimize the pain felt by animals during these accidents or procedures. There can be genuine pain and suffering sometimes. There has been a concerted effort in the veterinary community and among farmers to mitigate the pain of these routine procedures with local anesthetics and systemic analgesics. These are worthy endeavors. But I wonder sometimes if they achieve their intended goal.

Pain is unavoidable. Sooner or later, we all must endure it. Cattle feel pain, but tolerate it and maybe even hide it much better than other species. And the adage that states "This is going to hurt me more than it hurts you" may be more applicable in cattle than we know.

New Truck Smell
8-9-11

I log a lot of miles in my truck; during the course of a year, I average about 40,000 miles. If you assume that my average speed is about 50 miles per hour, that's 800 hours a year spent in my truck. My odometer is just shy of 213,000 miles.

The time has finally come for a new truck, so we broke down and got another practice vehicle last week. It's very nice, but I'm not quite sure how to deal with having a new vehicle. It really rides quiet; so quiet, in fact, that I can hear my equipment rattle. You couldn't hear any rattles in my old truck over the hum of the tires. And if I did hear a rattle in the old truck, I'd just turn up the radio. That would usually take care of it.

But the new vehicle smell is what worries me the most. I haven't had a new vehicle in a long time and I've become, over the past couple of days, quite fond of this smell. It's much more pleasant than cow poop. My old truck smelled like a cow's rear end.

My work truck doesn't get cleaned out very often. I really don't see the point of cleaning it out when it's just going to get dirty on the next farm call. So, after I transferred all of my equipment over into the new truck, I took a trip down memory lane as I cleaned out the old truck.

I found that piece of Pop Tart I lost several months ago. It still looked surprisingly fresh – almost like I could have enjoyed a small snack as I was cleaning the truck. I guess the preservatives are working.

Then there was the coffee stain on the upholstery from the day my thermos sprung a leak and I lost my entire days worth of coffee. That was a long day, but it did temporarily cover up the barn smell in the truck.

I found a lot of remnants of a bale of alfalfa hay that I brought home for the goats one day. This hay was pretty good quality. So good that it all but fell apart before I cut the strings. Bits and pieces of hay don't vacuum out well from vehicle carpeting.

Fortunately, I didn't find any samples destined for the lab in my truck. I must have turned them all in. I did, however, find some stuff in between the cushions that could have passed for a high school science experiment.

Sunflower seed shells seem to have been overrepresented in the back on the cab. I must not have very good aim when it comes to spitting them out the window.

I finally got everything vacuumed out and cleaned the windows and dash board with soap and water. I used the better part of a roll of paper towels in the process. By the time I was done, I expected the inside of the truck to be free of the cow smell, but alas, it still stinks. I don't know why I expected different. About 800 hours a year over 5 ½ years with me in the truck definitely took its toll. I'll have to hang an air freshener, or 10, from the mirror.

So now I have this new vehicle smell to deal with. I've been being extra careful not to drag any poop inside the new truck. I've always gone through a lot of coveralls in a day since I don't want to drag anything contagious from one farm to the next. But now, I find myself taking the outer layer of coveralls and my rubber boots off before I leave the farm and get in the truck.

Dirty clothes go in the vet box, not in the cab as do the rubber boots. So far, after two days, the cab doesn't stink... yet. I expect that if I'm diligent, I can probably get to about the middle of the second week of August before the truck begins to take on the characteristic smell of a cow vet's truck.

Barn Swallow
7-29-14

I don't often get called to treat a cow with milk fever anymore. "Milk fever" is a condition dairy cows get right around the time of delivering her calf and begins her copious milk production. It is caused by low calcium levels in her blood. Milk is high in calcium, but you already knew that.

But as the cow is making that milk, she pulls calcium out of her bloodstream and puts it into the milk faster than it can be replaced. She tries to replace it either from her diet or from her bones, which are also high in calcium. But, if her blood calcium falls below a critical level, she gets milk fever.

Ironically, cows with milk fever usually don't have a fever at all but their temperature is usually low. And they usually can't stand which is the primary sign we use to make the diagnosis. We treat them with intravenous calcium. If you have a medical background, you might think that's risky. Indeed it is. Many a cow has died of a heart attack during the treatment. Which is why, until recently, most cows with milk fever were treated by the veterinarian.

But farmers have become very skilled at recognizing cows with milk fever and also treating them effectively with intravenous calcium solutions. So effectively that I rarely get to treat one anymore. But occasionally, I still do.

While most cows get milk fever around the time that they calve, some cows get an atypical milk fever well into her lactation. So recently I got to treat a few cows for atypical milk fever, which is kind of a treat on a nice summer day.

The calcium solution has to be administered to the cow rather slowly, over at least 15 minutes, to minimize the risk of a heart attack. So, it leaves me some time to ponder as I hold the bottle of calcium, regulating its flow rate.

I usually don't think of anything in particular. Maybe sometimes I consider the surroundings, maybe recent cases or even upcoming calls. On one morning I found myself treating a milk fever and contemplating the barn swallow. No doubt it was because I was watching them swoop and dive all around me.

The barn swallow is a favorite bird of mine. They seem to defy the laws of physics, especially Newton's laws of motion. It's like they can stop in midair and start up again without falling an inch. I'm not a bird watcher, but I appreciate birds a lot. There is no bird that I'd rather sit and watch than the swallow.

They are prolific consumers of bugs, which makes me happy. I'd like to think there were hanging around me this morning to help eat the flies that were bothering me and this poor cow.

Barn swallows like to build nests in the rafters of barns where they lay their eggs and rear their young. In the late spring as the hatchlings are still unable to leave the nest, the adult swallows terrorize the barn cats as they make their way up the alley in search of a mouse or maybe a free meal of milk. They nose dive back and forth toward a cat to remind it that what is in the nest is off limits.

I was exiting a barn one morning and noticed a young swallow on the ground. I made sure I didn't step on it, but assumed the cats would find it before too long. It sounds harsh, but it happens. As I made my way to my truck I noticed the farmer pick up the helpless bird and remove him from harm's way. He told me that they make a little bit of a mess, but the pile of droppings underneath their nests represent bugs. I like that thought.

As I finished treating the cow that morning, I mulled over how the swallows always escort me as I mow my grass or brush hog the field. I guess I stir up some grub for them and they provide me with a little eye candy.

That's a little glimpse into the brain of a cow vet treating a milk fever with 15 minutes to think about nothing in particular. And as I left the farm, one solitary barn swallow escorted me down the road; I suspect just to show off some maneuvers.

C-Section by Cellphone
4-15-14

My paternal grandmother lived to a ripe age of 98 before she passed away some eight years ago. I still marvel at the changes that she witnessed in her long life. She had surely spoken with people that actually fought in the Civil War and she was alive herself during both world wars. She saw the transition from horse transportation to automobile, proliferation of the electrical grid, the invention of the radio, television and finally the internet. She was never afraid to use any of this technology and she would correspond with me by email until a year or two before her passing.

I'm not quite half way to 98 yet, but I'm starting to feel that I've seen quite a few advances in my life as well, both in medicine and technology. I was reading an article yesterday about a calf in Texas that lost both of its hind legs to frostbite this winter. Veterinarians were able to amputate the legs and fit the animal with permanent prosthetic limbs. I can't seem to recall going over that procedure in veterinary school.

Scientists have mapped the entire genome of the bovine, among other species. Now, we can take a blood test from a week old dairy calf and analyze its genetic make-up. With that information, we can predict with a reasonable degree of certainty how productive that animal may be in two years once she delivers her first calf and begins to make milk. We don't have to wait the two years to find out anymore. This technology is not only possible, but it is now common and being used by farmers from all across the country to improve their herds. Again, when I was in vet school, the genome hadn't even been mapped yet.

Scientists have cloned cows, sheep and a multitude of other beasts. In vitro fertilization (test tube babies) was unheard of when I was in school but is now an accepted and commercially available technology used by farmers to improve their herds.

And does anyone dispute how the development of the internet has changed our lives? Communication with colleagues half way around the world can be as easy as punching a few buttons on a keyboard. The computer can even translate for us in the event that the colleagues don't speak a common language.

Wireless internet on our phones has made communication even easier yet and continues to improve our lives. Having trouble finding a farm? No problem, the GPS on the phone will lead us straight there. Need a registration number on a bull from Italy? No problem – just look it up on the smartphone. Doing a Cesarean section in the middle of the night and need additional light? Just reach for the phone and open the flashlight app.

Wait a minute... Open the flashlight app?

If you appreciate irony as much as I do, you'll probably enjoy this one.

A client called late one night recently to help deliver a calf. The calf was way too big to be delivered naturally, so we decided in order to save the cow's life, we should deliver it by C-section. Now despite all of the fancy technology invented by human kind, we still have to do the hard work sometimes. C-sections are rarely easy and they are certainly more difficult in the middle of the night in an emergency situation.

It was just the farmer and me that night and I found the only corner of the barn that I felt comfortable positioning this heifer for surgery.

She had been in labor for some time and was a little wobbly on her feet. We usually do C-sections with the cow standing under local anesthesia, but I was afraid she might try to lie down during the surgery unless she was positioned properly. So, we had to look for the right place to tether the patient.

Unfortunately, it was pretty dark at midnight in this corner of the barn, but we plowed forward. After delivering the calf, I must have made some comment about a bat's vision because the farmer took out his cellphone and turned on the flashlight app to double as a surgery light. There we were; the farmer has a tail in one hand and a phone, er…, surgery light in the other and I was elbow deep in the belly of the cow trying to close her up. It was a night to remember.

I spoke with the farmer a few weeks later and he told me the cow is doing fine, thanks to the help of modern technology. I think my grandmother would have been impressed.

The Jeep
11-1-16

Many folks my age eventually have a mid-life crisis. I won't divulge my age but let's just say that I'm playing the back nine already. I've avoided the crisis for some time now but, alas, it has finally hit.

I bought a used Jeep.

Well, maybe it doesn't rise to the level of mid-life crisis. It's not a sports car and it certainly isn't marital infidelity. But it still is sort of a guilty pleasure.

For nearly 20 years, I've been a Jeep person. My wife and I have had, in one form or another, a Jeep vehicle since 1998. But the elusive soft top Wrangler had eluded me-until now. It doesn't have many creature comforts and I wouldn't want to drive all the way to California in it. I love it nonetheless.

Ok, you're probably thinking about now, where's the connection to farmers or cows or veterinary medicine? It might be a stretch, but I'm considering making it my practice vehicle.

Now before you scoff, I've seen more unusual practice vehicles in my days than a Jeep. There once was a veterinarian who would show up in our area every summer driving a hearse. Imagine calling the vet and having the mortician show up at the farm. I can't imagine it would exactly engender confidence in his clinical skills.

So, in that context, the Jeep as an ambulatory practice vehicle doesn't seem that impractical now. Indeed, I think it could actually be a winner. There are many advantages to the jeep.

The sole purpose of a practice vehicle is to transport the veterinarian, his or her equipment and some medicine to the patient. This is because the patient weighs about 1,500 pounds and is impossible to drive to the vet without a stock trailer. So, I asked myself, what equipment could I fit in the Jeep?

Jeeps are known for their ability to go anywhere in any weather, but cargo capacity, admittedly, is not a strong point. Well, I need some surgery packs. That's easy since bovine surgery packs are no bigger than a phone book.

And I'll need a bucket to wash up my boots before leaving the farm. That's easy too. It will fit on the floor behind the driver seat.

I'll need some medicine and some syringes and needles. No problem, they can go in a storage container in the back seat. I still have room for my portable ultrasound and some ropes and consumables.

Surgery pack –check. Bucket – check. Medicines and syringes – check. Ultrasound, ropes and consumables – check. Yes, this seems more and more plausible.

Livestock don't avoid getting sick when the roads are bad in the winter time. So even during a winter storm, we can get called out to attend a calving or suture a laceration or just treat a very sick cow. And the Jeep, I'm sure, will never let me or the farmer down if there's snow or ice on the roads. That's a big advantage.

But getting to the farm is only half the challenge sometimes. Cows, by nature, are outside animals. They eat outside, they sleep outside and they get sick outside sometimes. Occasionally a cow gets sick enough that she can't even walk back to the barn for the vet to look at her.

I've packed the back of a farmer's 4WD side by side full of medicine and equipment many times to get to the back 40 and doctor a cow. But with a Jeep as a practice vehicle, I could tell him, "No need to bring the Gator, my practice vehicle is up to the task!" In fact, driving the Jeep around is reminiscent of many instances of hitching a ride on the all-terrain utility vehicle.

And finally, perhaps the biggest advantage has yet to be discussed. Since the top can be removed, I finally have a way to deal with a pesky problem that all large animal veterinarians deal with. Within several weeks of breaking in a new practice vehicle, the interior gradually takes on the aroma of the rear end of a cow. It is totally unavoidable, and it makes for some awkward moments when a passenger climbs in the truck for the first time.

I figure the best way to deal with that is to just go topless. I mean the vehicle, not me or my passengers. That would just be weird.

Double Dipping
4-14-15

Since all dairy cows have to deliver a calf to make milk, there are a lot of calves born in our area. But since cows don't schedule these with us in advance, whenever assistance is needed, it is usually at an inconvenient time. If it wasn't for this fact, I think delivering calves would be one of my favorite things to do. No two calvings are the same and the outcome is always immediately known.

We see such oddities as deformed calves, twins trying to be born at the same time, an odd number of appendages coming at one time or no appendages coming at all in the case of a breech birth. Some farmers have become quite skilled at fixing these irregularities and others are still learning under our guidance. But regardless, whenever I get to attend a calving, it is usually bad news. I rarely get to deliver the easy ones.

Early last month I got one of those calls from a farmer to help him deliver a calf. This is one of those farmers that has delivered his share of calves and when he calls me, I know it's going to be a doosy. There are very few calves that he can't get born. To make matters worse, the calf to be born was an embryo transfer- specifically an IVF embryo transfer or a test tube baby.

He said that it was a big calf trying to come out of a small cow. They had a dozen or so of these calves born so far that month, all of them alive so far, and he wasn't about to lose this one on his watch. He figured we'd be doing a C-section.

When I got there, I sized up the situation and decided that the calf would likely fit through the birth canal, with a little bit of effort on our part. I recognized the potential value of the calf, so I wasn't going to jeopardize anything. If we weren't making progress after a few minutes, I'd go for the surgery kit.

I placed my ropes used to provide traction around the strap attached to the calf's feet and ran the other end around the post behind us. When we are trying to deliver a large calf, one trick we use is to pull one leg at a time. If we ease one shoulder at a time through the birth canal, we can deliver all but the largest calves. I removed the handle from the calf's left leg and started on the right leg. I grasped my rope that was attached to the calf's right foot to secure it and the cow decided to do the unexpected – she lurched forward.

That was when I felt the calf's right leg fracture. It was one of those moments where you hear words come out of your doctor's mouth that you never want to hear… "Oops." We began making the arrangements for the C-section since pulling with the calf's broken leg would have made repair impossible.

The farmer saw it fit to give me some grief, probably deservedly so. It was I who transferred the IVF embryo into this cow that got pregnant. He got a bill for that. And it was I who now got to do the C-section. He got a bill for that one too. He was muttering something about me double dipping as we were prepping the cow for surgery.

Eventually, we delivered a live calf by C-section without further incident but we still had the broken leg to deal with. Fractured legs are not an uncommon occurrence in calves. We see a few of them a year from difficult deliveries. I've learned that it's best to wait a few hours to set these since we have to sedate them to place the cast. And since newborn calves should get a healthy dose of colostrum, the first milk from the cow that's rich in antibodies, it's not good to sedate them with a full stomach. I had other calls waiting on me that morning, so I left instructions for the calf until I returned a few hours later.

By the time I had returned, the calf was good and dry and there was some moderate swelling around the fracture. I knocked the little girl out with a sedative and took a good look at my fracture. It felt like a growth plate fracture which usually heals pretty easy. The growth plate is the area of a long bone that actively grows adding length to the bone as the animal matures. Don't worry; long bones have two growth plates and if one is broke, the other will compensate.

I placed the cast which took about a half hour and it seemed to come together nice but it's buried in a cast. Short of taking an x-ray, there's no way to know for sure. Unlike a calving, the outcome of a fracture will take a month to be known.

I removed the cast the other day and the fracture healed nice. But since the calf never had the opportunity use the leg properly, she did look a bit pathetic with three one-month-old legs and one day-old leg. She will eventually figure it out and gain some coordination. And the farmer and I both hope she will stop contributing to his veterinary bill.

Nervous Ketosis
4-3-10

Once in a while I get a call from a farmer to treat a cow with a very dramatic illness. Such drama includes lacerated udder veins, prolapsed uterus and bloat. The cow with nervous ketosis, however, takes the cake.

Dairy cows get ketosis when they are using more calories to produce milk than they can physically eat. Making milk is hard work for the cow. It's the metabolic equivalent to a person running a marathon-every day. To make that much milk, she needs to eat a lot.

Usually, shortly after a cow delivers a calf and starts a new lactation, she can't physically eat enough to support her level of milk production. To make up the difference, she loses weight. Those calories get converted eventually into milk.

The cow will burn both fat and protein to support her milk production. When a cow burns too much fat at one time, she gets a condition called ketosis. If fatty tissue is broken down quickly in animals for energy, the body turns some of it into chemicals called ketones. Acetone, the active ingredient in most nail polish removers, is a ketone. Acetone is actually one of the ketones the cow produces.

Cows can further metabolize the ketones for energy, but not very efficiently. The problem comes when the ketones build up in the blood. They have a secondary effect of causing reduced appetite and weakened movement in the muscles of the digestive tract.

Ketosis is very common in dairy cows and has been for a long time. Nervous ketosis is not so common. What it lacks in frequency it makes up for with drama.

The reason this condition is so dramatic is that the affected cows are, well, crazy. They can be aggressive, sleepy or appear drunk. But, the most consistent feature is licking.

Now, I have a golden retriever that likes to lick. He'll lick the floor, my hand, the other dog and sometimes himself. But he has nothing on the cow with nervous ketosis. They are obsessed with licking. They lick the rail in front of them; lick their fur, their neighbor or the veterinarian treating them. If you tie a halter on one so she can't open her mouth, she will sound like she is licking the roof of her mouth. They just can't quit.

Many times a panicked farmer has called me when I'm on call to ask if his cow has some exotic disease because she won't quit licking. I once saw a cow with nervous ketosis lick raw a 12-inch by 6-inch spot on her flank. We don't know why some cows with ketosis get nervous and others don't, but it probably has to do with the level of ketones in her blood.

Fortunately, most of these cows recover in a couple of hours after giving them an IV infusion of sugar. Sugar, an energy source, breaks the cycle of rapid fat breakdown and ketone production. After a couple of hours, the cow is able to rid her body of enough of the ketones that she sobers up. And, hopefully, she won't have a hangover the next day.

Ancient Medicine
10-26-10

A number of years ago, a friend of mine from college found an old book titled "How to treat Common Ailments of Farm Animals" published by W. D. Hoard and Sons in 1945. This publisher is also well known for publishing a biweekly dairy magazine. I found it on my book shelf a few weeks ago and took a browse through it.

While I am not really a history buff, I do find it fascinating how different life is today compared to the recent past. As challenging as today's world is, it is nothing compared to just a couple of generations ago.

The same can be said of the cows. As you might imagine, things were done a little different in 1945. All but one or two of the drugs we have available to us today were not yet discovered in 1945. The description of the diseases and their causes, though, are surprisingly not much different than they are understood to be today.

While browsing through the book, a few of the descriptions caught my attention. Ketosis is a condition dairy cows have struggled with since well before 1945 and it does get mentioned in the book.

Ketosis is (and was then too) caused when a high producing dairy cow can't physically consume enough feed to supply the energy needed to make the vast amount of milk she is capable of producing. The cow compensates by burning calories from energy reserves, mainly fat.

One of the byproducts produced by rapid fat metabolism is ketones. Ketones, in high levels, will suppress a cow's appetite and slow down the movement of her digestive organs. As feed intake drops, the cycle worsens and milk production will eventually fall to low levels.

Fortunately for the cows in 1945, the recommended treatment was an intravenous infusion of purified sugar. It is still the recommended treatment today.

A second condition which made me take notice was the description of milk fever. Now, even though the name of the condition contains the word fever, it really has nothing to do with a fever. Milk fever is low blood calcium.

It happens in dairy cows just before or after they deliver a calf. As she is preparing for lactation, calcium is drawn from the blood to be put into the mammary gland to make milk. If the cow can't compensate quickly by drawing on her reserves in the bones, her blood calcium falls below a critical threshold and she becomes weak. Many times she becomes even too weak to stand.

The treatment today, as well as in 1945, is an intravenous dose of calcium solution. Many farmers are skilled at treating this condition, but we still do treat a cow for milk fever occasionally.

My book made reference to an old treatment that is no longer practiced today, thankfully. It describes the inflation of the four quarters of the udder with air until they become tense. This practice was wrought with danger since infection of the mammary gland was a common unintended effect.

But the condition that really got my attention is called congestion of the udder; we call it udder edema today. Udder edema is common when the cow delivers her calf. As anyone who has ever had a baby can attest (according to my wife), the mammary glands become quite swollen and painful. The cow is no exception.

The cow's udder can become so congested that its supporting ligaments will tear. To prevent this catastrophic injury in severely affected cows, we can treat the condition with a combination of diuretics and anti-inflammatory drugs. In 1945, however, a bizarre combination of concoctions was used. Quoting the book, "In the evening rub in a mixture of one part turpentine and fluid extract of poke root and eight parts of lard or sweet oil."

Yikes – I wonder what the milk would taste like after the udder has been bathed in turpentine for a few hours? It reminds me to be thankful that today, despite the news reports, our food supply is as safe as it has ever been.

Vet Wrapper
1-6-15

I was tending to a cow's sore foot one day last month. After cleaning the lesion and applying some medicine to the cow's hoof, I pulled out my roll of "vet wrap" to apply a bandage. The farmer must have been in a jovial mood that morning because he started teasing me about being the "vet wrapper." He told me that I should consider a new profession as the "vet rapper."

Now, I can only hope that he was not making that suggestion because of the way I treated his cow. Hopefully, I am welcome back on his farm in my traditional capacity as cow doctor. But, he got me thinking about the "What if…"

I am, by no means, a big fan of the rap music. On the other hand, I wondered, how hard could it be? So I took a few minutes and scratched out a rhyme or two. It goes something like this.

I'm a cow doc and I cannot lie,
I like my job but I'm now inclined
to take a farmer's advice
not because he thinks I'm nice
but on account of the function of the rhyme.

Break it down for me sister… MOO MOO MOO

OK, that's a good start. This rhyming thing might just have potential. Maybe I can come up with some more.

Sometimes farmers think that I am fly
So much so that they'll bake me a pie
I'm not a cowboy poet
And I think you know it
I'm just the Vet Rapper in my spare time

Let me hear it there, sister... MOO MOO MOO

There we go. I'm on a roll. Here's a little more.

It's the farmer that I work for
And his stock that I care for
People often think
That there's a stink
'Cause the stock makes a lot of manure

Sing it for me again, Sister... MOO MOO MOO

Unfortunately, this media leaves a lot to the imagination. Newspapers have yet to incorporate the technology of the singing greeting card. But if they had, you might get the next verse.

Now by this time you gotta wonder
The beat of music that this rap's under
I hear the cow bell
And some tractors as well
Makin' noise to carry this number

Scratch it for me now, sister... MOO MOO MOO

I expect by this time that the record executives will be calling me next week for a lucrative record deal. The bidding war could get quite intense, I suspect. But, I like my job so I penciled out the next verse.

Do not despair I'm not gonna quit
Despite the fact this rhyme's legit
There's still broken cows

In some of the corrals
That my colleagues and I visit

Let me hear some more, Sister... MOO MOO MOO

I'm the Vet Rapper MOO MOO MOO
Yeah, I'm the Vet Rapper... MOO MOO MOO

Don't worry, I have no plans to quit my day job.

Is It Worth It?
8-2-16

Sometimes I have to ask myself if it is really worth it.

Emergency duty is perhaps the most taxing part of any job for which it is required. Doctors, plumbers, linesmen and anyone else who is tethered to an electronic leash after hours know what I'm talking about. It is a necessary, yet frustrating part of the job.

But there are times, for me at least, when I have to force myself to hide my frustration. Sometimes I do it well and sometimes I'm sure I don't do it well. Our clients can surely attest.

There are few true emergencies when it comes to bovine veterinary practice. Farmers know this and are very respectful, even apologetic, when they call after hours. What constitutes a true emergency depends on if the animal's life is in immediate danger if attention isn't given. The two most common emergencies are the prolapsed uterus and lacerated udder vein. Even a cow delivering a calf can wait until a person eats his supper to attend.

A prolapsed uterus happens when a cow's womb turns inside out and exits out through the birth canal. Shock quickly sets in and if not replaced within a couple of hours, irreversible damage will threaten the cow's life. A lacerated udder vein in a milk cow, however, can kill a cow in mere minutes.

To illustrate this point, think of a 10-gallon bucket with a hose attached at the bottom. Fill the bucket with water and open the valve to the hose. How long until the bucket is empty? That's how long a cow has to live if she lacerates an udder vein.

The cow only has a chance if the farmer actually observes her lacerate the vein. Otherwise, she will bleed to death before the farmer even knows anything is wrong. But if pressure is applied to the gushing vasculature immediately, she can survive until help arrives.

I was preparing to eat a late supper with my family recently one night, which seems to be a special occasion anymore. As we were saying grace, our answering service called. After the prayer, I called them back to learn that a client had a cow that had "cut her vein." I knew what it meant and was in my truck before you could say "Amen." I spoke with the client from my truck and he was indeed applying pressure to the wound in hopes she would last until I got there.

The farmer told me he watched the cow try to imitate an Olympian and high jump the barbed wire fence, only to find herself disqualified. One of the barbs caught her udder vein and created a gusher.

I arrived to find the cow tied to a post in the pasture with the farmer holding his hand on the laceration in the rain. Darkness had now descended, making visualizing the blood-soaked udder even more challenging. I threw a clamp on the laceration, dodged a flying foot from the ungrateful patient and returned to the truck to get her a cocktail. I figured it would be best if she would relax a little as I was working on her.

Once she had lied down, I threw a couple of stitches in the two wounds that had penetrated the half-inch diameter vein. Now recognize that a cow's udder is the lowest part of her body that receives substantial blood flow when she is standing. This raises the pressure in her veins because of the effects of gravity. This is not the case when she is flat on her side so to rightly evaluate the success of the stitches, we have to see her standing.

I gave her a shot of medicine to reverse the sedation and allowed her a couple of minutes to stand. Sure enough, once her blood pressure went up in the udder, we found another squirter that needed addressed.

I am not a spring chicken. As I have aged, it seems that both my belt and my arms have shrunk. To compensate for my shortening arms, I've invested in some reading glasses which come in handy when it's dark and I'm hunched over trying to patch a hole in an udder vein. It's frustrating not being able to see and it's frustrating feeling the aches and pains when working hunched over. It was still raining and as I was hunched over squinting at this blood-soaked udder trying to stab it with some suture, a big drop of rain fell from the leaves above me and landed squarely in my ear canal.

It is during times such as this that I often ask myself, "Is it really worth it?" The new profession smell had ceded to the smell of cow poop years ago after countless emergency calls. I didn't cuss and I hope I hid my frustration after getting plunked with the rain drop, but honestly, it was a difficult moment. I took a breath and finished the stitch.

After straightening up and regaining my balance, I gave the farmer instructions on the cow. He apologized profusely for dragging me out on a difficult night and I assured him it was OK. And as I watched him lead the cow safely toward the barn, I found the answer to my question.

CHAPTER 3
Seasons

A distinct advantage to having a weekly newspaper column is the opportunity to write timely articles when it comes to seasons of the year. Topics that may be dated to a particular season don't necessarily, however, make good fodder for a book. Since a book can be read in the spring, summer, autumn or winter and at Christmas time or Halloween, I felt compelled to include some nevertheless.

I write about farmers and farming, and the weather is always foremost in my mind. When the weather is ideal, it is an opportunity to brag a little about how good things might be for a farmer. When the weather is bad, it provides an outlet to vent.

All farmers are at the mercy of the weather to some extent, some more than others. In regions that rely heavily on irrigation, at least the risk of drought is mitigated. But there still must be sunshine and warm temperatures for the crops to thrive. Other areas are completely dependent on Mother Nature to cooperate if they want to harvest a crop. Too wet or too dry can be a bust for these farmers.

Crops aside, the weather can wreak havoc on livestock operations, especially cattle farming. Too cold in the winter can kill calves. Too hot in the summer can stress cows. Too much mud in the springtime can stress everyone. And since the weather is rarely perfect in any season, there is always something to write about.

By and large, the weather is the safest topic anyone can discuss. The weather is never offensive or controversial. It's why the weather is the first thing we bring up when conversing with someone we may not know well. No matter what I say about the weather, it isn't controversial. I don't aim to be controversial, but neither do I aim to avoid it. Some of the most interesting topics can be controversial, so weather is just one topic of the seasons.

Holidays are seasonal and I find the temptation to discuss holidays like Halloween, Thanksgiving and Christmas too great to pass.

And finally, the rhythm of life on the farm follows the seasons. So, when it's time to haul the manure to the field, I feel obligated to explain why this necessary inconvenience to the motorists occurs. Yes, we might get stuck behind a manure spreader and sometimes we may even run over a bit of cow poop on the roads, but it has to get to the fields. There is no other option. Farmers are sensitive to this and do the best they can under the circumstances.

The rhythmic nature of farming continues throughout all seasons of the year. Preparation for planting may be started as soon as the harvest is over, even though the actual planting may be months away. The seasonal cycle of planting, cultivating, harvesting and preparation never ends and has a rhythm all its own.

Photo by Regina Hissong

January
1-9-19

It's cold. That's not really news for anyone reading this. But this year, misery gets company.

A lot of people have asked me how livestock handle these frigid temperatures. Their concern is not without foundation. Indeed, outside pets can succumb to hypothermia if precautions are not taken for them. But don't despair for the outside farm dogs. There are some with whom I'm acquainted that refuse to sleep indoors, even when given the opportunity. A thick fur coat and a wind break is all some of them desire.

As far as livestock are concerned, the sub-zero cold isn't near as big a burden as you might think. And farmers know what they will tolerate. Adult cattle acclimate to the cold with virtual ease. They have two things that you and I don't.

First, they enjoy a thick, insulating fur coat. Once the daylight length begins to decrease in autumn, cattle grow a thick undercoat. In the spring as long nights yield to long days, they shed this same undercoat. Cattle in the winter are so well insulated that snow will lay on their back for hours without melting.

Second, they have an internal furnace. The rumen, the largest compartment of their complex four chambered stomach, generates heat during the digestion of their feed. This fermentation chamber produces heat directly during the process of converting the fibrous feed into simple molecules that can be easily digested by the cow. The heat produced contributes to the maintenance of her body temperature.

So cows, even though you and I might shiver, actually prefer the weather to be a little on the chilly side. In fact, their thermoneutral temperature is about 40 degrees Fahrenheit. The thermoneutral temperature is the temperature that an animal expends no calories to either stay warm or cool.

Cows hate mud, though. Fortunately for cows, there is no mud right now. It has all been converted to ice by the polar vortex. You might have noticed some cows lounging on the frozen ground on days where the sun is up, but the temperatures are down. Mud will suck the heat out of them. Frozen mud provides a nice place to lie down.

But on windy days, cows will seek shelter. An open barn or even a group of trees can provide sufficient shelter from the wind and snow. Cows really do prefer to be outside, though. Barns can become quite stuffy with all those cows exhaling their moisture laden breath.

Stuffy air leads to pneumonia. In lieu of a building for shelter, some farmers will simply feed the cows supplemental grain to provide more calories. Cows will maintain their body temperature regardless of the weather, but they can lose weight in the process. Supplemental feed helps prevent the weight loss.

The baby calf, on the other hand, can encounter some problems when the winter temperatures arrive. Farmers know about this and do what they can to avoid any problems.

Newborn beef calves are a hearty lot. Once a calf is born, she is licked dry by mama. This gives the calf a good start. A calf is born with a supply of brown fat into which it taps to supply the energy to stay warm. And a generous first meal of colostrum from mama's udder provides further calories to keep its body temperature at the target 101.5 Fahrenheit.

But there can be a minor complication when the temperatures become especially frigid. The calf's ears are relatively exposed and poorly perfused with blood when it's cold. The ear tips can easily develop frostbite severe enough to kill the tissue completely. Once frostbitten, the tissue will dry out and slough, leaving the calf looking like a furry version of Shrek. And don't worry, the other calves don't even think of poking fun of the ones with the short ears.

Baby dairy calves may be a little more burdened by the cold than their beef cousins. But again, farmers know this and take precautions to avoid problems. Calf blankets are often provided to offer a little extra insulation during the winter. Extra milk is offered to maintain growth and the energy necessary for a healthy immune system to function. And farmers will bed their calves a little deeper to make sure they stay dry and insulated.

Please notice that I didn't say anything about bringing the calves inside when it's cold. In fact, this may be one of the worst things that a farmer can do to a healthy calf in the winter. The air is better outside. And once acclimated to the warm confines of the barn, it will be that much more stressful for the calf once put back outside.

If a cow or calf is sick, all bets are off. The frigid weather can literally suck the life out of a sick animal. But if things are firing on all cylinders, outside in a calf hutch or calf condo is the best place for a calf to be.

So, don't worry about the cows and calves outside in when the polar vortex sets in. Cold and dry can be happy times for the bovine.

February
2-24-15

What is the melting point of cow poop?

I'm not sure if physicists have that one worked out yet, but I have a pretty good idea of where it is. You see, I spend a lot of time at the business end of cows where the brown, stinky stuff is produced. I consider myself an expert in all things cow poop (as I'm sure many of my readers do, especially the variety that emanates from the bull.) I spend time there when it's hot, temperate, and the entire range of cold. Cow poop indeed acts differently at different temperatures.

These last couple of weeks have made me think a little deeper about how frigid the cold temperatures affect daily life, especially life in the barn. Equipment doesn't work as well, especially manure handling equipment. Diesel fuel gels in the fuel lines rendering engines useless. Baby calves struggle to maintain their body temperature unless farmers feed them extra milk. The cold spells that we experience every January and February make everything harder.

But the response of cow poop to these temperatures is something to behold. In the summertime when it's hot outside, cow poop wants to dry out. As soon as it contacts a wall, protective bib overalls or even my ultrasound machine, the warm sunshine starts drying it out almost immediately. It can then be scraped away with ease.

In spring and fall, cow poop tends to remain at, well, poop consistency. It stays wet and slimy on my rubber boots almost indefinitely. It tends to make a mess on whatever it contacts. It is, however, the most trouble free kind of manure.

Since cows poop a lot, upwards of 200 pounds per cow per day, just leaving it lay where the cow deposits it is a bad idea. So farmers have developed all kinds if innovative ways to deal with this byproduct of forage digestion. From slatted floors to scrape alleys to flush systems, I'd bet that more time has been spent developing manure handling systems than putting a man on the moon. In the spring and fall when the poop flows properly, these manure handling issues are no problem.

But when the temperature starts to dip in the winter, varying degrees of difficulty are encountered depending on the wind chill. When the temperature stays around 20 degrees Fahrenheit for any extended amount of time, the cow poop begins its transformation into a poop-cicle. Note that it is different than a pop-cicle.

At 20 degrees, cow poop takes on the consistency of a slushie. It isn't too inconvenient yet; it still can be scraped around and still flows down the pipes that move it to the collection pond.

But at around 10 degrees, it begins to become difficult to deal with.

It begins to lose fluidity and large chunks of frozen manure begin to accumulate in inconvenient places, like the pipes that transport manure to storage. This creates a dilemma for the farmer. If it isn't constantly scraped from the cow alleys, it will freeze solid and remain there until a spring thaw arrives. Dealing with frozen poop starts to eat into the farmer's already stretched time budget.

Once the temperature reaches 0, then it becomes a big problem. At this temperature, poop almost freezes on contact. Bedding packs begin to resemble a moonscape with a lot of dingle-rocks. Motorists worry about black ice; farmers worry about brown ice. Prolonged temperatures as we have experienced recently cause hazards for both cows and farmers. Once frozen at this temperature, manure has roughly the structural strength of concrete and is nearly impossible to break without the aid of a jackhammer or TNT.

But on some farms it can be worse than an inconvenience. There are several farms in the county that employ manure digesters. These digesters produce methane gas that can be used to produce heat or even electricity on the farm. Once the flow of manure is interrupted to the digester, things can get even darker and colder.

This is a disgusting subject to some but a fact of life nonetheless. So what exactly is the melting point of the stuff? Cow poop begins to melt again at around 25 to 30 degrees. I pray that it begins to melt soon.

March
3-23-10

Thank goodness, winter appears to finally be over. Now begins the busiest time of the year for my dairy and beef clients. Dairy farmers are getting prepared for spring planting. Most of the beef herds are full bore into calving season. You probably know of rabbit season, turkey season or baseball season, but you may not have heard of calving season.

Calving season in most areas of the country is in the spring, although there are herds that do it in the fall. It is the time of year when all the beef calves are born. It is also an especially busy time for large animal veterinarians who assist the beef farmers when a cow gets into trouble during delivery.

Calving season usually begins late winter and runs through the middle of spring. There are a number of reasons why a beef farmer would want to have all of his calves born during only a few months out of the year. First, since the cows have to be watched particularly close during calving, it concentrates most of the work into a few months.

For commercial herds, the product they produce for sale is calves. Calves are generally sold at weaning in the fall to be fattened for slaughter. A producer can fetch a premium price for the calves if he can produce a group of calves of uniform weight. This is only possible if all of the calves are born around the same time of year.

If the calving season is limited to two or three months out of the year, then the breeding season will also be limited. Bulls can be pretty ornery and downright dangerous. A defined breeding season can limit the farmer's risk of having to keep a bull. It also allows more efficient use of artificial insemination if the farmer wishes not to have a bull on the farm.

Spring calving herds can also vaccinate and control parasites with greater efficiency to the groups of animals that receive the most benefit. Calves should be vaccinated just prior to weaning to get the most benefit. If a farmer weans a couple calves every month out of the year, vaccinating would be a year round job.

But the most important reason for a spring calving season is grass. Since pasture doesn't need to be mechanically harvested like hay or silage, it is much less expensive to feed. And cows need to eat a lot of grass when they are nursing a calf. Just like a dairy cow, beef cows require a lot of energy to make the milk to feed the calf.

If timed right, the cow's peak milk production happens when the grass is lush and most abundant. Her milk production usually peaks around 60 days after calving, which is hopefully around the middle of May. As the weather gets drier and the calf gets older, the mama cow won't have to make as much milk, conveniently around the time when pasture is less available.

I love the change of seasons, especially when the winter season ends and calving season begins. By the end of calving season, I'll be happy to see it end too.

April
4-21-15

Thank God for springtime. Believe it or not, that sentiment is shared by many of the dairy farmers for whom I work.

Winter, with all of its complications, is a relatively slow time for dairy farmers. Yes, there is some equipment to maintain and there are cows to milk. There is also the annual arctic blast or two that freezes everything up and requires attention. But by and large, winter is almost like vacation. Dairy farmers even have enough time to attend an educational meeting or two. Their workload might be reduced to a mere 12 to 14 hours a day.

But when springtime comes, the vacation is over in a hurry. There's so much to do and so little time in which to get it done. There's manure to be hauled to fertilize the fields. There's fence to fix. There's ground to work. There's enough work to keep a farmer busy for the next few months. Long days are again becoming the norm.

Beef farmers aren't immune to the extra work either. Spring is calving season in our area. It's when most of the beef cows deliver their calves. Farmers plan this for a number of reasons, but mainly it's to coincide with the spring flush of pasture. Beef cows need a lot of nutrition to feed her hungry calf all of the milk that it desires. And there's no better way to feed a cow to feed a calf than to let her graze to her heart's content. The best grazing is in the springtime.

But calving season is a lot of work for the farmer. The cows have to be watched constantly to see whose going into labor next. Once the calf is born, it needs identified by an ear tag. It also needs and a good meal of colostrum, the mother's first milk that's rich in antibodies and vitamins. That first meal will support the growing calf over the next couple of months. Farmers have to make sure these things get done.

But when a beef cow has problems, the farmer has to deal with that as well. Sometimes the calf doesn't want to come out the right way and the farmer has to intervene. Hopefully it is an easy fix otherwise, I get the call to come and help. Other times, a cow can deliver her calf but complications arise afterwards. Occasionally, a cow will push her womb inside out immediately after delivering a calf. If a farmer doesn't catch this right away, it could be fatal for the cow. Beef and dairy farmers alike will give us the call to make those repairs.

But despite the work associated with calving season, I've never met a beef farmer who longed for the dead of winter.

Is it any wonder that we love spring? The temperatures warm up enough to make spending time outside enjoyable. The smells of spring, including the newly fertilized fields, remind us that summer is close. The serenade of the spring peepers is more pleasant than whatever music any human can compose.

But the workload certainly does increase for the farmer. Dairy cows eat an incredible amount of feed so farmers have to find a way to store up enough of it for the cows in time for the inevitable return of the next winter. Corn, hay, soybeans and other crops soon may be in the ground but the farmer still won't have time to relax.

All those crops have to be maintained. There are a multitude of pests that would just love for the farmer to be on vacation. Weeds try to choke the crops out before they get a foothold. Insects seek to feast on what should belong to the cows in a few months. There's no rest for the weary.

Springtime gives us hope that, once again, the rhythm of life on the farm will continue; the rhythm that farmers are well acquainted with. The rhythm that doesn't stop, that is, until the dead of next winter.

May
5-14-13

One of the disadvantages of a Tuesday column is that it's almost too late to write about the past weekend's activities but too early for the upcoming weekend. It was Mother's Day this past weekend and I heard a lot of moving tributes to mom at church and on the television and other media outlets. The tributes were all very nice but I can't recall seeing a recent tribute to the "foster mothers of the human race," the cow. Unfortunately, I'm just getting to it today.

Maybe Mother's Day isn't the best time to pay tribute to the cow anyway, but I'll go ahead and climb out on this limb. On the other hand, I recall a barn that I used to frequent that had a sign on the wall that read, "Treat each cow as a mother should be treated." Both quotes are attributed to the 19th century dairy farmer, W. D. Hoard.

Please don't misunderstand my intentions. I don't mean to compare our mothers to cows. THAT IS NOT MY INTENT. I simply wish to pay tribute to my second favorite mammal, the cow.

Beef and dairy breeds alike have brought forth food, draft power and leather for human benefit. As technology advanced, draft power from the ox was obviously replaced by machinery but nothing could replace the meat, milk or leather.

The dairy cow today is simply a metabolic marvel. The amount of calories a lactating cow burns to produce an average day's yield of milk is staggering. Pound for pound, it is more than a man uses to run a marathon; and the cow does it every day and even year after year with a two-month vacation between lactations.

And she accomplishes this feat this while eating stuff that is indigestible to people like grass and corn silage. The dairy cow is also very "green." She can eat cull potatoes, bakery waste, citrus pulp left over from juice production and a myriad of other byproducts that would likely end up as garbage if not fed to cows.

But dairy cows obviously shouldn't get all the credit. In fact, beef cows are selected, in part, based on their ability to "mother" a calf. A good mother first delivers her calf without assistance. Once on the ground, a good beef cow stays with her calf and stimulates it by vigorously licking it and muzzling it to get it to stand. A strong calf will be on its feet within 30 minutes or so if encouraged my mama.

Once on its feet, a good cow will be ever so patient as the helpless calf searches for its first meal. The cow is most certainly under pressure before the calf's first meal and undoubtedly sore. Yet she doesn't budge as the calf finally latches on to the teat and takes its first drink.

A good mother will then hide the calf from predators during periods of the day as she goes to the pasture in search of lush grass. She needs the nutrients to support her milk production if she is to be a good mother and feed the calf what it needs to grow.

But, of course no Mother's Day tribute would be complete without a mention of my two favorite mothers. Don't fret; I'm still going to completely avoid the pitfalls of comparing them to cows. My mama didn't raise no fool, you know.

I gave my mom no shortage of grief when I was a child but she never showed me a shortage of love. Nor did she show me any shortage of disciplined instruction when I needed it, which was more often than I'd like to admit. A good mother is able to love tenderly whenever possible and love toughly when needed. Mom knew which one was needed and I'm who I am today because of it. Thanks, mom.

The mother of my children, my wife, is my hero. While I'm busy being a veterinarian, she has the thankless task of getting the kids off to school (on time, every time) helping at the school, going to the store, maintaining the household, doing the household chores, getting the kids off the bus, taking them to soccer, dance and scouts and making sure their homework is done. When I get home at 9 or 10 p.m., (sometimes several times a week) she never complains that my schedule is too busy to help with the kids. As a result of her efforts, we have two well adjusted, healthy, happy children. Thanks, my lovely wife, and happy Mother's Day.

June
6-18-13

It's Father's Day weekend (I usually write my column on Sunday afternoon) and I recall that I took the time to list the attributes of a good mama cow recently on Mother's Day. Unfortunately, there isn't much to thank the bull for after the moment of conception has happened. In reality, the vast majority of cattle born as a male become steers (get castrated) and will enter the beef business as soon as possible. As for the lucky ones that remain as bulls, there is no "fathering ability" to consider.

Many farmers do not even like to keep a bull around. They are big, destructive and can be downright dangerous. The aggressive nature of the male is exemplified in the bull. Bulls, however, are a necessity if a farmer wants to continue to propagate his herd. After all, it takes two to tango. The form a bull takes, though, is open for discussion.

On many beef farms, a breeding age bull is kept with the brood cows during the mating season, which is about nine months before when the farmer wants his calving season. (The gestation length of a cow is just over nine months.) Once the breeding season is over, many of the bulls' time on the farm is done and, they too, may change careers. Occasionally, a bull may last for a couple of years on a farm.

The other form that a bull takes is that of a straw frozen in liquid nitrogen. Most dairy cows are bred by artificial insemination. This process has undoubtedly had more impact on the genetic improvement in the dairy breeds than any other innovation. With traditional breeding, a farmer would have to either select the best bull from his herd and mate him to all of the cows, regardless of whether it was a good match or not.

In the 1950s, however, the process of artificial insemination became commercially available. Here, only the best of bulls in the country would be used to inseminate cows. A farmer in Pennsylvania could breed one cow to a bull from Michigan and another from Wisconsin and so on. The improvement in genetic merit came rapidly, but it was not without some growing pains. Since we evaluate the ability of a bull to transmit genetics through the performance of his daughters, it takes at least three years to be able to begin to evaluate a bull's true merit. As a result, many bulls that were used heavily turned out to be rather poor genetics.

Newer technologies like improved data evaluation, consistent record keeping and even genomic technology will continue to push the envelope forward. I'm certain that there will be more growing pains and unintended consequences. But even more progress will be made with the added benefit of not having to keep a bull on the premises.

Artificial insemination is commonplace in many of the beef herds as well, but its use never really rivaled the extent that we see in dairy herds. There are still live bulls used in some dairy herds, both out of convenience and economics.

The bull has but one job; pass on his genes. Beyond that, he really has no other redeeming qualities.

As I was reminded again during the Sunday homily this morning, fathers in our culture take quite a beating. The popular culture sees the father, at best, as a bumbling fool with the "man cave" as his top priority. At worst, he is seen as expendable. I feel pity for those who feel that way.

As a man, I guess we learn from our own father's how we are best to do the job of parenting. Not being the type to draw attention to himself, this may embarrass my dad. But I think you should know his story.

My dad loves agriculture and went so far as to earn a master's degree in ruminant nutrition. He used his knowledge to teach at an agricultural college near Philadelphia for several years. My parents made the difficult decision to move home so my brother and I could know our grandparents as we grew up, even though there were no agricultural schools in our native Westmoreland County. In fact, there was little opportunity to make a living there with an agriculture degree. Consequently, my dad took a job in a rock quarry to put food on the table and helped part time on several local farms, including his brother's small beef farm. He sacrificed greatly for the good of his family.

I'm certain that my passion for agriculture comes directly from him. I can only hope that my ability to make selfless decisions is as good as his as well. Thanks, Dad. Happy Father's Day.

July
8-3-10

My kids and I fulfilled a summer ritual this past weekend. The blackberries and huckleberries are in season now and every summer, we drive to my in-law's property near Rockwood to snatch as many as we can before the bears get them. The blackberries are big and juicy and the huckleberries are near prime.

Like every summer, we faced the typical pitfalls that every hunter-gatherer faces. Biting and stinging insects, snakes, oppressive heat and thorns were the easy part. The constant, "Dad, are we done yet? Can we leave now?" was the hard part. Like any parent, I tried to make it a teachable moment.

To encourage them to pick faster, I jokingly told my kids, (Bena, 5 and Nolan, 8) that the first one to fill their bowl wins and the winner gets to drive us home. That greatly concerned my daughter so she kept putting the berries she picked into my bowl to make sure her brother didn't get to take the wheel. Fortunately, my son ate as many berries as he put in the bowl, so my victory was never in doubt. Now before you think I'm a bad father for telling them that, I didn't quit there.

As we were toiling, I asked my kids if they have a new appreciation for farmers that grow, nurture and harvest our food. They replied with an enthusiastic "Yes!" My daughter then asked me, "You mean farmers grow these?"

In the constant effort to reduce toil, farmers are always looking for ways to increase efficiency. These efforts benefit the farmer through higher yields and the consumer through lower prices.

Technology plays a large role in this battle against toil. More efficient and stronger machinery, better fertilizers and pesticides all contribute. Higher yields, in addition to reducing toil, also reduce the amount of land necessary to grow food. At first glance, technologies like fertilizers and pesticides may seem like a detriment to the environment; however, their use allows millions of acres to be left as wild lands and forest.

The dairy industry also widely utilizes technology to reduce toil. Only 60 years ago most cows were milked by hand. Today, milk is almost exclusively collected with a vacuum driven milking machine. Imagine how much toil it would take to milk the 8.7 million cows in this country twice a day. Milkers would have forearms the size of tree trunks.

One of the more controversial technologies used by some dairy farmers is recombinant bovine somatotropin (rBST) or bovine growth hormone. This hormone improves milk production over the course of a cow's lactation by about 10 percent. It allows farmers to ship the same amount of milk while feeding, bedding and milking 10 percent fewer cows. It also reduces the amount of land needed and the amount of manure produced.

While rBST's use has brought widespread criticism from activist groups, the milk from treated cows is both physically and chemically indistinguishable from that of untreated cows. It is also controversial within the dairy industry itself. Many farmers swear that they would never use it and some think that the extra milk it has produced is responsible for a surplus of milk. When there is a surplus of any commodity, it lowers the price farmers get paid for that product.

In the interest of full disclosure, I don't own even a single stock in Elanco, the company that sells rBST. It is undeniable, though, that technology like this reduces toil. Every year there are more people in the world to feed, but there is no more land on which to produce food.

In the future, farmers will have to rely more heavily on technology to meet the growing demand for food. There is nothing high tech about picking wild berries, though. And as long as I can continue our summer ritual, I will.

August
8-30-16

Last week concluded an annual rite of summer, the Somerset County Fair. Besides the comfort food, the games and the rides, there are some important life lessons to be learned at the county fair. Hundreds of animals from pigs to dairy cattle are put on display with pride by their handlers, the 4-H and FFA members.

Granted, it is a long week for the kids and their parents. The animals are checked in a full week before they are allowed to leave. The responsibility for feeding, watering and bedding the livestock lies squarely on the shoulders of the kids responsible for them. Besides netting them a hopefully large profit after the livestock auction, there are a plethora of life lessons available to the kids at the fair if they are willing to accept them.

It works something like this. The kids decide what animals to show and begin the process by purchasing the animals, or even better, picking the animal from their family's own herd. The beef cattle are usually started nearly a year before the fair and the pigs, lambs and goats around six months prior. The kids get a taste of what it is to be a farmer, albeit only a small slice of the pie.

Farming is much more complicated than picking out a choice steer and feeding it, grooming it, keeping it healthy and selling it for a profit. But the kids get an appreciation for how difficult that single task is to raise a steer and a couple of pigs. Maybe for the more ambitious ones, there might be a lamb or a goat thrown into the mix also.

They learn there is no vacation from the responsibility of raising livestock. If there is a family vacation planned, arrangements must be made for someone else temporarily to tend the animals under their care.

And there are rules to follow, just like in farming. The meetings must be attended, the proper vaccinations must be given, the right documents have to be completed, animals must be identified with an ear tag and once at the fair, show times must be adhered to. While uniforms might not be mandatory for the show ring, looking like a slob will reflect poorly on the competitor and may mean the difference between first and second place.

Showing livestock at the fair fosters an attitude favorable to competition. While some people are naturally competitive and others are not so much, nobody likes to lose. Competition encourages self-improvement. It nurtures a healthy pride when successful and drives the kids to get better when success was beyond their reach. The winners are elated and the losers are not. And, if you are wondering, there are no participation trophies in livestock competitions.

The process of raising livestock for the county fair teaches kids about hard work. The animals have to be tamed down which takes time. They have to be taught to lead with a halter or in the case of the swine, walk with the handler. The kids have to ensure that the animals have feed, bedding and water every day. And when it comes time for the fair, the livestock have to be groomed and fitted for the show.

And there are parameters that must be met. Animals have to make weight in time for the show. If they are too light, they are ineligible to show. And in the case of pigs, they can't be too heavy or they are disqualified also.

The ultimate purpose of this entire endeavor is the livestock sale. The ribbons are nice, but the payday, I'm sure, is paramount on the minds of the kids. While the livestock auction isn't a perfect analogy to the real world, it does reflect that if you sell a good product, people are willing to pay for value.

And, just like in real life, a nice sales figure doesn't necessarily guarantee profitability. Some of the animals were purchased months ago by the participants at a healthy price and the sum of that price and cost to raise them may exceed the selling price. Hopefully, this lesson teaches the virtue of living within one's means.

And finally, we get to the ultimate lesson of the whole experience. After the ribbons have been awarded and the auction is over, the realization sets in that these are food animals. They have been companions for months and most of them are about to fully comprehend their final purpose as a food animal.

There were surely many tears shed as the realization set in that these animals are on their way to the slaughter house. What lesson could that possibly teach? It teaches detachment.

Detachment is an understanding that this world is fleeting, along with all of its inhabitants including livestock. Food animals were put here for a purpose, to become food. They don't make good pets and they are expensive to keep. That doesn't mean that kids don't enjoy them; they do. But at the end of the summer, their purpose is fulfilled. And their beneficiaries are both the kids and the people fed by them. Some of the best lessons are the hardest.

September
9-25-12

I love silage. No, I don't mean for myself but as a feed for cattle. Cattle love silage too. I've written about silage before but since it fascinates me so, please afford me the opportunity to indulge and repeat myself. Silage is feed that is chopped wet and packed to allow for fermentation. Sauerkraut could possibly be considered cabbage silage since it is a wet feed that undergoes fermentation; although sauerkraut rolls off the tongue a lot nicer. There are a plethora of types of silage, but corn and hay silage are by far the most common.

You have, no doubt, seen the many trucks and forage wagons traversing the countryside over the last several weeks delivering chopped corn from the field to the silo. Their cargo is not yet silage and it won't be for several weeks. It is still chopped corn.

Hay silage is made by first mowing the hay and allowing it to wilt in the field for some time to allow the moisture level to reach a critical level. If it gets too dry, it won't pack in the silo correctly and becomes unstable. Instability leads to heating. It could even heat to the point that it burns. If it is too wet, the packing process will squeeze out the moisture like wringing out a wet sponge. Along with the water go the nutrients.

Corn silage, on the other hand, is almost always chopped as it stands in the field. The problem with this is that since there is no wilting process, harvesters are at the mercy of the moisture content of the corn plant. When the corn plant dries to about 65 percent moisture, it is ready to chop. If it gets too dry, it doesn't pack well and heats or spoils.

It seems that all of the corn in the county that is destined for corn silage is ready to chop right now. That's why you see some mud on the roads as the trucks and forage wagons hastily exit the fields on their way back to the silo. Farmers are quite busy right now ensuring that all of the beautiful corn turns into beautiful, stable corn silage.

So, what makes the silage "stable," you might be wondering? Stability happens in several steps during the fermentation process. In fact, fermentation, like a fine wine, will continue for years, but stability happens after just a couple of weeks. When the silage has adequate moisture and sugar and is packed so that air cannot get to it, bacteria break down the sugar and produce lactic acid as a byproduct. The lactic acid eventually kills the bacteria that produced it and the plant and its nutrients that remain will not decompose. After about two weeks, stability ensues and the chopped corn becomes silage. If there is inadequate moisture or inadequate packing, oxygen enters the environment producing the opposite of silage- compost.

Since many of the farmers are very busy chopping corn right now, veterinarians who spend a majority of their time working on dairy cattle usually don't have much to do. If this didn't happen every year and we didn't know better, we might feel downright unloved.

But since silo capacity is usually at a premium on many dairies, often the new corn silage must be fed to the cows before it becomes completely stable. This fermenting corn silage can cause bellyaches, indigestion and even twisted stomachs in the cows. Dairy veterinarians feel the love once again when farmers start calling about their sick cows.

I don't know who invented the process of making silage, but it must have been quite a leap of faith to do it the first time. I can imagine that trial and error must have resulted in mostly error and probably a lot of either sick or hungry cows. Today, silage production is very, very high tech. New corn hybrids, powerful choppers and novel storage methods have allowed farmers to improve the quality and quantity of the silage that they harvest for their herds. The cows, I'm certain, appreciate it.

October
10-30-12

I was watching Phineas and Ferb with my kids the other day (don't laugh…) when a commercial came on previewing an upcoming episode. This episode featured the "Were-cow" just in time for the Halloween season. Without a beat, my son said, "Dad, I'll bet you could fix the were-cow." I immediately had a flashback to the original were-cow.

This were-cow is not just a legend, you see. I've seen her up close and personal and, believe me, she's not a pretty sight. Her name is 61 and she's big, black and white, and meaner than snot. She and I first crossed paths about four years ago on a farm in right here in Somerset County. She was a recently purchased first calf heifer that had just delivered a set of twins. (Heifers are females that have never delivered a calf and first calf heifer describes the cow just after delivering her first calf.)

The twins should have been my first clue. Heifers that survive delivering twins are simply too hateful to die. Normally, a twin pregnancy in a dairy cow is full of danger to the cow and in heifers, it is even worse. Too many times it's a death sentence for the heifer. Young heifers lack the body capacity to account for the metabolic strain that the complicated pregnancy puts on her.

But this cow was the exception. She survived the calving, but she soon quit eating. The farmer asked me to look at her to figure out why she wasn't eating. I danced more during that exam trying to dodge flying hooves than I danced at my wedding. Of course, she had a twisted stomach, so I told the farmer that she needed surgery. But since she had just delivered twins, it was unlikely that she'd survive. The number 61 were-cow needed surgery and, to my disappointment, the farmer wanted me to try to fix her.

Good old number 61 must have heard me tell the farmer that I didn't think surgery was a good idea because what I encountered during the initial exam was just a warm up for the surgery. She could reach places with those back feet that would make a contortionist stand in awe. I wasted no time in reaching for the tranquilizer cocktail.

The cocktail I use is a combination of three different intravenous sedatives called the "standing stun." I gave 61 enough to kill an elephant and, by golly, it did take the edge off just enough to get the local anesthetic in and start the surgery.

The "standing stun" cocktail usually gives the patient about 45 minutes worth of pleasurable consciousness alteration – more than enough time for the experienced surgeon to fix the twisted stomach. The 61 were-cow, however, can really hold her sedatives. She was bright eyed and light footed again in about 20 minutes. I tried to get the last layer of sutures in without another round of cocktail, but alas, I gave in and returned to the bottle.

After that surgery, the 61 were-cow's picture was burned into my mind. She is notorious in her barn for whacking anyone that dares to stand beside her. Our assistant became acquainted with her as soon as she was well enough to be vaccinated after the surgery. The black and blue mark on his leg lasted for about two months. Her picture is burned in his mind too. To this day, she rarely misses whoever is in her sights.

The were-cow number 61 is the stuff of which legends are made. Unfortunately, she is all too real and still kicking. On certain nights, when the air is still and the feed bunk is empty, you can hear her angry "moo" from miles away. After my flash back, I thought, "I've already fixed her, son. Unfortunately, I've already fixed her."

November
11-29-11

Ugh. Another Black Friday has come and gone with the typical reports of shootings, pepper spray and near riots. I feel pity for those people that find it necessary to participate in this new American spectacle in the hopes of saving a few bucks on a television. It does remind me, however, of predictable animal behavior that farmers have to deal with.

Livestock can be pretty aggressive toward each other when it comes to their favorite things, namely food. When cattle are lined up at the feed bunk, they can be downright nasty. This can become a real problem in dairy cattle especially since they require a lot of calories to keep healthy. If anything interrupts her calorie intake, she is susceptible to developing a number of metabolic diseases.

Typically, in any dairy herd, there are several boss cows. There are also some timid cows and everyone else in between. The boss cow will clear herself a path to the feed bunk and any other cow in the way will get a swift whack from her 100-pound head.

Now you might wonder, if a timid cow is chased away from the feed bunk by the boss cow, why doesn't she just go to the bunk when the boss cow is done? Cows, being herd animals, like to do everything together at the same time. There is a big, fat scientific name for this behavior- allelomimetic. So, when the boss cow is done eating, everybody is done eating. It reminds me of the saying, "If mama's not happy, ain't nobody happy."

So, what ends up happening is the boss cow eats her fill, but the subordinate cow doesn't eat what she needs. The effect on the subordinate cow can range from less than expected milk production to severe metabolic disease. There is one group of cows on any dairy that is at highest risk for the severe complications. These are the cows that are within several weeks of delivering a calf. These girls need to eat enough calories to grow the developing calf inside of her and, at the same time, gear up to make milk.

These cows, almost universally called "close up cows" because they are close to calving, are big and pregnant and not very ambitious. When the boss cow says, "Get off my turf," the subordinate cows oblige. If she is prevented from eating what she needs the result can be diseases like ketosis, retained placenta or even a twisted stomach.

Farmers have figured out the key to preventing the boss cows from wreaking havoc on the rest of the population. The key is adequate bunk space. In general, it is pretty well recognized that these "close up cows" need at least 30 inches of bunk space per cow to prevent competition at the bunk. Not enough space means nowhere for the subordinate cows to hide and the end result is a lot of sick cows.

This behavior is not unique to dairy cows; it happens in most domestic livestock. The reason it is such a problem in dairy cows is they are metabolic athletes. The effects seen in dairy cows would be akin to starving a marathon runner before he embarks on multiple marathons on consecutive days. Beef cattle, sheep and goats are much more resilient.

In fact, I see this behavior in our goats every evening when I feed them. I pour their grain in the trough and they knock each other over to be the first at the bunk. Once they line up side by side (they don't have enough bunk space,) the boss goat will growl at her neighbor, then give her a swift head-butt. It's as if she was saying, "Let go of that flat screen or you'll be snorting pepper spray."

December
12-19-17

Our world is a broken world. It seems so often that what's right is wrong and what's wrong is right. Political correctness and group think have supplanted righteousness and common sense. We have a lot to be anxious about.

Even the memorial of the Nativity of our Savior has been altered by commercialism and materialism; we are all very much aware of that fact. "Merry Christmas" is taboo in some circles. As an aside, I find it more than a little ironic that some get bent out of shape when a retail company orders its associates to proclaim, "Happy holidays" instead. Retail shopping, after all, isn't really what this season is about.

But now is the proverbial season of joy. We all want joy, not just during the Christmas season.

Joy can be hard to find in this world, unless we know where to look. My clients, mainly dairy farmers, probably have more reason for sorrow than most. They are in the midst of an economic downturn in the milk, beef and crop market that has lasted for nearly three years, and there is no end in sight. Consumers are demanding that they change the way they do business or get out of it. They work long hours and are constantly at the mercy of the weather.

But many of them have joy, and not just during the season of joy.

Joy is greater than happiness. When I get a Christmas present that I like, it makes me happy. But that soon fades. When I fix a broken cow or deliver a calf successfully, I'm happy. But that also fades as soon as I'm presented with my next challenge.

Joy is much deeper. You can find joy even in unhappy conditions. It seems paradoxical, but joy doesn't need to fade.

Which brings be back to one of the upside down, mixed up, paradoxical natures of our earthly existence. We reflect each Christmas season that the God of the Universe, in perfect humility, was born in a stable to the Virgin Mary in a little town occupied by the mighty Roman Empire a couple of millennia ago in order to make right our broken world.

He is God. He didn't have to do it that way. He could have arrived in a great spectacle. But he was born in a barn, among the animals and the lowly.

And to whom did the Angel of the Lord appear to first announce the Good News? The lofty Pharisees? The powerful Roman Emperor? The rich and privileged? No, it was the shepherds.

The shepherds didn't lead a glamorous life. They were at the bottom rung of the social ladder. They slept in the fields with the sheep. They were dirty and probably stunk like sheep. But the God of the Universe found it appropriate to provide them the joy first.

"Now there were shepherds in that region living in the fields and keeping the night watch over their flock. The angel of the Lord appeared to them and the glory of the Lord shone around them, and they were struck with great fear. The angel said to them, 'Do not be afraid; for behold, I proclaim to you good news of great joy that will be for all the people. For today in the city of David a savior has been born for you who is Messiah and Lord. And this will be a sign for you: you will find an infant wrapped in swaddling clothes and lying in a manger.'" Luke 2:8-12.

That seems upside down and paradoxical to me. A manger is something from which a cow eats. And, believe me, cows are sloppy eaters. But, it brings me joy that a cow may have been one of the first creatures to have taken gaze upon the Baby Jesus. Yes, that probably means more to me than most.

Were you ever asked when you were younger, "Were you born in a barn?" when you left the door open? Well, He was born in a barn. And He's left the door open for any of us that want to enter. If that's not reason for joy, then nothing is. Have a joyful Christmas.

CHAPTER 4
The Culture

Photo by Roger Latuch

The American experience is probably my favorite topic to write about. With our diversity of cultures, opinions, ethnicities and backgrounds, there is always material available. Perhaps I take some liberties and I hope I haven't offended anyone, but it's always fun.

In reality, there is not one American culture, despite what some would wish for. There is a rural culture that is distinct from city culture. There is northern, western and southern culture that are distinct from each other. And there are ethnic cultures that are so distinct that many of us have trouble just getting along.

If I could have a second chance at another profession, I'd consider sociology. Not because I'd ever make a good social worker; indeed, I wouldn't. But what makes people tick within society is fascinating.

I try never to attribute motives to the actions of others because I am not a judge. We will all be judged in the end and that's good enough for me. But when I poke fun at societal quirks like animal rights, transgenderism, social media, Madison Avenue or pot smoking, I do it in the context of society as a whole, not individuals or their motives. We are a complex people and I could never know what's really in someone's head. I probably wouldn't want to anyways. On the contrary, it probably gives the reader a glimpse of what goes on inside my head. Maybe I ought to apologize for that image, but I won't. It is what it is.

We have such a diversity of opinions; no two persons' worldview is exactly the same. And with the growing popularity of social media, many different opinions are on display for anyone in the world to gawk at. Some of these opinions are, frankly, just weird to those of us in rural America. The idea that security is more important than opportunity is foreign to many of us who have an entrepreneurial bent. The fact that so few people have a basic understanding of how our food is grown is scary. And the notion that cows should have more liberties and rights than people is weird, at least to those of us who make our living with cows.

I love the American opportunity and the promise that we can live among whatever culture we so choose. Would it be hard for a city person to uproot his life and move to a small town, remote from the amenities of the big city? I'll try not to generalize, but I would imagine he would feel as awkward as I do every time I go to Chicago. But many city dwellers do eventually relocate to the country in the hopes of a more peaceful existence. And who could blame them?

I would imagine that every one of them are surprised once they get to the country and begin to lay down roots. Rural America has a high level of sophistication, albeit different than one would find at the opera or art museum. I've been to both of them and they are sophisticated, but they're not for me. Rural sophistication involves the appreciation of wide open space, the grandeur of springtime, the harvest in the fall, the complex network of farmers, the infrastructure that allows for the marketing of commodities and the incredible financial risks taken by farmers.

The rural culture takes its share of hits in the media. Farmers are often portrayed as slow witted, toothless, tobacco chewing hayseeds. I doubt many of us take great offense to that, but maybe I'm a little thin-skinned with respect to how farmers are portrayed. It's probably because I know that they are intelligent, hard-working, entrepreneurial, and have sophistication that many don't understand.

Farmers raise their children to carry on their legacy. Some children, once they grow up do follow through, but many others leave the farm. It's probably for the best since life on the farm isn't for everybody. That life has to be in one's blood to endure the risk, the hours, the danger and work. Programs like Future Farmers of America and 4-H, in addition to what farmers teach their children, provide for the continuance of the rural culture. They also deliver a divergent view of how things may exist on other farms.

I wish more people could appreciate the diversity that exists within the profession of farming itself. In every sector, there are multiple ways of raising poultry, livestock and growing crops. What works for one farm might not work for another. Every farmer is an entrepreneur and is charged with determining what works best within the facilities, infrastructure or capital in which he or she has to work. I'm sure it's the same with other endeavors, and that's my point. Farming is essentially at a level of sophistication comparable to a manufacturing business in the rust belt or a technology company in Silicon Valley. The only difference is the product or service offered.

I've made a conscious decision to live in rural America because that's where I feel useful and comfortable. I don't have animus towards other cultures. But when I'm in the country, I am home.

Cow Wisdom
5-26-15

I spend a good portion of my waking hours in the company of cows. It's a good thing I like them. In fact, I've come to learn a few things from cows. Consider it, if you will, barnyard wisdom.

When I was in veterinary school, the clinicians used to impress upon us students the significance of close observation. Animals that can't communicate with us still could give us clues to what ails them by subtle signs. By the same token, healthy cows, if we pay close attention to them, can teach us a lot. A lot about them but also a lot about ourselves.

Be protective of your loved ones. Most cows are instinctually very good mothers. While dairy calves typically are not raised by their mama, beef calves almost always are. The instinct of a mama cow is to protect her baby from predators. If you've ever handled a beef calf in the presence of her mama, you'd appreciate the intensity by which she fulfills her duty. She aims to protect her baby at all costs. She takes nothing for granted. She even suspects the farmer of being a predator at times.

We live in a world full of predators ourselves. There are the literal predators, sure, but there are also subtle, figurative predators. There is the predator on the television that subtly whispers into our children's ear that disordered behavior is not only normal, it's praiseworthy. There's also the predator that seeks to elevate fame and riches above God and family. If we would safeguard our children with the same veracity that a cow protects her calf, we would send the predators running with tails tucked between their proverbial legs.

Get along with others. Cows are social beings. They have a hierarchy and a pecking order. Cows form cliques too. Researchers have actually followed groups of cows around a barn with a camera and discovered that cows have friends, acquaintances and those with whom they don't get along. If a new animal or animals are introduced to the group, the social order has to be reestablished.

To reestablish the order, the boss cow goes around and reasserts her authority by pushing around all the others. She is a bully in the truest sense of the word. She eats when she wants and lays down when she wants. All the other cows avoid her. Nobody likes the boss cow except for the boss cow herself. Such is the case with bullies.

Make meal time a regular occurrence. Cows love to keep a schedule. If a farmer delays feeding the cows by even an hour or so, the cows will let him know by standing at the bunk and bawling. And since cows are social critters, they like to all eat at the same time. And when meal time is over, it is over for just about everybody, with the exception of a few stragglers.

I think it's been pretty well established that meal time in families is important for family closeness and bonding. Unfortunately, we live in a day and age that's busy for everybody and family meals are too often eaten separately or on the run. We would be wise to take this hint from our cloven hooved animals.

Laziness might get you fired. All dairy farms are run on a tight budget. The difference between profitability and red ink can hinge on the productivity of just a few cows. That's why farmers pay attention to the milk production of every cow in the barn. And if a cow is a low producer, i.e. lazy, she just might get fired. A dairy cow that gets fired usually ends up with a different career as a beef cow, a very short lived career if you get my drift.

Now people who are lazy don't get turned into hamburger, fortunately. But I would do nobody any good to suggest that laziness is virtuous. On the contrary, there is great dignity in hard work and doing a good job. Sloth, on the other hand, leads nowhere but to a path of self-destruction. In more than one way, cows remind me of that every day.

The grass is always greener on the other side of the fence. If you drive around the back roads this time of year, you surely can't miss the sight of cows grazing in the pasture. The lush green grass is growing rapidly and providing the cows a welcome reprieve from preserved forage like hay and silage. But if you're observant, you'll see that some cows are never satisfied.

They push the literal boundaries of the pasture. They might stick their big head under the fence to get that bite of grass that's just out of reach. Or they might try to reach over or through the fence. Even though there's still perfectly good grass in the pasture, the cow wants that which she can't have. It sort of reminds me of the strong inclination of a lot of people, myself included.

Despite these lessons, I don't believe cows really are wise. They're sentient beings that are bound by the chains of instinct. Wisdom is certainly not a bovine attribute yet I think we still can learn a thing or two from them. But only if we pay close attention.

Cow Eggs
3-19-13

I had an interesting conversation with my daughter the other evening. I had just received a package in the mail and I was looking over my new purchase as she was doing her homework. Seeing the opportunity to procrastinate, she looked at me holding the shiny object and asked, "What are you holding, daddy?"

I was holding a 1-pound block of solid aluminum that I had just purchased from eBay. By the way, when I looked on eBay to see if any poor desperate souls were trying to pawn off a chunk of aluminum, I didn't really expect to find anything. But I did venture a quick search for the sake of completeness.

What I found shocked me to no end. There were no less than 50 different cuboidal blocks of aluminum and aluminum alloys available for auction or purchase from a myriad of different sellers. In addition, there were also a plethora of various chunks and shapes of aluminum that conceivably has some value to somebody as more than just scrap to recycle. I shouldn't have doubted the effectiveness of a free market economy. But I digress.

When my daughter asked me what I was looking at, I answered, "A chunk of metal."

She didn't come right out and say it, but I reckoned she had that much figured out. Then she asked, "Why?"

I saw the opportunity to have a little fun. Does that make me a bad parent? Anyways, I told her that I bought it to keep my eggs warm. Now, I could just about hear the wheels moving inside her head as she pondered how in the world that hunk of shiny metal would keep eggs warm.

Her mother told her to ask me where my eggs are, and she obliged. "Where are the eggs at, daddy?"

I replied, "Inside the cow." If the incredulous look on her face wasn't enough, then the white smoke that was starting to waft from her mind gave away the fact that I had her completely stumped. I think she was trying to picture how a cow egg might fit under this piece of metal.

Let me explain. I've been working on a project that involves aspirating oocytes, or "eggs" from a cow's ovary. We ship the oocytes overnight to a lab half way across the country to be fertilized and cultured in vitro to become embryos.

Incidentally, the first time I shipped the incubator back to the lab, the nice lady at the FedEx counter asked me what was in the box. I let her know that it was an incubator. Her eyes lit up and she asked, "Are there live animals in there?"

I replied, "Well, kind of."

Then she said, "Are they eggs? What kind of eggs are they?"

I found it odd that she knew I was shipping oocytes to the lab, as this type of technology is really pretty new. When I told her that they were cow eggs, she gave me the same look that my daughter gave me.

The resulting bovine embryos are then returned to me the next week for transfer into recipient animals. This project has been one of trial and error to see what works best. We do know that the eggs are very intolerant of cool temperatures.

To get around this problem of temperature, we have a warming plate that is made of metal with a sensitive thermostat that keeps the metal plate's temperature exactly the same as a cow's body temperature. Any metal block placed on this plate will assume the same temperature within just a few minutes. The metal block I purchased is destined to have multiple holes drilled into it to accommodate the test tubes that will contain the cow eggs so we can keep them happy.

My daughter was apparently not done and came back for one more question. "How will that thing keep your eggs warm?" Seeing an opportunity to give a quick lesson on one of the laws of thermodynamics, I told my daughter that metal is perhaps the best conductor of heat, much more efficient than wood, glass or air, and that the cow eggs needed to be kept nice and warm. It was at this point that she gave up and went back to her homework.

What is Poop?
4-18-17

I am a journeyman. Cyclic, but not always busy. I begin my cycle in the dirt and end in the dirt. I am elemental and fundamental, but never temperamental. As the soil warms, I move. Incorporated into plants, I fulfill my purpose. Some people hate me, but others think enough of me to pay a hefty price to utilize what I can provide. Some are offended by my mere presence. Yes, I can pose a danger if not properly handled, but the circle of life simply cannot continue without me. I am poop, and here is my story.

I come from different places. Sometimes from the majestic cow, sometimes from swine and even from the vast collections of fowl raised for food. I begin as a necessary by-product of eating- livestock can eat a lot. The average dairy cow may produce in excess of a hundred pounds a day. The above average dairy cow produces even more.

Once on the ground, so to speak, I must be stored in bulk, away from the investigating young stock. Yes, I am necessary, but I've been known to carry disease. If not stored far away from the curious livestock, who tend to investigate with their mouth, I might do more harm than good.

Farmers have developed some of the most innovative ways to provide me with boundaries, so I don't become mere runoff. I can be scraped, pushed and pumped into vast storage containers called pits. Some of these are just that- pits in the ground. Some are above ground steel or concrete barriers. These are the most sophisticated. As the winter progresses, solids separate from the liquid fraction in the pit and I must be agitated. At the same time, the neighbors become agitated since the stirring of the pot creates a bit of an odor.

If my entrance into the world by exit from an animal occurs on a bedding pack, I lose my ability to be pushed around. Instead, storage serves two purposes. The bedding soaks up the moisture while allowing firm footing, yet soft accommodations in which the animal can lie and rest. Storage happens without effort, but removal and travel to the field takes considerable effort.

Some farmers have even figured out how to quickly compost me as I provide a comfortable place for the livestock to live. The composted pack must be tilled up twice a day lest it becomes a sloppy mess. Heat produced during the compost evaporates moisture and kills pathogens that pose a danger to the residents.

And I have even been given credit for saving the planet. Some larger farms have installed storage systems that can harvest the methane released as I wait for the spring and fall removal cycle. The methane fuels powerful generators providing heat and electricity for the farm, homes and businesses nearby. All that's left is a fluffy, semi-moist, nutrient rich powder that can be applied to fields at the farmer's convenience.

After I have been accumulated enough to fill a wagon, a tank or even the large pit, my true purpose begins. I am taken from storage and sent to work in the fields. This is sometimes where I offend people, but only because my intentions are misinterpreted. Indeed, it stinks sometimes. But the volatile funk that accompanies me is transient. If there is a south wind and you live north of a cornfield in the spring, I offer my sincerest apologies. But in the fall when the cornfield is thick with ears providing a bounty for the livestock, I will have done my job. No gratuity is necessary.

You see, there simply is no other option. I provide nitrogen, phosphorus, potassium and other building blocks for the growing plant. What else could I do but be used to fuel the crop that will become the feed for next year's herd? Besides the minerals, I contain organic matter. The cellulose and other carbon containing compounds will enrich the soil, allowing it to retain more moisture to feed the growing plant. I'm not taking credit for the rain, don't misunderstand. But the spring rain would not be as effective without me.

The smell of spring is in the air right now, but you already knew that if you live next to a crop field. As the spring season progresses, I become part of the crop. Elements like nitrogen, potassium, phosphorus, calcium, magnesium and chloride help the plants grow strong. I don't do all of the work myself, mind you; synthetic fertilizers supplement what I can't provide. But I do the heavy lifting.

I am a reality. I am necessary. I am poop.

Dairy Princess
4-30-13

I had the privilege to attend the coronation of the 2013-2014 Somerset County Dairy Princess last week. For those unfamiliar with the Dairy Princess, I'll briefly explain. Every year, a new county Dairy Princess is selected to promote the value of consuming dairy products. She is a young lady commissioned to visit public events and schools in order to educate and answer questions about dairy foods and the farms that produce them. It is, by and large, a volunteer effort on the part of the Princess, however, a small stipend is provided.

Many counties in Pennsylvania have a Dairy Princess and she works diligently to promote dairy foods. The coronation of the incoming Dairy Princess is done with much fanfare and with many dairy farmers in attendance. You see, she will be their representative to the community for the next year.

I got to thinking about the Dairy Princess program after the festivities were over and its implications on the lives of the dairy farmer. It is part of a larger marketing program, advertising, if you will, that is undertaken by the farmers themselves- like they don't already have enough to do.

The Dairy Princess program is operated with funding, in part, by the sometimes controversial dairy check off program. While an exact dollar figure to market dairy cannot really be quantified, I'm going to take a stab at it.

The dairy check off program is funded by withholding a portion of what is paid to dairy farmers for their milk. These proceeds then go to promote dairy products. (The popular "Got Milk?" campaign was a result of this program.) This check off program is loosely analogous to the leviathan that is Coca Cola's marketing budget of $2.9 billion in 2010.

Economists marvel at the success of Coca Cola and the magnitude of its advertising budget. About 40 percent of all soda sold in the United States is produced by Coca Cola, which isn't too shabby. Anyone who has read my column with any regularity knows that I like to dig deep into the numbers, so let's take a look.

The dairy check off program was good for about $196 million dollars in 2011, according to its own website. Also in 2011, according to USDA statistics, Americans consumed around 21 billion (based on 604 pounds per capita consumption) gallons of milk in one form or another (fluid, cheese, ice cream, etc.) So how much money is spent to market one gallon of milk? Not quite one cent per gallon.

Americans consume, on the other hand, around 50 gallons of soda per person per year, depending on who you read. Coca Cola has about 40 percent market share of that which is about 20 gallons per person per year (that's 6 billion gallons of Coca Cola total.) So how much money is spent to market one gallon? About 48 cents is spent per gallon of Coca Cola. Coca Cola out spends the dairy industry by about 50 to 1.

So, as the new county Dairy Princesses assume their reign, we probably shouldn't let them know that the odds are stacked against them. We have complete confidence, however, that they are up to the task because, first, dairy products are superior to soda. Second, they have hard working farm families to back them up. And finally, Coca Cola might have a huge budget, but we have a princess.

Nostalgia
7-19-16

There are days when I become nostalgic about the past. I can't help it. I was younger, fitter and had more hair where I was supposed to and less where it doesn't belong. I feel nostalgia for the days before the aches and pains arrived resulting from the daily grind. I miss the time when there were enough hours in the day that I could actually get caught up on my work.

I guess it's OK to feel a sense of nostalgia for a time less complicated. We all do it as we age; I'd like to think. I've been party to many conversations where the topic of the recent past has come up like the worry about a lack of family friendly programming on the television or the coarsening of the culture.

But I'm starting to wonder if dwelling on the past just might be a crippling quality. Change happens whether we want to be a part of it or not. Sometimes the change is for the worse, but often it is for the better.

I suppose the culture may be coarsening. And watching television with my children indeed can result in some awkward moments, like when the commercial for the little blue pill comes on. "Daddy, what is E.D.?"

My parents, I'm sure, felt the same way whenever we would watch such family friendly programming as "Three's Company" or "Seinfeld." Is the culture really coarsening or the is coarseness just on brighter display since the advent of social media? I, personally, miss the days before social media.

At any rate, we can't control the culture. We can only keep it from controlling us.

There was a time, however, when the agricultural community was a lot simpler as well. Farmers planted the crops and raised the livestock without much hassle. The work was hard and the days were long, but there wasn't much hassle. Eventually, though, things got complicated. New technology continues to emerge that makes life easier for farmers, but scares consumers.

The irony is that new technologies like the much maligned genetically modified organism (GMO) makes life easier for consumers as well. By making it easier to raise crops with fewer inputs, consumers don't have to spend as much on food. One of the reasons we enjoy the standard of living we do in this country is because of the availability of plentiful, affordable and wholesome food.

But I'm not sure the standard of living of many of America's farmers has kept pace. Don't misunderstand me; this isn't a call to action to provide price supports for farmers or meddle in the market in any way. It is what it is. But farming does get more and more complicated as time goes on.

Innovative farmers are constantly looking for ways to become more efficient and reduce toil. They are looking for ways to work smarter and not as hard. Don't confuse the desire to reduce toil for laziness. We all wish to reduce toil. The vacuum cleaner was invented to eliminate the need to hang the carpet on a line and beat it with a stick. It is still work to vacuum the carpet but less work than beating it with a stick. This desire to reduce toil has resulted in the ever changing landscape of agriculture.

Should we long for the good old days or embrace the present? I don't really know. My answer probably depends on the day you ask me.

The question on the minds of many dairy farms is whether to go the non-GMO route or not. Like the manufactured controversy over treating cows with growth hormone that raged 10 years ago, GMO feeds fed to dairy cattle are rapidly becoming the new scapegoat. As soon as the first company claims the moral high ground that their milk is produced without GMO feeds, other companies feel obligated to follow suit.

I miss the days before "sustainable agriculture" became a buzzword for an anti-technology agenda. Sustainable agriculture has always meant to me that we could sustain a population of people on this planet by continuing to increase food production.

I fear that once consumers realize how much additional pesticides will be needed once GMO feed is taboo, they will wax nostalgic for genetically modified crops. Once no-till practices are impossible because GMO is no longer an option, we will be nostalgic for the topsoil that washed down the river. And eventually, as the price of food goes up because yields are cut, many will feel a sense of nostalgia for the good old days.

Transspecies
4-28-15

Our American culture is not what it used to be. I've all but dropped out of the culture but it seems that whenever I do tune in, the topic of transgender seems to always come up. I don't remember it being like this a generation ago.

But I was watching the news recently and a family and their 4-year-old transgender daughter, now son, were profiled in a story. It reminded me of something bizarre I witnessed in a barn recently.

A farmer and I were making the rounds through his barn full of dairy cows. I was doing the typical pregnancy checks with my ultrasound when I heard a very distinct and loud "OINKKKKKK, OINKKKKK!" coming from the other end of the barn. This particular farmer's son is a very accomplished breeder of pigs and so it's typical for there to be some pigs in his barn. Call it diversification, if you will. I just figured his sow (a sow is a mature female pig) was upset about something and was venting some frustration.

But it was strange that this oinking sound originated from an area of the barn that does not usually contain his pigs. But I barely gave it another thought and moved onto the next pregnancy check.

As we progressed through the herd, we eventually passed by the area from which the loud and distinct oinking originated. My vision was mostly obscured by my ultrasound goggles so I didn't take notice of the noisy pig. But out of the blue once again, "OINKKKKKK, OINKKKKK, OINKKKKK!" I looked up to catch a glimpse of the frustrated sow and was absolutely shocked at what I saw. The poor critter was very confused about its identity. It was actually a cow that was squealing like a pig!

When I say it was a cow, I mean that literally. She had four feet, four teats and weighed about 1,400 pounds. It was not a pig with black and white paint; she was 100 percent cow, except, that is, for her lack of "moo."

I've seen a lot of strange things in my veterinary career and this was one of the strangest. Without saying a word, I looked at the farmer with an obviously puzzled look on my face. He confided in me that my reaction was typical. His hired man thinks that this cow may have recently eaten a pig and this was the result; it was a pig trapped in a cow's body. I don't think that to be the case literally; I just think that she has a species identity issue.

I suspect that if this farmer ever let her out of the barn, she might wander off and find someplace to wallow. She might even root up the pasture. And if she ever gets pregnant again, I'm afraid she might have a litter of calves. That will be a mess unless we intervene.

I know there are a lot of medical doctors and psychologists, none around here I'm sure, which capitalize on, I mean, treat gender identity confusion in people. I'm starting to think that there could be a market for veterinarians to take advantage of this burgeoning species identity confusion as well. Seriously, I think we could actually surgically transform a 1,400 pound cow into a 1,400 pig. Do you know how much bacon that would be? I'll be rich!

But, of course, it's not about me. It's about these poor, confused species. I'm pretty sure that we could perfect the transformation with a little bit of practice. To complete the conversion would likely take a few years. It should start with some porcine origin hormone therapy. Don't worry, that's really nothing new. Diabetic people for years used porcine origin insulin, a hormone, to control their blood sugar. Until, that is, the superior human insulin could be manufactured through genetic modification.

After the hormone therapy has done its job, we can intervene surgically. I can shape the cow's muzzle into a snout. Then we could we could transform her udder with four teats into something any pig would be proud of, at least 10 more teats. The series of operations would conclude with a reticulumectomy. That's a fancy doctor word for removing the part of the cow's stomach that is responsible for cud chewing. No self-respecting pig should have to chew its cud.

I'm sure there will be some resistance to my idea at first. In fact, I wouldn't be a bit surprised if I got some hate mail over it. But in a generation, I could see this idea of trans-species being acceptable to most progressive farmers. And in time, it will be no more absurd than encouraging your four year old to become transgender.

Security
4-11-17

Centuries ago, the bovine was domesticated by early humans. I was taught in high school that the relationship between man and this beast is considered mutually beneficial. Man benefits from the food, fiber and draft provided by the bovine while the bovine benefits from the security that man provides. It's hard to know how that relationship came about for sure, but one can speculate.

Before cattle became domesticated, we can assume they roamed the vast plains and grasslands in search of food. Cattle were free to migrate at leisure, eat what was available and reproduce on their own terms. Shelter wasn't a concern since migration took them to where the climate was tolerable.

While they were free, it was hardly a bovine utopia. Migration took effort. In times of drought, there may have been starvation, limiting the size of the herds. There were predators that shadowed them, harassed them and eliminated the weak from the herd.

On the other hand, in addition to the wolf, saber tooth tiger and the lion, man played the part of predator. Early tribes conceivably followed herds of primitive cattle as they roamed in search of fresh forage.

One day, some innovative person must have considered that it would be good to have some control of the situation and stop this roaming. From the perspective of the cattle, they must have looked forward to some security as well. The migrations, after all, took them sometimes to where there was drought. The lifestyle was inconsistent, at best. But if man and beast could enter into a mutually beneficial arrangement, they could rest a bit and even make merry occasionally.

And so it happened. Man tamed a few of the wild cattle and a partnership was forged. The cattle must have been tickled to get some help with their pesky wolf problem. Man had a vested interest in defending the cattle since every one that a wolf gets is one less for the tribe.

Granted the cattle weren't thrilled about the whole "slaughter" thing, but it was easier than dying at the jaws of a hungry pack of wolves. Heck, the wolves don't even wait for them to die before chowing down. At least with the humans, death was quick and, relative to the wolves, painless.

Over time, the security had to become tighter, though. The cunning wolves had adapted and man didn't want to be on watch all the time. So, the fence was built. The fence was originally sold as a means to keep the predators out. But what the domesticated cattle found out soon enough was that it also acted to keep them in. Eventually the cattle accepted it as a necessary part of life and went about their grazing.

The fence had another unforeseen consequence. It was so effective in keeping the predators out that the cattle population soared. Grazing land was at a premium and the cattle clamored for forage. Man had to devise a way to feed the hungry cattle, so they baled hay, stockpiled grain and ensiled forage. This made the cattle happy- and also fat.

But soon the cattle needed some kind of shelter since the fence prevented them from escaping the difficult weather. Also, since the cows were eating so much now, the inevitable byproduct (manure) littered the ground making conditions difficult. In the interest of the environment, the farmer convinced the cattle to accept this new housing.

Large complexes of barns arose. But now, different groups of cattle like feeders and springers needed to get from one barn to another so mass transportation in the form of trucking was developed. This hastened the practice of grouping cattle based on their productivity.

Not long after, cattle started becoming sick from disease. All of this comingling and stress allowed infections to devastate the herd. The cattle were in need of medicine and the farmer heard their call. Farmers provided the medicine for the cattle at the farmer's own expense. The cattle, for their part, didn't really have much say in it. They, after all, couldn't pick their own veterinarian since they don't have opposable thumbs with which to dial a phone. Instead, they relied on the farmer for their health care. Many cows still got sick.

As the relationship between man and the farmer evolved, the farmer saw that some cows were way more productive than others. Some bulls when bred to cows produced calves that were very productive. Other bull's calves, however, were not so productive. So, the farmer saw it necessary to sterilize the bulls that were, let's say, at the wrong end of the bell curve. Only the best bulls were permitted to propagate.

Eventually, the farmer learned that some cows produced inferior calves even when mated to the best bulls. These cows weren't allowed to have calves of their own either. Instead, they would be surrogate mothers for the most productive cows. And once the farmer saw the genetic code of cattle decoded, that decision could be made much earlier in the cow's life. A farmer could just take a saliva sample from a calf and get information on genetic diseases, likes and dislikes and even ancestry of the calf. It was like they finally had total control.

Wow, it's a scary time to be a cow. At least they have security...

Face-Snap
6-20-17

I readily admit that I'm naïve when it comes to the universe of social media. I was taken to school by a veterinary student recently about the vast expanse of social media. I was amazed like a city dweller would be when he sees the country sky at midnight. I just don't ever see much of it, social media that is, but I still believe the night sky is more beautiful.

Our family hosted an exchange student this year and he left for home last week. Indeed, it was a quiet ride home from the airport that day. Not wanting to say goodbye to him forever, my son asked several weeks ago if he could get one of those social media apps for his phone. I understand that social media has replaced traditional text messages where he lives, so I relented.

At the airport, I concluded that I didn't want to say goodbye to him forever either, so I asked my son where I could get that face-snap application, or whatever it's called. He looked at me like I was out of touch, then quickly found it for me on my phone.

I opened it up trying to find both my son's page and our departing guest's as well, with no success. I had to ask for help yet again. At the speed of a megabit, both profiles were attached to my phone. Now I can keep in touch with him through this snap-book app, or whatever it's called.

When we got home that evening, I was playing around with the app, mainly out of morbid curiosity. I found a lot of stuff that I wasn't expecting, like its ability to download my address book and names of my friends, family, colleagues and clients who also have face-chat on their device, or whatever it's called.

I clicked on all the names I recognized, which wasn't all of them since many have handles that I've never been introduced to. Within seconds, I got replies from a half dozen or so friends that linked to my device. Maybe this face-snap thing isn't all that bad, or whatever it's called.

I also got replies from colleagues with whom I am acquainted because of their professional work that I've never actually met. I know that many professionals utilize these social media platforms as a means to market their practice. Even our practice has a Facebook page, but I certainly don't know how to navigate it.

But this snap-chat thing, or whatever it's called, is kind of like a quickie, Facebook-lite. You take pictures, or video, and post them to your profile. People linked to your page can view them, for a short time and only once, then they're gone. If you're under 25, I'm not telling you anything you don't already know; if it's even accurate.

But I contemplated for a moment after my epiphany. What a great opportunity to post pictures of my day, with full consent of the client, of course. If I'm delivering a calf, my friends can watch. And if I mess something up, they can't replay it. It's perfect.

I can have the farmer hold the camera phone while I'm saving an animal's life during surgery. I'd hold it myself, but I should remain sterile and I need both hands to tie a knot. If the bleeding rages out of control, it can't be used against me in a court of law. Sign me up.

My daughter, who is still forbidden to play with social media, taught me how to alter the pictures. I don't know how she knows, but apparently you can alter your appearance with the app by putting on a mustache or shrinking your face. Apparently, this can't be done on cows as far as I know. That's a bummer.

The veterinary student that introduced me to this says there are famous veterinarians who became famous through social media. I don't know any of them. On second thought, maybe I don't want any of that. My wife thinks I'm already over exposed.

I remember when I was a child; the teacher told us that one day we would have the ability to make phone calls where we could see the person to whom we're speaking on a television screen. It was almost prophetic. I wonder if she knew the extent to which this technology would invade our lives. And if you know how to work this chat-book thing, I'm there now. Or whatever it's called.

Uncle Sam
10-13-15

Sam began as a farmer. He maintained a herd of dairy cows and beef cows, chickens and a few pigs. He took great pride in the diversification of his operation, but he was most especially proud of his dairy herd as they were the backbone of his farming venture. Without the productivity of the dairy cows and the income they generated, the rest of his farm could not exist.

Sam did right by his dairy cows and they did right by him. In fact, he was more of an uncle to the cows than a farmer. He maintained their infrastructure well with the income generated by their productivity. They had everything they needed to be productive. Sam treated his dairy cows like they were very important because they were.

And the dairy cows consistently returned the favor. His dairy cows were productive as long as Sam left them do what dairy cows do best, make milk. It is in her nature for the dairy cow to make milk and a lot of it. Of course, some cows were more productive than others, but that was natural too. Nobody expected all cows to be equal in either potential ability or actual production; not even Sam.

Now it should be made known that dairy cows can only be as productive as their feed allows them to be. Some farms have excellent feed quality and allow their cows access to as much feed as they care to eat all of the time. It's like a 24-hour buffet. Some even feed the most productive cows extra goodies to ensure they maintain their milk production. Think of it as incentive if you wish, but it works every time it's tried.

Sam's best and most productive cows were always fed the highest quality feed that he was able to produce. And Sam made sure that the highest producers had access to whatever they needed to be productive. All farmers know that if they withhold feed, the productivity of their livestock drops precipitously.

But at one point at the urging of other interests on the farm, namely the chickens, pigs and the beef cows, Sam thought it would be best to interfere in the dairy cows' business of making milk. The other interests saw how the dairy cows were rewarded for their production and they complained.

At first, since the cows ate the most feed, Sam fed all cows less than what they had been getting before the complaints came in. The dairy cows responded as one would expect; the highest milk producers just couldn't keep up with their strong pace while eating less feed. The highest producing cows began to suffer, lose weight and productivity.

Some of the cows rebelled and tried to maintain their feed intake by refusing to give up what they needed to maintain production. At the urging of the other interests again, Sam hired a firm and gave them authority to enforce his new feeding program. They went by the name of the Intake Regulation Society.

But the other interests weren't satisfied yet since the dairy cows were still getting much more feed than the other animals. Their persistent complaining eventually convinced Sam to have the Intake Regulation Society place rules on the dairy cows. They could only work when the pigs did, which was only a few hours a day. They could only enter the milking parlor as often as the beef cows did, which was only once a day instead of the 2 or 3 times a day to which they had become accustomed. And the chickens, well, the chickens were given free access to the dairy cow's feed any time they wanted.

Sam's farm started to lose money, but he didn't know why. He knew the dairy cow's milk production was starting to slip, so he undertook an ambitious borrowing venture that he thought would improve cash flow. Sam figured that after his cows had produced several more generations of calves, his farm would be able to pay the money back. He wasn't overly concerned about the debt anyways because he reckoned he'd be long dead before the bill was due. His heirs could take care of it.

But the more money he borrowed, the more money the pigs wanted to produce their pork. The chickens, even though they aren't the smartest of God's creatures, knew the accounting didn't make any sense. They were still afraid, however, to speak up. The dairy cows, meanwhile, tried their best to be productive despite the other interests raiding their feed.

Sam began to panic when the cash flow situation worsened. He dug deep into the numbers and saw that the dairy cows, even though they only made up 20 percent of the farm's livestock, still ate 80 percent of the feed. Sam figured this disparity was the reason for the farm's decline. He did what the loudest of the other interests prodded him to do; he took more feed away from the dairy cows and gave it to the other interests. The other interests just didn't think it was fair.

Eventually, the dairy cows just couldn't go on any more. It's not that they didn't want to; they wanted desperately to be productive again. But they couldn't both follow the rules set forth by the Intake Regulation Society and also maintain their productivity on the same amount of feed meant for a chicken. Seeing that the dairy cows were no longer producing milk, Sam forced them to change careers and become beef cows. And with that, Sam's farm ceased to exist.

Medical Marijuana
12-12-17

A movement has been afoot for a decade or so to legalize marijuana. Some states have already shunned federal authority and decriminalized the weed at the state level. Others will surely follow.

The Associated Press has reported that even my own profession has joined the chorus of those seeking to legitimize pot. The claim is that animals can benefit, too, from medicinal properties of pot.

I, personally, don't know about this. I am not, and have never been, a pot smoker. And I'm not convinced that it is good medicine.

There is a slight problem with the premise that marijuana has medicinal properties in animals, though. There is no research to support it.

There is no research because the federal government classifies marijuana as a schedule 1 controlled substance. A schedule 1 controlled substance is the highest classification of control that the federal government can place on a drug under the Controlled Substance Act of 1970. A schedule 1 drug may not be used for any purpose, even research. And since federal authority supersedes state authority, marijuana is actually still illegal in all 50 states. Since there has been no research on medicinal pot, there is no research to support its use.

Some in my profession, and others, seek the reclassification of marijuana from schedule 1 status. This would open the door to legitimate research on the drug for the benefit of domestic animals.

But my clients, I'd reckon, might anticipate a benefit from this. Where do I start?

To begin with, some beef cows can be a bit squirrelly at times, especially just after they deliver a calf. Maternal instinct kicks in and they get quite protective of their 80-pound mooing bundle of joy. A little bit of relaxing Amnesia Haze variety could make her just a bit easier to handle to process the calf.

And dairy cows can be touchy as well, also around the time they deliver their calf. The first-time mother, especially, can be just a little nervous upon her first visit to the milking parlor. A hit or two of the Lavender variety can calm her down just enough to convince her that the milking unit really can't suck an entire cow into the bulk milk tank.

One of the largest bottlenecks in terms of profitability on a dairy farm is the breeding program. Cows only breed in a short window during a three-week cycle and if the farmer doesn't know when she is fertile, she will miss the opportunity to become pregnant to artificial insemination. But a drag of the Barry White variety can put that twinkle in her eye so the farmer knows to call the artificial breeder.

And, most certainly, farmers encourage their cows to eat more since the more she eats, the more milk she makes. I think there is where the real potential lies. Farmers can lace the ration with a pound or two of pot to encourage the munchies; any variety should suffice. Their cows will make so much milk that they won't be able to store it all.

But I can foresee some complications too.

It will be difficult to teach the cow how to hold a marijuana cigarette with her hooves. And cattle have limited lung capacity as it is. Too much smoke and she could get a case of pneumonia that could land her on the back 40. Obviously, smoking in a barn would be a disaster waiting to happen since there is a lot of dry hay stored.

Besides, what farmer would want to go to the barn every morning and have to listen to the sound of The Grateful Dead blasting from the speakers? And perhaps the worst complication could happen if the cows see a Doritos truck driving down the road by the farm. It could result in an all-out stampede.

But if the farmer can manage these side effects, it could very well be the difference between a profitable year and a losing year. Farmers, after all, are in a tight spot right now. Prices for nearly all farm commodities are pretty low and many are having trouble making ends meet.

Fluid milk consumption continues to decline and some think farmers need a sound marketing plan to boost the sale of milk. I, for one, think that there is opportunity here.

What self-respecting hippie wouldn't go for bowl of Ben and Jerry's ice cream made of milk from cows fed a little bit of weed? The psychoactive compound in marijuana would surely be passed on in the milk. They could even market new varieties of ice cream like Purple Haze or Animal Cookies and Cream.

And when the research shows that medicinal pot has no benefit in cows, who better to supply the cash crop to Colorado than the American farmer?

Five Freedoms
3-29-16

We hear a lot of discussion about freedom today in the context of politics. One politician wants to take away our freedom to bear arms while another wants to safeguard our freedom of speech. Politicians like to talk about freedom.

Conservative politicians are especially fond of the topic of freedom. Liberal politicians, on the other hand, prefer to solve society's ills through government intervention, paying less attention to freedom itself.

I am not a liberal, but I'd like to take a moment to suggest that, as a society, we take up the mantle of providing freedom for our neighbor. These freedoms might not be what you think. There are five of them that should be considered.

Freedom from hunger and thirst. As it stands today, there is no true safeguard against hunger and thirst. All people need to eat, and in a country with abundance like ours, we should see that all are free from the bane of hunger and thirst.

Freedom from discomfort. As a compassionate people, we should all cringe at the thought of our fellow citizens living in discomfort. Whether it be temperature or accommodations, people should have the ability to live in comfort.

Freedom from pain, injury or disease. Indeed, people should enjoy freedom from pain, injury or disease in a country with a health care system as advanced as ours. There are ample medicines and technology to accomplish this goal; all that is needed is the will.

Freedom to express normal behavior. Well, this one could get a little controversial, depending on what the definition of normal is. But we should be free to act in such a way that we are at ease. Normal behavior for me is to get up early for work every day and express my opinions once a week in print. That might not be normal behavior for another, so let's just leave it up to the individual to express him or herself as he or she sees fit.

Freedom from fear and distress. All people should be allowed to live free from fear and distress. We should be free from fear of violence, terrorism or crime. And distress should never encroach on any of our citizens for whatever reason.

Do these seem like lofty goals? Do they seem utopian or do they seem like a parody? Well, I am not the first to propose them. They have been well known and discussed in some circles for some time, but they aren't really intended to apply to people. You see, they are the Five Freedoms of Animal Welfare as first described in 1965.

Even the most liberal of politicians have never proposed a welfare state as comprehensive as this for mere humans. But for our furry friends, it has already been proposed and cited regularly in animal rights circles.

But to take it a step further, these freedoms weren't intended for our pets but for livestock. They were developed for and continue to be cited today as standards for livestock.

Now at first glance it might seem reasonable to keep farm animals free from hunger. But there are times when it is good for animals, particularly dairy cows, to be a little bit hungry. If left to her own devices, a dairy cow would eat until she becomes fat. A fat dairy cow ends up as a sick dairy cow. Preventing freedom from hunger could cause pain and disease.

And I'm not quite sure how to ensure freedom from discomfort. Most cattle become uncomfortable anytime a person is within five-feet of them. Freedom from pain, injury and disease is simply an impossible standard to aspire. While I like to think that I'm a pretty good veterinarian and our practice does a fine job, there are still patients of ours that experience pain, especially after a surgery to save the animal's life.

And if we were to allow cattle to express normal behavior, like using their horns to fight, it would certainly violate the third freedom again. And freedom from fear is impossible since livestock instinctually fear humans.

Keeping livestock healthy and comfortable are primary goals of every legitimate farmer because unhealthy and uncomfortable livestock are simply unproductive. The stated goal of the animal rights movement isn't to make livestock comfortable or keep them healthy, however, it is to eliminate meat consumption by humans.

The Five Freedoms is neither a Utopian pipe dream for communal life nor is it a realistic goal for raising livestock. Besides a means to frustrate livestock owners, I'm not sure what it is.

Political Party for Cows
1-19-16

I am a casual follower of politics, although in previous days I took it more seriously than I do today. The presidential race, however, is inescapable. I don't dwell on it, though, because I'd rather not invest emotional energy in something that rarely changes. It seems that many politicians care more about their own power than the citizens they govern. Not all of them, but many.

That editorial comment aside, I was asked recently if cows had political views, where would they stand? My answer was, "It depends on the cow."

First, there are the conservative cows who believe in limited control by the farmer. They can be ambitious, yes, but are content to go outside and forage for themselves. These cows have a strong independent streak and are upset at the very mention of change. They are rule followers by nature; law and order types if you will. If a cow in the barn gets out of line, they demand swift justice, like a visit to the electric fence or week in the pen.

They tend to work a lot but believe they pay too much in taxes. Conservative cows believe in traditional roles and eschew progressive farming practices, like group raising of calves and artificial insemination. They support Ted Cruz for president.

But on the other end of the spectrum are the liberal cows. With these girls, the very boundaries of society are called into question. They like to experiment with social mores and have fun, a little too much fun, at times. They have been known to go on a several day grain binge and pay the price afterward. The liberal cows believe in strong intervention by the farmer, like the stockpiling of feed now and worrying about the consequences later. They even will go as far as to "tax" the feed of the rich cows and distribute that feed to the cows that have little.

Liberal cows band together to form unions with other cows to stymie the farmers into giving more perks and benefits, like a longer dry period or more grain at feeding time. These cows support Hilary Clinton for president.

But not all cows fall into these traditional categories. There are some cows with populist tendencies. These cows reject the notion that riches result from achievement. Instead, they view the rich cows (cows with deep pedigrees or impressive milking records) as sinister. They feel slighted and call for the rich cows to take care of the others.

These cows are usually the ones protesting near the milking parlor. The disruption garners them attention from the farmer and other cows who may be sympathetic to their cause. These cows would probably support Martin O'Malley for president, if they had ever heard of him.

There are also the pragmatist cows. They believe that getting things done is the ultimate goal. It doesn't matter what gets done, as long as something gets done and everybody can get along. They support John Kasich for president.

And then, there are the socialist cows. The farmer really has to keep his eyes on these girls, as they tend to cause the most trouble. They think that the farm doesn't belong to the farmer, but the cows. Socialist cows promote the idea that the worker cows should rise up and seize the farm and all of its assets from the capitalist pig farmer. Well, not the pig farmer but… you know what I mean. The inequality is just more than they can bear. The socialist cows support Bernie Sanders, obviously, for president.

I can't neglect to mention the establishment cows. They are the ones who think that the well-oiled machine is clicking along just fine, even though the clicking noise actually means the machine is running out of oil. These girls support Jeb Bush for president.

And not to be overlooked are the agitator cows. These cows, usually

Jerseys, will do anything for attention, even if it means offending the Holsteins, Ayrshire and Brown Swiss cows. They overlook any faults of their favorite candidate, as long as he continues to tickle their ears.

These cows want to live in closed herds where no other cows are introduced that might be contagious and cause disease. They support their candidate no matter what, as long as he continues to throw bombs at the establishment. As if there was any doubt, they support Donald Trump for president.

Thank goodness cows can't vote.

Politically Incorrect
8-4-15

Sticks and stones may break your bones, but words will cause irreversible emotional harm. So much harm, in fact, that there is great justified outrage whenever a person in the public eye mutters something that may be offensive. This outrage has made many people carefully consider their next sentence lest he or she incur the wrath of the nation, even the world.

Universities, corporations and government bodies have strict rules about making offensive remarks and violations often result in the offender being ostracized. It's unfortunate, but rarely do we see the same indignation when somebody makes an offensive statement about cows. The time for inclusion is now and I've compiled a list with which to start.

I recognize that there will undoubtedly be more remarks in the future and we can expand upon it according to the whims of social media trends. Punishment for uttering these offensive phrases could include having to eat only salad and tofu for a week or the dreaded 20 wags of a finger from smart people.

"Milk it for all its worth." Obviously, if I were a cow (and I'm not this time) I would take great offense at this. Milk isn't worth much right now, as evidenced by dairy farmers' paychecks. Whatever it is, it's probably worth more than milk.

We should refrain from referring to anyone as a "bull in a china shop." Just because a bull is big and sometimes in a nasty mood doesn't make him bad. We should be more compassionate toward the lumbering beast wandering among the fragile dishes and saucers. He really doesn't mean any harm. I'm sure he would say he was sorry of he could talk.

We also ought to be careful about mentioning anything about "the cows coming home". If the cows left, especially on a stock trailer, chances are they aren't coming home… ever. Do you know why they aren't coming home? I don't even want to mention it. And this is especially scary to the cows that do leave on a stock trailer on their way to the prestigious cow shows. They must surely think the worst. No, there's never a need to use that phrase.

I've also heard some inarticulate people telling others not to "have a cow." This is offensive in so many ways. What's wrong with the cow and why should we not want to have one? Since having a cow is derogatory toward the cow, the use of this phrase should be stopped immediately.

If another person is asked if he or she was "raised in a barn," the wrath of the twitterverse should rain down like fire and brimstone. Many fine cattle have been raised in barns, including the ones that made the milk you had on your cereal this morning. Since when did a barn become a bad thing?

"The grass is always greener on the other side." Yes, I recognize that it isn't necessarily specific to bovines but, let's be honest. We all know what it means. Those cows on the other side of the fence without access to the finest grass must surely want the best also. We should just quit reminding that the best is out of their reach.

And finally, we have to stop using the phrases "holy cow" and "sacred cow." This is most offensive to those who don't believe there is anything holy or sacred. There is, remember, separation of church and speech. We must not mention it or we risk offending those with nothing to believe in.

I'm sure there are some slick agenda driven people out there that would milk this politically correct paradigm for all its worth. They truly are as destructive as a bull in a china shop. I'm sure we'll be fighting this battle until the cows come home. We all know that the grass is always greener for the sacred cow. And don't have a cow, man; I wasn't raised in a barn. I'm able to use these phrases only because I'm in tight with those of the bovine persuasion.

CHAPTER 5
The Outdoors

I used to be an avid hunter and fisherman. I am still an enthusiastic hunter and love to fish; I just don't take the time to enjoy them as often as I might like. But on occasion, I took the opportunity to write about the subject. It's a natural fit as many of our clients are also avid outdoorsmen, and women. I asked one client while on his farm how he had done in deer season. He confided in me that he didn't hunt since he was too lazy to hunt and not lazy enough to fish. Being a dairy farmer, I knew he wasn't too lazy to hunt but was probably just too busy for both.

Many of the farmers we serve are very serious hunters. They get up extra early to have a chance to bag the big buck during deer season. Many of them even bow hunt, which requires even more time and dedication. But they always wait until the chores are done to sneak a few moments in the woods.

As we get older, our responsibilities increase and usually the first thing to get replaced is the time in the tree stand. Work is substituted for a stint in the woods. Priorities trump the pursuit of a trophy. Even so, I doubt anything could ever replace the hope of a deer hunter.

Parallels
11-5-13

I am an avid bow hunter. I thoroughly enjoy all things that have to do with bow hunting. And right now, as my fingers crank out these words on the computer, the much anticipated rut is underway. This column that appears weekly in this newspaper, unfortunately, has nothing to do with bow hunting. But maybe, just maybe, I can make this work.

Now before anybody jumps to any false conclusions, I am not looking to take over Tim Resh's slot. On the contrary, I am not much of a mountain man. And I'd have a better chance of hitting a deer with a flintlock if I threw the gun at it than to try and shoot it. But I really enjoy hunting with the bow.

I've actually been bow hunting longer than I've been doctoring cows, so I'm hereby claiming to have some kind of credibility in the realm of the bow and arrow. In fact, the sport of bow hunting has sort of made me the cow veterinarian that I am today. Let me explain.

I've learned many life lessons in the countless hours I've spent in the woods in the pursuit of brown furry critters. Here are just a few.

Practice makes perfect. Admittedly, I don't practice enough. So, my mantra is practice makes better. A bow hunter can't expect to kill a deer with an arrow from 25 yards away unless he practices repeatedly, and repeatedly and even some more. The same is true with the practice of my profession. Some think that we "practice" our profession because we never achieve perfection.

Patience is a virtue. Even the most successful bow hunter doesn't expect to bag a deer every time out. Like bow bunting, surgery and other technical procedures take time to master. It is frustrating to a veterinary student or a new graduate when the degree of difficulty of the procedure he or she is trying to master is exceeded only by the lofty expectations of the one in the process of learning. We see this in many of the students that rotate through our practice. But patience and persistence will serve both the bow hunter and the veterinarian well.

Nobody likes homework, but those that finish it will be rewarded. Leading up to the season, the serious bow hunter will do his homework in the woods. He will take the time to study the trail camera pictures and spend time in the woods looking for good stand locations. The veterinarian will also spend time doing homework, even after the last final exam has been passed. Journal articles, continuing education meetings and conversations with colleagues all bear the fruit of knowledge.

Knowledge of where the deer are, as any bow hunter will admit, is not enough to seal the deal, nor is it enough for the astute veterinarian. The successful bow hunter has the wisdom not only to put himself in a position to get a shot but also to draw the bow without being seen and place the arrow behind the elbow. Book knowledge, while important to the veterinarian, isn't enough. Wisdom in the form of common sense and the ability to communicate will see the veterinarian through the tough decisions like whether to perform exploratory surgery, wait and observe the patient or even euthanize an animal when appropriate.

Stealth is an indispensable quality of the bow hunter. Deer have very acute hearing and a twig snap from a hundred yards will give the hunter away every time. The stealthy veterinarian also holds an advantage over the usually flighty cow. A loud voice, no matter what the situation, is like an alarm bell for the cow. It alerts her to the possibility of a shot or maybe an arm up her rear end to see if she is pregnant. Indeed, it's easier to sneak up on a cow than it is to chase her.

The serious bow hunter is detail oriented. Wind direction, stand placement, scent control and concealment can be all wrong if the details aren't right. The same is true for the clinician. Details during surgery like sterile technique, suture selection and pattern and animal positioning can be the difference between a successful and unsuccessful surgery.

The successful hunt ends with some tasty meat and maybe some delicious jerky or bologna. And in the case of an exceptional hunt, maybe even a trophy on the living room wall. The successful outcome of a sick cow may be a little less dramatic for the veterinarian, but the gratitude of a satisfied farmer makes it worth all the practice, patience, homework and effort undertaken.

Meat
11-29-16

It's the most wonderful time of the year.

Of course, I'm talking about deer season. Once again, hordes of hunters across the commonwealth have taken to the woods and fields in search of the elusive whitetail deer. Some are hoping to tag a trophy; others are just hoping for some meat in the freezer.

Non-hunters think it's easy to get a deer. I've heard the charges.

"Arm the deer and it will be a challenge."

"How hard can it be to shoot a defenseless animal?"

Granted, the use of a weapon makes getting a deer less hard than without. But it still doesn't make it easy. Throw into the mix defined hunting seasons, property boundaries and mandatory regulations like antler restrictions and it becomes downright difficult to put some meat in the freezer.

Speaking of meat, I'm a meat hunter. I go in search of the elusive whitetail for the sole purpose of enjoying venison. Big antlers are a nice bonus, but not a prerequisite. Without venison, there could be no venison jerky, venison bologna or venison tenderloin roast.

Deer hunting indeed is challenging. But when a hunt is successful, the reward is great. When a hunt is unsuccessful, it's still enjoyable. The beauty of recreational hunting is that even though we might not bag a deer, we still have the opportunity to enjoy meat- thanks to the American farmer.

Thanksgiving has just passed and how many of us enjoyed the large, succulent holiday turkey? Most of us did, I'd be willing to bet. Now, how many of us shot that wild turkey during this year's fall turkey season? Probably a few, but not many. And I'd also be willing to wager a deep-fried turkey wing (my favorite part of the bird) that the farm raised turkey tasted much better that the wild variety.

Turkey farming makes it possible for millions of Americans to enjoy a few slices of white meat and maybe some dark meat as well on Thanksgiving. Without farmers, we would either have to successfully hunt for one or grow our own. I don't know which one is harder.

Turkey is good, but a bird only has maybe 10 pounds or so of meat on it. If you want to talk quantity, let's talk beef.

A properly processed deer may contain 50 pounds of meat for the average size deer. But a beef may yield upwards of 500 pounds or more after processing. That's a lot of meat. It's so much that most of us buy beef by the half, or even individual cuts of meat at the store.

Beef farmers and ranchers are very good at what they do. Beef farming is somewhat specialized today because of its complexity. Cow-calf farms produce the calves that will eventually be fed out for slaughter. Background and stocker farms take the weaned calves and grow them some more until they are ready for the feedlot. Finally, a calf ultimately winds up in a feedlot where it will be fed as much as it wants to eat. These calves may gain four pounds or more a day until they are heavy enough for slaughter. That's even more weight that I gain during the holidays.

For deer hunters, the hard work starts after pulling trigger. At the very least, the hunter has a short drag back to the truck after gutting the deer. But many of us haul the deer home and butcher it ourselves. But thanks to farmers and butchers, getting beef for a meal is as easy as a trip to the grocery store.

My point is that meat is a luxury in many parts of the world. Yes, hunting is enjoyable, but it is also both challenging and a lot of work.

And if you hunt like I do, it is also unreliable. But thanks to the American farmer, meat is accessible, affordable and easy. Deer season for the hunter indeed is the most wonderful time of the year. But for the everyday consumer of meat, every day is wonderful.

Warning Labels
12-3-13

We live in a risk free society. Or at least that seems to be the expectation of some based on the warnings we receive on the products we buy.

It seems that nearly everything we buy has a warning label. The vehicle I drive has a multiple warning labels all over it. The gasoline pump I go to has a warning label reminding me that gasoline is flammable.

Really? I'd never have figured that one out.

I purchased a two-person tree stand so that I could hunt deer from a good vantage point with my son this year. It not only came with a warning label, it came with a warning DVD.

The video warned not to climb the tree stand without a safety harness. OK, that's sound advice. I never climb a tree without a harness. If you don't have a harness, hunt from the ground. I continued to watch for some more pointers.

They warned me never to climb a tree stand if I'm drowsy. I'll readily admit that when I get up at 4 a.m. to go hunting, I get a little drowsy. If you are drowsy, hunt from the ground. Maybe I'll just drink some more coffee to keep me alert.

Then I became a little concerned. Don't hunt from a tree stand if you are sick, have a heart condition or spinal problems, they said. If that is the case, hunt from the ground. Well, I'm generally healthy and my ticker is fine, but I inherited a terrible spine from my family. But I've been hunting through my back problems for years, so why quit now?

Finally, I was warned not to climb the tree stand during inclement weather like rain, snow or cold temperatures as it may make the tree stand unsafe. Wait a minute, am I the only one who finds it silly? This isn't southern California, you know.

"Warning: this coffee is hot." Well, I hope so. "Warning: cigarettes are bad for your health." No kidding.

I really got to thinking about all the obvious warnings concerning almost every facet of our lives. Maybe it's the threat of lawsuits or maybe it's a lack of common sense. But there seems to be no escape from the warning labels- except on our food.

It's a little surprising that food doesn't come with a warning. I can see it now. "Warning: may cause weight gain. If eaten with hot sauce, it can cause acid reflux. If eaten with beans,…" well, you get the point.

On the contrary, the other side of the package could come with a different label. "Warning, if you don't eat, you could starve." What are we to do?

But considering the number scary foods in the news, we might expect to see warning labels soon. From "pink slime" to hormones, we should all be expected to cower in fear, warning labels or not.

Being a person who likes to look at the evidence in the numbers, I decided to take a look at the Centers for Disease Control (CDC) statistics concerning foodborne illness. What I found didn't really surprise me.

In 2011, there were about 9.4 million cases of foodborne illnesses from known pathogens. That sounds like enough to justify warning labels, right? Well, consider this.

If the 300 million people in this country all consumed two meals a day, a conservative estimate, in a year's time that would be 219 billion meals consumed. That works out to about one case of illness per 23,000 meals. I eat about 1,000 meals a year, so I can expect to get sick about every 23 years.

Foodborne illness is a serious matter and I am not making light of it. My point is that our food is not only affordable, plentiful and wholesome in this country, it is incredibly safe. So safe that sickness occurs not monthly or weekly as in some parts of the globe, but it is measured in decades. There may be risk, but it is incredibly small.

Risk free is an unattainable goal; unless it concerns tree stands. You see, my son and I will be hunting from the ground this year.

Deer Season
11-28-17

It's opening week of deer season. A year of anticipation finally concludes with the festivities on the Monday following Thanksgiving. I'm going to bag a big buck worthy of hanging on my living room wall. A successful deer hunt, as any successful hunter knows, takes preparation. This preparation often begins with the conclusion of the previous season. Food plots, trail cameras and spotting scopes precede sighting in the rifle to make sure it can drive a tack at a hundred yards.

Anticipation of killing a monster buck can almost consume an avid hunter. The scenario gets played over and over again in his mind. He sees the monster emerge from the brush. He counts, one, two, three…, ten. A ten point is wandering right towards him. A relaxing exhale steadies his hand before squeezing the trigger and… Boom! He hits the rewind button and replays the scenario again on the night before opening day.

The morning of opening day finally arrives. The hunter jumps out of bed way before he is used to; the alarm clock is unnecessary this morning. His gear has been packed and he begins the trek to the big woods. Anticipation is still palpable as he has forgotten all the previous opening days when he left the woods empty handed. He crawls into his stand and it's game on.

In most years, opening day comes and goes without fulfilling the hope imagined before dawn of opening day. We leave the woods disappointed, yet still hopeful that the two-week season can produce a trophy. Sometimes we settle for a smaller buck, tasty nonetheless. There are some years that we don't fill a tag. But the anticipation brings us back again next year.

For the fortunate few, the trophy buck materializes and everything falls into place. A well-placed shot brings the majestic buck down and the work begins. The story is recounted to his buddies over and over again just like it played out in his mind before opening day. He had a big bill from the taxidermist, yes, but it was well worth it.

I used to hunt a lot more than I do now. A busy career, adolescent children and a plethora of other responsibilities have distracted me from the thrill of the chase. Some might even argue that my enthusiasm for deer hunting has been replaced by my career.

The majority of my professional time recently has been devoted to the practice of embryo transfer. Out of a single cow, we can recover multiple fertile embryos and transfer them into surrogate cows called recipients.

This practice has some peculiarities. First, donor cows are the best of the best and their offspring can fetch ten times the normal market price for cattle or rarely much more. Since cows don't have litters, this procedure allows the farmer with a superior cow to take advantage of her genetics. Second, some donor cows are more prolific than others. This disparity is well known among farmers who utilize this technology. Roughly 30 percent of the donor cows produce 70 percent of the embryos. Individual yields can vary even more.

A successful embryo collection requires preparation. This preparation often begins with the conclusion of the previous collection. The donor cow must be in a good state of health and the proper shots have to given at the right time to prepare her to make multiple embryos.

Anticipation of a successful collection is inescapable. The farmer knows that a donor has the potential to give him 20 or even more fertile embryos. The night before the collection, the farmer thinks about all of the calves that are to be born in nine months from this collection. The recipients have been prepared and the donor is ready. Will it be five embryos? Or maybe he hits the jackpot and the donor produces a bigger yield of 20?

Collection day arrives and the farmer has to get up even earlier than usual. In addition to trucking the donor to the collection site, he still has the normal routine of chores to do. But the alarm clock is barely necessary since the anticipation brought him around before it was time.

He has forgotten all of the previous collection days where his donor cow didn't produce anything. But he remembers vividly the day one of his cows made four times the average yield of viable embryos. This day has the potential to be even better. He can feel it.

Most collection days come and go without fulfilling the hope of breaking the record of embryos in a single collection. Sometimes he settles for an average yield, which is still profitable. And there are the days where the donor is one of the 20 percent of unfortunate cows that doesn't yield a single embryo. It's disappointing, but there's always the next time.

But for the fortunate few, the cow fulfills on the hope of a big score. She may even break a record or produce the embryo that becomes the best cow in the breed. I can imagine as the farmer looks at the calves once they are born, he recounts the day the embryos were collected and his cow set the record. He had a big bill from the veterinarian, yes, but it was well worth it.

It's funny, but I've just developed a bit more empathy and understanding for my clients.

Good luck this deer season. I hope you get to pay a taxidermist!

Catch and Release
6-6-17

I like to fish. So much so that if I ever live on the bank of a river, this column would cease to exist. At least it would when the water wasn't frozen over. Unfortunately, I don't live on a river and my busy schedule prevents me from getting the rod and reel out very often.

So, when I fielded a call the other day about a steer with a fish hook stuck in its mouth, I jumped at the chance to mend the poor critter. After all, I hadn't had much opportunity to remove any hooks from my catch this year. At least this time, I could play a role in the catch of the day.

Something definitely smelled fishy about this case, though. I wondered just how such a thing could happen. Did some ne'er do wells go trolling for some combined surf and turf? Maybe the steer was named Gil and he got confused? At any rate, the steer was certainly in troubled waters and needed help.

When I arrived at the farm, I asked the farmer to get the steer restrained in the chute. The chute could barely contain him and I almost went for my net. He was putting up a pretty good fight, but he finally settled down and we landed him.

When I opened his mouth, the problem was worse than I initially thought. He was caught pretty good and wasn't going to be the one that got away. He had eaten a diving crankbait with two treble hooks. One was caught in his gum below his incisor teeth and the other was not visible because he couldn't open his mouth.

Having removed my share of hooks from the mouths of fishes, I knew what a treble hook can do. This was a real beefy catch, but still no match for a treble hook. Fortunately, I came prepared with a heavy duty set of wire snips since I didn't think I could remove the barbed hook intact. I didn't have a gaff with me, so we placed a nose lead in him and slowly opened his mouth.

I tried to grab onto the lure, but as I did he shook his head, probably trying to throw the hook. I thought better of it a second time since only two of the three hooks on the treble were embedded in his jaw. If the other hook landed me, I'd surely drown. Well, maybe I wouldn't drown but I didn't want to get caught up in that mess.

I eventually located the split ring that attaches the hook to the lure and could get my wire snip on it. After a couple of snips, the first hook came free and fell on the ground. I picked it up and handed it to the farmer for disposal.

But there was still the matter of the other hook still attached to the lure. When I opened his mouth to look for it, I couldn't see it. I panicked for a second and thought maybe it went down his gullet. But instead, the hook was stuck under his tongue.

I've had the displeasure of having more than one hook stuck in my finger, and I know it hurts. It must hurt even worse to have it stuck in your tongue, at least that's what he had me believing. So, I didn't want to waste any time getting him free.

Not wanting to make the same mistake of almost losing the lure again, I attached a pair of needle holders to it. I tried to locate an appropriate place to cut the hook, but it was tangled up like a rat's nest in the tongue. Finally, I rotated the hook and saw my chance. I picked out one of the barbs and snipped it.

It was almost free, but still loosely attached. The steer had struggled for a few hours and turned the area into sushi, or hamburger, or… Well, let's just say there was a lot of tissue damage. I couldn't find anywhere else to snip and I still had the last hook on the needle holders. I thought I had one chance to do this right and I gave a good yank. Out popped the hook and the lure.

Just for the halibut, I gave a thorough feel under his tongue for any remnants of the hook and it was clean. I thought the steer was a keeper, but the farmer convinced me that he was in favor of catch and release. I guess that's only fair.

I asked the farmer just how the steer ended up with a lure in his mouth. Apparently, the neighbor kids were fishing in the farm pond and lost a lure. The steer found it as he was grazing on the bank. The kids are going to get their lure back now; I suspect with a verbal lashing also.

The steer will be fine, but he'll be sore for a few days. He was certainly a big one. And that's honestly no fish tale.

CHAPTER 6
Conversations with cows

Photo by John Higgins, VMD

The series of articles in this chapter is the result of a person who takes some liberties and pretends to speak for cows. Recognize, though, that there are some caveats to my intent. First, they were inherently fun and entertaining to write. Second, I've spent enough time around cows that, sometimes, I think I can read their minds. Maybe it's just the voices in my head telling me that, but the sentiments expressed by the cows make perfect sense to me, and hopefully others as well. Third, there is deeper meaning embedded in the points the cows are making, mainly as it relates to their nature and how that nature is often misunderstood by people.

I have, on occasion, been pretty critical of the practice of anthropomorphizing animals. It can imply that animals are capable of emotions only experienced by people. Animals don't love people. My dog acts like he loves me sometimes, but he's really just hoping I'll take him for a walk or give in to his mooching. Love, after all, is an action, not a feeling. Animals can't hate people either; they are bound by the chains of instinct. Animals can only do what their nature allows them to do. Nonetheless, I took some liberties and had a lot of fun with it. I hope you also have some fun with them.

Interview with a cow.
1-10-12 to 1-24-12

Ms. Cow, thanks for taking the time. How do you like to be addressed?

Well, some call me Peanut, some call me 4804, while others call me 23WBC5437. But, please call me Nut.

23WBC5437? Could you please explain that one, Nut?

Sure. That's my official identification, sort of like your social security number. The 23 indicates that I'm from Pennsylvania and the WBC5437 is an identifier as unique as I am.

As fascinating as identifiers and official identifications are, it isn't really what I was planning on talking about. Let's get to the heart of the matter, Nut. Do you like your farmer? We've heard rumors that the man is keeping you down.

Why do you assume my farmer is a man? My farm is actually a family and, yeah, I guess I like them. I mean, they feed us, give us a place to live and help us get rid of all this milk twice a day. They even give us medicine when we're sick. I don't like getting shots, though. I hate needles. In fact, sometimes, when he or the vet tries to give me a shot, I try to squeeze them in the corner. Once, I even kicked him in the knee.

Ouch! What did he do then?

Well, he called his buddy over and he pushed my tail straight up in the air. I just froze. I was like, what the…, then, I got the shot and didn't even feel the needle. I learned after that – no more kicking the farmer.

So, Nut, tell me, what is your favorite time of day?

For sure, it's after milking time is over. I am always the first one in line to be milked so I can get back in the barn and pick the most comfortable stall. Then I'll lie down, chew my cud for an hour or so and then take a short nap. That is by far, my favorite time of day.

Do you have a least favorite?

It's the mad dash to the milking parlor. Those cows from the west side of the barn are always trying to bully me and my girlfriends. Those girls are such… well, let's just say I don't like them. Don't like them at all.

What types of things do they do to you and why do they do it?

Well, first of all, they'll butt me in the ribs with their big heads, and then they'll try to cut in front of me on the way to be milked. If they can get in front of me, they will stall in front of the milking parlor entrance and slow the rest of us down. I think the farmer is fed up with them too because I overheard him say they are gonna have to change careers if they keep this up. I'm hoping by that he means they will soon be in the beef industry. That's terrible, I shouldn't think that way, but it's the inevitable result for most of us cows one day.

You bring up a disturbing topic to some, Nut. What about the slaughterhouse?

Yeah, I guess it probably is disturbing to some. Look, it's a part of life. The world was here for a long time before my mama gave birth to me and it will be here for a long time after I've fed a lot of hungry people. I don't really like to dwell on it.

On a lighter note, do you have a favorite food?

Oh, yes. It's corn – high moisture corn. Mmmmm. Some of my herd mates like the hay, or even the fresh grass, but I like the high moisture corn. It is to die for, literally. I had this friend once who jimmied open the lid on the grain cart and must have eaten about 30 pounds of the stuff. About 6 hours later, she was flat on her side having her rumen emptied out by the vet. She would have died if they didn't do that.

I thought corn was a staple of your diet. Why would she have died from eating that?

If she had eaten it in moderation, like 10 pounds or so, she would have been OK. But she ate a cartful of it. It all fermented in her rumen at the same time, like a whiskey mash, and gave her a bad case of rumen acidosis. It was more than just a few Rolaids could take care of.

What is your favorite color, Nut?

Black and white.

Black and white aren't really colors, are they?

Hey, I'm a black and white Holstein – what do you mean they aren't colors? Colored breeds, like Jersey and Brown Swiss and Guernsey, have all the eye appeal to some people, while we poor schleps are just grinding it out day in and day out trying to make a living for our farmer.

Don't get me wrong, I'm not prejudiced- some of my best friends are Red and White. But I'm proud to be black and white.

Are you a morning person or night owl?

I'm a cow and I only sleep a few minutes a day.

Oh, sorry, that was a poor choice of words.

Forget about it.

Nut, I have to admit, one of the reasons I wanted to do this interview with you was to discuss the whole anthropomorphism of animals trend that's been going on in the culture lately. What do you think of that and do you see any harm in it?

Is this off the record?

No, it's all on the record.

Oh. (Long pause) OK, I'll say it. I think it's stupid. We aren't people. We're cows. We look like cows. We smell like cows. We act like cows. And we think like cows. We don't think like people in that we don't care about tomorrow. People are always worrying about the future. I just don't have the freedom to do that; I'm bound by the chains of instinct. It has its advantages, don't get me wrong. I mean, instinct tells me to eat when I'm hungry, leave when I'm scared, lay down when I'm tired and moo when I have the urge to make noise. It's really no more complicated than that. My farmer takes care of my future and I really like it that way. Maybe my ancestors, centuries ago before they were completely domesticated didn't like it that way; I'll never know. But really, my farmer gives me food, shelter and free health care. I wouldn't have to worry about anything even if I could.

So, what harm could come of it? So what if people attribute human qualities to animals?

Well, first of all, surely you have to recognize the irony of you and me even having this conversation. I mean, really. I'll grant you that on the surface it might seem benign and some of it probably is. The danger lies when people with an agenda use it to try to convince others that we have human qualities. The animal rights activists, like PETA, are notorious for this. They try to portray the relationship between my farmer and me as akin to slavery. Sometimes they compare us to prisoners. It's not like that at all. I'll admit that there might be a few people who call themselves farmers that don't take good care of us. If you have a big enough tree, you're gonna find a few squirrels, if you know what I mean. But by and large, farmers know that they have to take good care of their livestock.

How can you be so sure, Nut? Haven't you heard of factory farms?

Come on, do I look stupid? I know I'm a cow, but I wasn't a calf yesterday. Listen, we know when we aren't being taken care of and if we aren't, we just don't produce. I understand my farmer wants me to work for a living and he knows that if he doesn't feed me properly and keep me comfortable, I won't work. You can't squeeze blood from a turnip, you know. We don't go on strike, mind you, we're a bit more subtle than that. And it isn't just dairy cows; it's also beef cows, pigs and goats.

What about sheep?

Well, sheep really are stupid. Seriously, the only thing dumber might be a bag of hammers. But they won't produce either if they aren't properly taken care of. Uh, sorry, that wasn't very politically correct. I hope Bo Peep and her minions don't picket my barn when this goes to print.

With all due respect, Nut, you didn't really address the question of factory farms.

Factory farms? What a stupid term, with all due respect. What constitutes a factory farm? Is it size? My farmer milks several hundred cows. That doesn't make it a factory. Do you mean if a farm hires employees outside the family that makes it a factory? My farmer isn't entitled to a day off once in a while? He's not a machine, you know. Maybe factory farms generate a profit? Does that make it a factory farm? Without the possibility for a profit, what farmer in his right mind would put up with the hassle? I reject the whole premise. It makes no sense to me.

It seems like I touched a nerve with the factory farm question. Why is that?

Sorry, it gets a little irritating after a while. People throw this term around but it's just empty rhetoric. So, I live in a barn with a couple hundred other cows. Technically, I'm confined, OK? So that makes it a factory farm? Well listen, the weather gets plenty miserable here and honestly I'd really prefer to be inside much of the time. That's where my stall is. That's where my food and water are. I have a respite from the wind in the winter and shade and fans in the summer. The flies are much less of an issue in the barn too. This might not be paradise, but, really, we've got it pretty good here.

As a cow, people think you'd want to be outside frolicking?

Have you ever seen a dairy cow frolic? I have and it's a disaster waiting to happen. I had this friend a couple of years ago, right? My farmer decided one day, since it was a pleasant spring day, we should all go out and get some exercise. When the barn door opened up and we went outside, my friend found it necessary to frolic. She kicked up her heels and do you know what happened? She tore a ligament. According to the vet, it was the median suspensory ligament, the one that attaches the udder to the body It wasn't a pretty sight and she was never the same after that. The last time my farmer let us out of the barn, we were lined up at the door within an hour wanting back in.

But don't you want to be outside eating grass like cows are supposed to?

It seems like you're trying to stereotype me. Look, I'm a metabolic athlete. When my milk production gets cranking and I'm in top form, I need a lot of calories. Pound for pound, I need more calories than a runner needs to run a marathon. And I do this every day. Do you think I could do this eating just grass?

So you don't like grass? I thought all cows liked grass.

Don't get me wrong, I like grass as much as the next cow. I just couldn't live on it. I need more goodies than that. I'm a dairy cow.

So, Nut, tell me what happens in the milking parlor? It seems like such a mystery to people.

Well, it's really no big deal. Once I learned the routine, it became quite easy. We just walk in and stand side by side with seven other cows. The farmer cleans us up really well, checks for any problems, and attaches the milker. After four or five minutes, we're done and I can go lie down, chew my cud for a while and take a snooze.

Does it hurt?

It hurts if we don't get milked, let me tell you. Ouch. Talk about being under pressure. The milking unit, if there's something wrong with the vacuum system, can be uncomfortable. You know what they say- "vacuum sucks."

Who says that? I've never heard it put that way before.

Oh, it must be a cow thing.

Note: The experiences of "Nut" the cow are the impressions of the author and are quite representative of the typical dairy cow. Neither cows nor rational people were harmed in the making of this interview.

An Open Letter from a Dairy Cow
7-21-15

To Whomever Thinks I'm a Victim,

You may wonder what in the world is going on that a dairy cow can be writing a letter. And you may also notice that open letters are usually "to" and not "from." But all is not what it seems to be.

Hardly a month goes by without some "undercover" video surfacing from an animal rights group highlighting the plight of the poor cow. Well, let me just say that they don't speak for me. I and my fellow cows are quite content, I must admit.

Are there some cows that are mistreated? I'd have to guess that there are. But frankly, I think you humans have a better track record of treating us cows than you do of treating your fellow humans, judging from the killings and wars and crimes committed that we hear about when the farmers talk. Those farmers that mistreat cows just aren't going to be in business for very long and here's why.

I realize that very few humans know just what makes a dairy cow tick. Truth is, dairy cows are metabolic athletes. Most of you like sports, right? Think of the marathon runner and what he has to endure to run the 26.2 miles in mere hours. He has to burn a bunch of calories. He might have a personal trainer. He probably has really comfortable shoes. And I'm sure he has to eat the right kind of food in the proper amounts to run that marathon a few times a year. He takes pretty good care of himself.

We dairy cows, pound for pound, need just as many calories to produce about nine gallons of milk as that marathon runner. But most of us do that every day. Some of us will double that amount or more when we are at peak performance a couple of months after delivering our calf. Do you think we could accomplish that if we weren't happy? Do you think you could run a marathon every day if you weren't fed right or were uncomfortable?

We get fed a specially balanced diet formulated from some of the smartest minds in the business. We get our feet trimmed and shaped on a regular basis. The farmer is constantly checking us for problems and when something goes wrong, we get medical attention.

We dairy cows were made for this; it is our purpose. We were bred to have a strong drive to eat to provide the calories necessary to produce that much milk. We were bred to have a sturdy frame to get around. We were bred to have strong feet to support our massive frame. Of course, there are some unfortunate cows that come along that just can't keep up with the rest of us. The farmer has no choice but to cut them from the team. It's nothing personal; it's just business. It makes the rest of us better.

As time goes on, we dairy cows as a group get better and better. Every year, we make more milk than the previous year. If we didn't love our job, we simply couldn't keep improving.

Every year, farmers learn more and more about us and what drives us and how to make us better. Sometimes, they might add a new ingredient to our feed. Or maybe they might try a new variety of corn. Often, they just try to make our accommodations better so we are more comfortable. Comfortable cows make a lot of milk. Farmers like cows that make a lot of milk.

So, please, we are not victims. We like what we do. If you ever get the chance to stop and gawk at a group of dairy cows, please take it. Look at us and decide for yourself if we look unhappy.

And it's normal for you to be able to see our ribs, OK? We are not beef cows. A marathon runner wouldn't make it past the first mile if he was plump and out if shape, right? Neither would we be able to keep up with the demands of the job if we aren't in shape. But please, no cameras. We don't want the farmer to think you are trying to exploit us and ruin our reputation like the animal rights folks.

Sincerely,
The dairy cow

Questions for a Cow
8-9-16 through 12-6-16

Social media has changed the way our world works. It has accelerated cultural changes and made our world smaller. It also leaves few secrets for those willing to bear their souls on the world wide web. Cows have a lot of secrets and they are usually unwilling to open up and be frank. Being the conservative type, they usually don't like social media. Plus, it's hard for them to type on a smartphone without thumbs. But, since I am an influential and respected member of the bovine's inner circle, I have been able to accumulate a unique insight into what cows think about and how they feel about people, their jobs and other cows. And I've done this without the help of social media.

To best communicate this insight to my readers, however, I feel I have to do something a little different. Have you ever come across one of those lists of questions passed by email or social media to get to know another person better? I mean questions like, "What is your favorite movie," or "If you could have lunch with one famous person, who would it be and why?" I have found such a compilation of questions that, if asked of a cow, would be answered something like this.

What is the number 1 song played on your iPod?

I broke my iPod with my hoof when I tried to download my favorite song, "The Dirt Road" by Sawyer Brown. But if the little music box still worked, that would top my play list, I'm sure.

If you could throw any kind of party, what would it be like and what would it be for?

It would be a simple party with some good food and plenty of area to lounge and chew some cud. The party would be for the cows when they come home. I keep hearing about the cows that are coming home when this happens or when that happens. When they finally make it back, boy are we going to have a big party.

Which celebrity do you get mistaken for?

Some tell me that I resemble… uh, wait. I'd better not take the bait. I'm a cow and I could end up getting somebody in trouble. Let's just say others have told me I should audition for a Chic Fil A commercial.

Have you ever had something happen to you that you thought was bad but turned out to be good?

Oh, boy, have I! Several years ago, I had this weird feeling like something was moving in my belly and my udder started getting really big. Next thing I knew, I felt this twinge and… well, granted it was a little more than a twinge. But this calf squeezed out of my back end! I was like, this isn't right; not right at all. And my udder hurt really,

really bad, like it was under pressure. But after the calf came out, the farmer cleaned me up, gave me a nice warm bucket of water to drink and relieved me of the pressure in my udder. And now he does this twice every day. I was told that the calf was my ticket to stick around in the herd. Without it, I couldn't make milk. Yeah, I thought it was bad for a bit, but it turned out to be the best thing that could have happened to me.

What was your favorite food when you were a calf?

Cow's milk. I don't guess I have to elaborate.

If you could paint a picture of any scenery you've seen before, what would you paint?

Every morning after milking time, I hurry back to my favorite stall to lie down and chew my cud. It's my favorite stall because it has the most spectacular view of the hollow. There is the state road down below with the traffic and the hills and mountains. If could paint, and I can't because I don't have thumbs, that's what I'd paint.

What do you want to be when you grow up?

I can tell you what I don't want to be. I don't to be a sheep. They're not real bright, you know. And I wouldn't want to be a sow, either. You know they have litters of piglets; as many as a dozen and a half at a time I only have four spigots. No, I'm content to be a cow.

What was one of the best parties you've been to?

A couple of years ago, the hired man forgot to latch the gate to the barn. One of my friends found out and called a breakout party. We made it known to the whole pen that the gate was open and one by one, after the sun went down, we snuck out into the hayfield. It was the most fun. We ate so much grass that half of us had the bloat. Somebody called the farmer about 2 in the morning though and, whew, was he mad. After getting his whole family out of bed, they all walked through the field and herded us back to our barn. By the time we were back in, it was time to milk and we were all dead tired. We sure can't party like we used to.

What is your favorite quote?

"Don't have a cow, man!" – Bart Simpson

If you could choose to stay a certain age forever, what would it be?

I would be 5. At that age, I was at peak performance. When I was 5, I began my third lactation. I will never be as strong or make as much milk as I did then. But who wants to live the same age forever? I like the progression. With age comes seniority. I get the better stall now. I get to take advantage of the early bird special now at the feed bunk and I have the respect of all the fresh 2-year-olds. That's what we call the girls that have just have had their first calf. But 5, yeah, that's the best age.

When you have 30 minutes of free-time, how do you pass the time?

Whenever I get a half hour, I go to my stall, lie down and chew my cud. It is so relaxing and I don't think my description can really do it justice. If you look up content in the dictionary, you'll likely find a picture of a cow chewing her cud. To chew a cud, we ruminants will regurgitate a mouthful and chaw on it for a spell. Once we've ground it to a pulp, we'll swallow and repeat, over and over. It's healthy for us too; it allows us to extract more nutrients from our feed and it helps us buffer our rumen. My rumen is the largest chamber of my complex forestomach. It needs buffered to keep me from getting a sour stomach. It might sound disgusting, but take it from me, it's an acquired taste. But you simple stomached critters will just never really understand.

What was the last movie, TV show or book that made you cry or tear up?

A few months ago, my farmer had the door to his office open and "Old Yeller" was playing on the TV. I was glued to the story, since I like all things about animals. But at the end, I teared up so bad that the farmer thought I had pink eye. He called the vet. By the time the vet got there, I had settled down and the vet told him that he must have caught the wrong cow. To this day, I don't think he ever figured that one out.

What's your favorite indoor/outdoor activity?

I already talked about my favorite indoor activity. My favorite outdoor activity is grazing. Except when it's hot out then I don't like to do anything outside. I'd rather be in the barn where the fans are and the flies are under control.

If you knew the world was ending in 2017, what would you do differently?

Well, the Mayan's sure blew their prediction a few years ago, didn't they? But I'm a cow and the world could, in fact, be ending in 2017. Some people get all excited and worried that cows end up as beef at the end of their days and, well, it's part of being a cow. If cows aren't supposed to be food animals, then why are we made of meat? No, I don't think I'd do anything different.

"What would you name the autobiography of your life?"

The Cream Always Rises to the Top: The Life Story of an Udderly Incredible Bovine." Does that sound too presumptuous?

What was the hardest thing you've ever done?

I entered the "dry period." That's when the farmer quits milking me and gives me a vacation from lactation. It's hard because I like my job and I'm comfortable with the cow cohorts in my barn. And I won't even mention the pressure I'm under once the milking routine stops. But they tell me a dry period is necessary to allow my udder to regenerate in time for my next lactation in two months.

What chore do you absolutely hate doing?

To be honest, I really don't have any chores. I get milked twice a day, I eat when I want and I chew my cud when I want. My farmer prepares my meals and cleans up after me. If you think about, I have it pretty good.

If you could pick anyone, who would you choose as your mentor?

It would be Gigi, no doubt. Gigi, for those of you who don't know her, is the world record holder for milk production in a year. She produced nearly 75,000 pounds on milk in one year. That's about 8,680 gallons, or well over 23 gallons a day. Gigi knows how to do her job.

If your farmer could play a walk-out song for you, what would it be?

"Milk Cow Blues" by Johnnie Lee Wills

What was the last experience that made you a stronger cow?

When I had my calf last time, I came down with a condition called milk fever. I was absolutely overcome with weakness to the point that I couldn't even stand up. Luckily, the farmer recognized that I wasn't right and called the vet. What happened next certainly made me stronger, although I didn't really like it.

The vet took out this big needle and stuck it in the vein in my neck. Then he attached a bottle of medicine to it and ran it straight in my vein. I couldn't fight much because I was so weak, but I gave it my best try. Next thing I know, he's talking my halter off and I feel great. So great that I jumped up and made a bee line for the gate. Yep, that bottle of medicine made me a stronger cow.

What is your favorite form of exercise?

It has to be walking the hill out back of the barn. It keeps me healthy and I can go in search of some lush grass when I'm out there. Is that a conflict of interest, looking for some chow while exercising?

If you could witness any event past, present or future, what would it be?

I think it would be the day that people figure out all the excess milk produced in this country could be used to feed hungry people around the world. People have figured out how to make cheese from milk, you know, that is easily transported.

What did you do growing up that got you into trouble?

Oh, my. Well, there was this time when I was just a heifer and I was trying to get to the grass on the other side of the fence. The grass was greener over there, you know. So, I jimmied open the gate to the pasture and some of my fellow heifers and I snuck out after dark to eat. What I didn't know is that it wasn't grass, but alfalfa. I got the bloat so bad that the vet had to come out and stick a tube down my throat to relieve the pressure. We all got into trouble after that because the farmer moved us to a new pen and fed us nothing but dry hay and water for a week. The vet said it was for our stomach, but I think we were just in trouble.

What is your favorite time of day/day of the week/month of the year?

My favorite time of day is 3 a.m., 11 a.m. and 7 p.m. Those are the times during the day that I go to the milking parlor. I'm under a lot of pressure before milking time, if you know what I mean, and getting milked is quite a relief.

If you could learn to do anything, what would it be?

I think it would be to communicate with people. That way, I could let them know how much that shadow in front on the milking parlor scares me. That's why I hesitate to go in sometimes. And that one-inch depression in the concrete that holds water looks more like a bottomless pit to me than a puddle. Yeah, I think I would like to learn to communicate with people. Hopefully, you appreciate the irony in that answer as much as I do.

When was the last time you had an amazing meal?

About 45 minutes ago. Excuse me a second while I regurgitate a cud… Thanks. That meal was amazing for sure, as was the one before it and the one before it. They were all the same and that's the way I like it. I love consistency since it is easy on my digestive system. But every time the farmer opens a new silo of feed, we have to learn to like new feed again. But once we get used to it, it becomes amazing.

What is your least favorite mode of transportation?

The stock trailer.

If you had to work on only one project for the next year, what would it be?

Hmmm, well that's a tough one. What could I do, what could I do? I guess I could…, no, that would never work. Maybe I could work on that…, never mind. I know! I'll work on making milk. Sorry, I have a sarcastic bent in me sometimes.

What was the best and worst gift you ever received?

The best gift I ever received were this pretty, yellow dangling ear jewelry that the farmer gave me as a heifer. It hurt a bit going in, but I was the envy of all the younger calves. And then I found out that all the older heifers had the same jewelry, only theirs had different numbers on them. It was also the worst gift I ever got.

If you were immortal for a day, what would you do?

I would eat about 50 pounds of grain, but only if I was immortal. To mortal cows, eating more than 25 pounds of grain would mean a death sentence. It's not a capital offense or anything, but it just is bad for our system. All the starch in the grain ferments at the same time and we get a nasty case of acid indigestion, bad enough to kill a cow. But it's still so tempting to do it.

What do you miss most about being a kid?

Well, first off, I was never a kid. I was a calf. But what I miss most about being a calf was the ability to frolic. We could run around and kick up our heels without thinking twice. We don't do that anymore. Some people think I should have the ability to frolic if I want to, but it just isn't a good idea. You see this udder? If I jumped today like I did when I was a calf, I'd bust my median suspensory ligament and my career would be over. I miss it, but I know better than to try it again.

Cows Debating
9-27-16

Once again, we are in the midst of a presidential election season. We have progressed from the candidates' initial announcements, through the tough primary fights, to the debates that started last night and finally with the conclusion coming, hopefully, on Nov. 8 in six weeks.

So, I got to thinking the other day about what the debates might be like if we could substitute cattle for the candidates. It's weird, I know, but no weirder than what we've experienced so far.

Playing the part of the Republican candidate could be a crunchy old bull named Taurump. The Democratic party could put forth an equivalently old cow named Hilabov. And just to make things interesting, the Libertarian party might nominate a quirky steer named, of all things, Gary. I suspect the exchange might go something like this...

Moderator: "Mr. Taurump, what will you do to keep the herd safe from outsiders?"

Mr. Taurump: "This barnyard has been overrun by outsiders for the last eight years. Every cow, bull and heifer from outside our ranks have crossed our fences illegally and it has to stop and it will stop once I'm elected. These other cattle bring disease and lawlessness. I'll construct an enormous electric fence around the farm and I'll make the outsiders pay for it. It will be the best fence ever and it will work perfectly. No undesirable from the outside will ever be able to enter our herd without permission again."

Moderator: "Mrs. Hillabov, your response?"

Mrs. Hillabov: "Well, thank you Mr. Moderator. As you know, our administration has worked tirelessly to see that outsiders become insiders. I fully support a comprehensive reform to ensure that all those affected become better and moooooooove everybody forward. You know, as American Cattle, we all deserve to be treated with dignity and as president, I will see that my administration will work hard to guarantee that all cattle will be beneficiaries of the same benefits as the top 1 percent of cattle."

Moderator: "Mr. Gary?"

"Mr. Gary: "We are a nation of immigrants. I think expensive walls and amnesty are no good for cows. So, please go to my website and sign my petition dealing with the issue of immigration."

Moderator: "Mrs. Hilabov, our barnyard is experiencing much strife. The beef cattle and dairy cattle don't get along. And the black cattle and white cattle and the black and white cattle, along with the red cattle experience bias and mistrust not seen in decades. What will you do as president to bring our barnyard together?"

Mrs. Hilabov: "Well, thank you Mr. Moderator. As you know, our administration has worked tirelessly to see that we end discrimination. I fully support a comprehensive reform to ensure that all those affected become better and moooooooove everybody forward. You know, as American Cattle, we all deserve to be treated with dignity and as president I will work with black cattle and white cattle and black and white cattle and red cattle to ensure that we are all entitled to the same benefits as the top 1 percent of cattle."

Moderator: "Mr. Taurump, your response?"

Mr. Taurump: "Relations have never been worse between cattle in the history of our farm. I have reached out to the minority communities and have received endorsements from many, many powerful and influential leaders in those communities. I will restore law and order in the barnyard between the black and white cattle, and the black cattle and the white cattle and the red cattle and also the long horned cattle, by the way, which are some very, very good cattle. Some of my very best friends are long horned cattle. And the Wagyu cattle…"

Moderator: "Times up Mr. Taurump. Mr. Gary, you're on the clock."

Mr. Gary: "Do you have any Doritos…?"

Moderator: "Um, no. Mr. Taurump, other farms have been flooding our market with cheap products like meat and milk, putting many of your potential constituents out of work. How do you plan to address this problem as president?"

Mr. Taurump: "These other farms are taking advantage of us because we don't know how to negotiate. As president, I will negotiate deals with the other farms that will be in our favor. I wrote a book on making deals once, so I know how to do it. I will negotiate the best deals ever and our farm will be great again. My opponent negotiated the worst deal ever with that other farm with the nuclear weapons. I will renegotiate a new deal once I'm president after I tear up the old one and it will be the greatest deal of all time."

Moderator: "Mrs. Hilabov, would you care to respond?"

Mrs. Hilabov: "Well, once again, thank you Mr. Moderator. Unlike Mr. Taurump who has consumed milk from those other farms, our administration has worked tirelessly to see that this barnyard's cattle are protected from unfair trade practices from the other farms. But we also have to make sure that we comprehensively reform our negotiated trade deals to moooooooove all cattle forward. You know, as American Cattle, we all deserve to work with dignity and as president, I will see that my administration will work hard to guarantee that all cattle will be beneficiaries of the same benefits as the fat cats on Wall Street."

So, if you watched the debate last night, I'm sorry. That's a couple of hours of your life you'll never get back. Out of 350 million possible candidates in this country, this was really the best we could do?

CHAPTER 7
Goats

Photo by Angie Neer

About seven years after accepting my position at White Oak Veterinary Clinic, my wife and I realized our longtime dream of owning a house and a little bit of land in the country. As a large animal veterinarian, I felt a compulsion to own livestock, and we had been looking for just the right place to accommodate some critters for a while.

I had tried my hand at this several years earlier, only we had lived in the town of Somerset at the time. I bought a couple of beef cross dairy calves from a client to hand raise on a bottle until it was time to wean. I figured two calves didn't really constitute a herd, so I patched a couple more together and raised the four calves at my partner, Dr. Welch's farm. Every morning before calls, I'd drive to his farm and bottle feed the calves. Before I made it home for the day, I'd stop and feed them again. It seemed like a good idea at the time, but I soon realized that all the extra traveling created an inconvenience that I hadn't considered. Eventually, I weaned them and trailered three of the calves to my uncle's farm for him to finish raising and sold the youngest.

Obviously, I thought, when we have a place of our own, we could manage livestock a lot easier. But it was a good first lesson in both humility and the dedication necessary to own and raise livestock.

So, when we finally had a little bit of land of our own, one of the first things I did was resume my activities as a farmer. I use that word loosely, because I now realize that I wouldn't make a good farmer.

A client called me several months after we had settled in our new house and said that one of his Boer does had delivered triplets. She had gotten sick and the kids were now orphaned. He didn't have the time or the energy to hand raise these kids, which can be high maintenance, and wanted to know if I was interested. After a 30 second discussion with my better half, we decided to give it a go.

We bottle raised two of the goat triplets until the spring that year and, like before, reckoned that two animals didn't constitute a herd. Eventually, our herd of goats expanded to seven does and we rented a billy in the hopes that our herd would expand further. It did expand, along with the feed bill, our responsibilities and the manure pile.

Again, I realized just how much dedication it takes to be a farmer.

After three years among the ranks of those whom I admire most, I was forking manure and bedding out of the goat barn one Saturday afternoon in March. It had been a particularly harsh winter and it had not been possible to get to the barn with the tractor until then. By the end of the day, I had forked six loads of manure by hand into the spreader and hauled it to the hayfield below. By the evening, my back was so sore that I could barely walk and I vowed that before the next winter, I would relinquish my dream, at least temporarily, of being a farmer. We sold the goats that October.

I do not regret my foray into the world of farming. In fact, I learned more about the psyche of the farmer from that experience than at any other time in my professional life. Indeed, it is a labor of love and, well, I just didn't love it anymore. The following articles are some of our experiences with raising goats.

Goat Farmers
12-21-10

My family recently became goat farmers. Well, maybe it's a little presumptuous of us to claim to be farmers, so let's just say we came into possession of some goats.

The goats are actually a couple of orphaned Boer goat kids. Boer is a breed of meat goat. The doe (female goat) died shortly after delivering them, so they need to be bottle raised. I take on these challenges periodically so I can better empathize with my clients and their level of dedication to raising their stock. At least that's what I tell myself.

Bottle raising young livestock is not an easy endeavor. Almost all dairy calves are hand raised today since it would be dangerous for both the cow and the calf in modern farms to leave them together. Given the multitude of responsibilities of a dairy farmer, it can sometimes be a challenge to give the calves the necessary attention they need.

This is probably going to make me sound sexist, but women make much better calf raisers than men. Maybe it's because women are better at nurturing or maybe they have more patience than men; I don't know. I do know that when the wife and/or daughter(s) are in charge of feeding the calves, the calves do better. Nobody can convince me otherwise.

Dairy farmers are well accustomed to hand raising their calves. Meat farmers are not. It is indeed a chore to bottle raise a beef calf, a runt pig or an orphaned meat goat or two. Fortunately for our Boer goat kids, my wife has a much better developed nurture center in her brain than I do. She does most of the feeding.

A revelation came to me the other day as I was dehorning the kids. I mean the goats, not my children. Since the kids tend to squirm a lot when restrained, I needed some help holding them as I disbudded them. I enlisted the help of my wife.

Goats should be dehorned as early as possible since their rapid horn development results in big horns in a short amount of time. The bigger the horns are, the more pain the goat experiences when they are removed. Also, the risk of leaving some horn tissue increases which will result in scurs. I like to burn the buds off before the kid is 2 weeks old.

Burning the horn buds at this age, however, carries its own risk. Since the brain lies a mere 5 millimeters below the horn, if the iron is left on too long, permanent brain damage can result. How would you know if a goat has brain damage, you ask? Point taken.

My wife held each goat as I injected the local anesthetic and I could see her cringe with each needle stick. It must have been more traumatic for her than the goats. I make a living performing normal husbandry procedures on livestock that, to the non farm public, might appear as torture. We don't do these things because we are sadistic; we do them if they are necessary. An ornery buck goat with horns can leave quite a bruise on an unsuspecting person.

After the horn buds were numbed, I quickly burned them off with a butane heated disbudding tool. The kids (our children) didn't even hear the kids (the goats) bawl. But my nurturing wife must have felt every bit of it. "They're bleeding!" she said.

I replied, "They're not bleeding; they're oozing."

Again, she sounded worried when she asked, "What do we need to put on the wounds?"

"Nothing, let 'em dry up."

She didn't stop. "But what if they get infected?"

"They won't get infected," I replied in a slightly agitated tone.

Still concerned, she said, "But they look like it hurts them!"

"I numbed them. They don't hurt...yet." It was then that I had my revelation. I married a city girl. And now she's a goat farmer.

A Lesson Learned Once
5-31-11

After much deliberation and toil, the fence to contain and protect our small goat herd is complete. The deliberative part was to ensure that the right type of fence was used. And we had a plethora of options available to us. Do we go with high tensile, barbed or woven fencing. What type of posts should we use, T posts, locust or treated. And do we make it electric to deter the goats from attempted escape?

Of course, we went with the electrified high tensile because it is the most effective. Now, before some of you think we're mean for choosing electric, let me explain in detail. Electric fence is also the most humane.

The Gospel reading in church recently was the story of the Good Shepherd (John 10:1-10). My mother, incidentally, asked me if goats are like sheep and know their handler's voice. I really don't know for sure, but our goats are certainly not as stupid as sheep, so I have to assume they would recognize our voices.

Anyways, in Biblical times, there were really no fences. The shepherds would stay with the flock for days at a time. Often, sheep from different flocks would co-mingle and they would get sorted out by recognizing the shepherd's voice; hence the parable.

Obviously, I don't have time to stay out with our goats for days at a time, so I had to build a fence if I want to keep goats. I could let them roam, I guess, but they would likely become roadkill after eating my neighbors landscaping. Or even worse, they could eat my wife's garden and not become roadkill.

If you accept the premise that a fence is necessary, then what type of fence does the job at a reasonable price needing little maintenance without harming the goats? I could have gone with woven fencing, but I didn't like the testimonials that they tend to get their heads stuck in the fencing and hang themselves. I'd have a hard time explaining that one to the kids.

Barbed wire might seem like a reasonable deterrent to you and I, but our goats lack the ability to reason. Therefore, I'm pretty certain that after they tried to walk through the barbed wire, my suturing skills would be getting some practice.

High tensile without electric is just plain inadequate. I watched one of the goats as we were hooking up the electric to the fence crawl between the strands three times to get into the yard. And I'm certain that the coyotes looking for an easy meal could easily negotiate the high tensile wire.

So, electric it is. We wondered how effective it would be and, indeed, it is a miracle of technology. After we attached the fencer and plugged it in, the male goat walked right over to it and put his nose to the hot wire. SNAP!

"BAAAAAAAAAH!"

He isn't the smartest goat in the world, so a couple of minutes later, SNAP!

"BAAAAAAAAAH!"

The next evening, my wife and I were watching the pair of goats from our back porch. She kept saying, under her breath, "Stay away from the fence, stay away from the fence" as we watched the female let her curiosity get the better of her. SNAP! My wife jumped higher than the goat, and the goat jumped pretty darn high.

Since then, I don't think they have tempted the fence again. I'm sure it hurt. It probably hurt really bad, in fact. If it hurt them half as much as the last time I got it from an electric fence, they won't soon forget it. Which brings me back to my original point about the electric fence being humane.

They won't tempt the fence again. Even the snap of the fence against a wet blade of grass sends them in the other direction. And I'm pretty confident that if a coyote ever tries to investigate with his cold, wet nose, it will be something it never forgets either. The result: safe goats with a healthy respect for boundaries.

Dandelions
5-8-12

Our small goat herd is about to get a little bigger. Five of our six does are very pregnant and look like they are about to pop any day, now. As a result, they've been receiving a lot more attention lately; mainly so that we aren't caught off guard when the first one goes into labor.

I was spending a little time with them in the pasture the other day and observed something that one only notices this time of year. The dandelions have all but flowered and what are left are the puffy seed heads that form on the stalk that was formerly occupied by the flower. Last week, the hay fields, pastures and a lot of yards were blazing yellow with dandelion flowers. They are nice to look at as it is a reminder that spring is here to stay. On the other hand, they don't really do the hayfields any good. It seems that the dry, early spring we had this year must have been perfect for the dandelions as I can't remember a year when they were more plentiful.

I have a love hate relationship with the dandelion. I love the greens in a salad. Don't think of getting some now, though. Since the flowers have come and gone, the greens are tough and bitter. In the middle of April, though, the greens are delicious as a salad.

I also have wanted to make some dandelion wine. I have a recipe that was given to me by a client about 12 years ago and I keep telling myself that this is going to be the year it gets made. Again, the window has come and gone.

As much as I revere the dandelion for its potential to make some fine food and drink, it really doesn't do my lawn any good. As I was mowing this afternoon, I must have hit the peak of the puffy seed head stage. I was trying to entertain my mind as I was driving to and fro on the mower and I considered just how many seeds there might be in an acre of land. Judging by the vast numbers of the featherweight seeds that were hitting me in the face, I reckoned that it must be an astronomical number.

So, I did some quick math. There were roughly 10 or so of these seed pods per square foot on my lawn. (I know; I don't spend much time taking care of my lawn.) An acre contains a little more than 40,000 square feet, but to keep the math simple enough, let's just use the 40,000 figure. I estimated that, conservatively, there were about 100 seeds per seed pod. That works out to 40 million dandelion seeds per acre, give or take a couple. (Trust me, I did the math twice.) That's a bunch of seeds.

So, what does all this have to do with our fat, pregnant, uncomfortable goats? As I was watching them in the pasture, I noticed that the goats really dig the dandelion seed head. Goats, unlike cattle, are not grazing animals. They prefer to browse. Browsers, like goats, will walk along and pick and choose what they eat. They tend to eat the flowers and the more palatable parts of the weeds and grasses. Their grazing cousins, on the other hand, munch indiscriminately.

The goats will go out of their way to pick off the top of a dandelion seed head. Maybe it's a pregnant craving or maybe it's a seasonal delicacy. Personally, I hope they eat every seed head in the pasture but I'm sure a bunch of them will escape. Regardless, I can't seem to find a nutritional analysis anywhere of the dandelion seed head, so I guess I'll just have to have faith that the Good Lord has designed them to be good for our goats. Should there be any doubt?

Purpose
5-22-12

Our goat herd is in expansion mode. This is our first experience with delivering kids of our own, of the four-legged variety anyways. Our daughter, Bena, was more than happy to offer her assistance to the does in loving on the kids, but I reminded her that it would be best to let the mama clean the slime off of them first.

The mothering instinct of the does is really something to behold. One day, they are fat, happy and without a care in the world. In a moment's notice, it all changed. There are now a couple of mouths to feed.

As I went to the barn with my daughter the day after the first twins were born, from the pasture I heard an unfamiliar, high pitched "Baaaaaaahhhh." I looked at Bena and said, "Uh-oh." Through the window of the barn, I could see the new arrival standing as the doe was cleaning her off. As we approached them, there was a second, newer kid lying in the tall grass, not yet ready to stand.

I am in awe of the immediate transformation of the personality of the new mothers. The first doe to deliver was raised as an orphan, so she is all but a pet to begin with. I expected that she would make the transition fairly easy; and she did. But the second doe was a different story. She is a little on the wild side. I was concerned that she might not accept the kids once they were born, but thankfully, my concerns were unfounded.

Typically, when I approach this doe, her tail goes straight up in the air and she doesn't wait to see what my intentions are before she leaves. But once the kids were on the ground, everything changed.

She let me walk up to her as the first kid was trying to find the teat to take his first meal. I wouldn't attempt this with a cow since they are frequently aggressive protecting the newborn calf after delivery.

I moved the kid lying on the ground closer to her and the doe didn't even twitch. I firmly believe that mother's instinct has more wisdom than I, so I left the doe and her still slimy kids alone. I did, however, observe them from a distance on the other side of the fence just to make sure everything progresses as planned.

Now that the delivery was over, the next critical step in the new journey of the kids is to get a nice big meal of colostrum. Colostrum, the mother's first milk, is rich in energy, vitamins and even has a mild laxative effect. But most importantly, colostrum contains lots and lots of antibodies. The newborn kid, calf, lamb among others, is completely dependent on colostrum to get their immune system up and running. Without it, trouble in the form of infectious disease is sure to visit.

I watched as the doe planted her feet and allowed the kids to struggle to find the spigot that would dispense this magical first milk. I watched until I got bored so I decided to mow the lawn. At supper time an hour later, the doe was still standing patiently as the kids took turns at the teats. The story was the same after supper. In fact, she remained in the same spot until I finished mowing. The kids had apparently drunk their fill because their bellies were full and her udder had shrunk.

When my wife and I had our kids (the two legged variety) and left the hospital, we didn't have a clue. We received all sorts of advice from many different, well intentioned sources, but it was still an anxious time. Incidentally, the best advice I received was from a friend of mine who told me that I shouldn't feel guilty when I realize that the first two months stink. "It's OK," he said. "It stinks but it gets better." I still remember the realization to which my wife and I came shortly after bringing our first child home. It's not only about us anymore. Life now has a different purpose.

I put the kids in the clean maternity pen that was prepared in the barn and the doe dutifully followed them in. I noticed that she still had a good deal of slime on her rear and teats from the delivery process, so I thought it best to clean the slime off. Yesterday, if I had touched her udder when she wasn't looking, she would have jumped out of her skin. Now, she stood there and let me do what I needed to do. Instinct tells her to stand there and take it for the sake of the offspring. It's almost like she knows it's not only about her anymore. Apparently, that's what having kids does to you.

Instinct
6-19-12 to 6-26-12

I think there are some questions that, in this life, are just destined to remain unanswered. Answers to questions like, what happened to Amelia Earhart and what really goes on at Area 51 are just not available. One nagging question that puzzles me relates to the instinctual nature of animals. How do they know how to do what they need to do?

Instincts like those of the Monarch butterfly's habitual return to a tiny plot of land in Mexico for the winter and migratory birds' pinpoint navigation skills are nothing short of fascinating. No less fascinating is the instinct of a newborn.

By newborn, I mean those newborns like calves that, upon entry into the world, are raring and ready to go. In the wild, these prey animals must be able to get away from predators soon after birth if they want to survive. If it were as simple as just being able to get up and leave, it wouldn't be nearly as fascinating. There's a lot more to the miracle of this story.

We got to experience this miracle up close and personal this spring as our small goat herd had its first crop of kids. As a veterinarian, I get to deliver a lot of calves. With few exceptions, when I get called for a cow in labor, it is already established that something is amiss. Not all calves are delivered alive and when they are, I usually have somewhere else to be. Our goats afforded us the opportunity to witness the normal side of things.

Actually, the goats are pretty sneaky about the whole birthing process. We went from thinking delivery was a few days away to kids on the ground; a few pages of the story were missing. But the truly miraculous part was yet to come.

A lot of things have to happen correctly even after delivery in order to ensure a live calf, lamb, kid or whatever. First, the newborn has to take a breath. That's easy, right? Not so for a newborn. While still inside the womb, the lungs are completely collapsed. It actually takes a great deal of effort for the newborn to expand its lungs as it takes its first breath immediately after birth. The expanded lungs result in oxygen rich blood, the likes of which the newborn's body has never before seen. This increase in oxygen causes several physiologic changes to occur in the body, from changes to the very anatomy of the heart itself to altering the structure of hemoglobin in the red blood cells.

Once the lungs are working, the newborn needs to stand. Within a half hour or so, the newborn is up and at 'em. But they don't just get up; it's a tough process. First, they get up on their back legs then fall on their face. This is repeated several times until finally, a front leg is straightened. Then, they fall on their face again.

This is again repeated several more times until the last leg is straightened and all four feet are on the ground. The newborn will stand there and wobble back and forth as if it were on a john boat in the middle of the ocean with 8-foot seas. Finally, it garners the courage to take a step and boom- it falls on its face again. This can be painful to watch, especially to a control freak like myself. I want to help, but I know that this is nature's way of teaching. She is certainly a better teacher than I am.

Finally, the newborn gains the strength to successfully take a few steps. All during the process, mama is close by softly humming encouragement to the newborn. By humming, I mean just that. It's a very soft "moo," or "baa" sound made without ever opening her mouth.

As difficult as all of this does sound, none of it is learned behavior; it is all instinct. These instinctual behaviors are hard wired into the animal. Like a successful baseball player with good instincts for the game, the animals with good instincts will have a successful career. Usually, within an hour or so, the newborn calf is on its feet and ready to move. It is truly amazing that a calf, lamb or kid can stand and walk that quickly, but the truly amazing part has yet to happen.

If the newborn could think rationally, it might wonder if it was appearing in an episode of Mission Impossible, "If you choose to accept this mission…" The new mission is to eat some colostrum. Colostrum is the first milk from the mother. It differs substantially from plain old milk in that it is very rich in antibodies.

These antibodies in the colostrum, if ingested in a timely fashion, get absorbed intact into the newborn's bloodstream and serve to function as protection against infectious diseases. If ingestion is delayed, even by as little as a few hours, the absorption of the antibodies is decreased and the newborn's immune system isn't nearly as strong as it could have been. Lack of timely colostrum ingestion is nearly a death sentence for a newborn.

So, it is imperative that the newborn get a big meal of colostrum as soon as possible after birth. Standing and taking its first steps was no easy task for the newborn, neither will be finding the teat to take its first meal.

Obviously, the udder is the place to be for the first meal, but getting there is harder than it would seem. Since the newborn knows what it wants but isn't sure where to get it, it searches somewhat randomly on the mother. It might start on the neck, only to find it dry and unrewarding. Next, it might find the elbow. No colostrum there, either. The newborn bounces around until finally, it finds a teat.

Once it finds what it was searching for, it latches on in no time flat and begins to nurse. How it knows what it needs is no doubt driven by instinct. Then, without warning, the newborn instinctively gives a quick upward thrust with its head into the udder as if to say, "Milk faster!"

What I just described is the best case scenario and it doesn't always work out that well. There are some pitfalls that the newborn might encounter and one is a less than perfect teat to latch onto. These "balloon" teats happen commonly in some beef cattle and goats. It is a hereditary condition and is undesirable since the newborn has a difficult time latching on as the teat is too big for its mouth.

A couple of our does have a mild form of this balloon teat and it did create some complications. In one doe that had twins, one teat was normal and the other was slightly ballooned. The kids preferred the normal one, of course. This caused the ballooned teat to become even bigger and the normal one was sucked dry. I tried to trick the kids into latching on to the bigger teat, but their instincts told them it just wasn't right. They would have nothing to do with it. Eventually, I ended up just milking out the large teat into a bucket, just to remove the pressure.

And that is what originally got me wondering about the overwhelming strength of instinctual behaviors of the newborn. Why would they not take the large teat, even when I put the kid's mouth right on it? Is there a particular feel it needs to have, or is there a scent that attracts the kids to the teat or even repels the kids from things that aren't a teat? After I milked it out, I smeared a little saliva from one of the kids and some milk from the other teat onto the skin of the balloon teat and left it until morning. The next day, the kids had figured out how to nurse off of both teats, much to my relief and the relief of the doe.

All of our pregnant does have now kidded and, for the most part, the kids' instincts were good enough to get them over the hump. The does are now enjoying the instinctual behavior of the kids as they lay low in the tall grass to avoid predators. This gives the does an occasional respite from the harassment of the hungry kids. Sure, there are no predators in our pasture, but as far as mama is concerned, the kids don't need to know that.

Dilemma
11-12-13

I butchered one of our goats this weekend. In fact, it was actually the last of our goats, at least for the near future.

My son was ecstatic; he doesn't have to get up before the crack of dawn anymore and feed. My daughter, well, she was less than ecstatic.

If you are tempted to send me a nasty note (the email address is at the end of this article) about killing one of our goats, remember that they are meat goats; they are made of meat. It was born to be eaten.

Now, truth be told, I'd just as soon have sold the goat to somebody else than butcher it myself, but this goat was had a slight problem. Only one of his testes had descended from his abdomen at birth.

I had originally intended to castrate him and sell him. But when our vet student and I showed up one afternoon to do the deed, I made the discovery. I always count to two before making my incision and I couldn't get past one on this guy.

The condition, known as cryptorchidism, causes quite a dilemma in a food animal. Removing just the one that's accessible would be unethical since the other that remained would still function to produce hormones. (He would have been rendered sterile nonetheless.) The hormone production would make him stink like a billy-goat and possibly act aggressive. Doing abdominal surgery to remove the missing one is simply impractical in a food animal. Leaving him intact to be used as a breeder would be just as poor of an idea since many believe that this condition has a hereditary component.

So, I left him intact at the time we castrated the others and butchered him before he started to stink. My wife took the kids to Greensburg for the day and I took the opportunity to play the part of the grim reaper while they were away.

That evening as I was processing the meat on the kitchen counter, the curiosity was more than my daughter could bear. She strolled up to the counter and proclaimed, "Poor Bucky, I really liked him."

It's a lesson that we all learn at some point. Meat comes from an animal. We usually don't know that animal, but if we do, it does provoke some reflection.

Then she looked at what I was doing and grimaced. "Is that blood? Why is there so much blood?" I didn't waste much time hanging him to drain all the blood, so there was indeed more blood in the meat than she is used to. She sees me butcher several deer a year and I was impressed that she picked up on this.

Then she must have forgot about liking "Bucky" since she stood beside me the whole time I was processing the carcass. "What is that slimy stuff?"

"It's fat," I replied.

"Why are you cutting it out?" I explained to her that we don't want to eat that part of the fat since it comes from the shoulder and is rather nasty. "Why are you cutting the meat up into such small pieces?"

"So I can grind it into burger," I reminded her.

"You can make burger out of goat? I thought you make burger out of cow?" Then she asked, "Did you find the missing testicle? Was it nasty looking? I wish you would have saved it so I could see it."

And so the conversation continued. She'd ask a question and I'd give an explanation which would be followed by a coy, "Ewwww."

I was proud of her, but not really surprised.

Hershey's Back
4-29-14

Farmers are a diverse lot of folks. There are grain farmers, livestock farmers, vegetable farmers and even fish farmers. Some farmers diversify and raise several different crops or critters. Some are full time and others are part time. All of them are an asset to the rest of us.

I've often wondered what would draw a person to become a farmer. Is it his or her upbringing? Is it for the benefits of being self-employed? Maybe it's because they just like it. I don't think anyone could argue that it's for the financial security or stability. Whatever the reason, I'm glad that there are people who want to farm.

While I never claimed seriously to be a farmer, we used to raise some meat goats. They were nothing fancy, just something to keep the pasture mowed down. We sold the herd a while ago and, after this winter, I'm grateful that they weren't here.

It's not that we didn't like the goats; we did. My schedule doesn't really afford me the time to devote to the care of livestock of my own. I learned that lesson after a couple of winters. Forking the manure and bedding out of the barn, carrying bales of hay down to where the goats were housed and making sure the water didn't freeze took most of the fun out of it for us in the already busy winter.

So we made the decision to sell the herd so that someone else can benefit from them. We had them for several years and, admittedly, I was glad when were gone. I probably don't have it in me to be a farmer, but I think I understand why someone might take up the profession of livestock farming.

One of the goats that we got rid of was an orphan. We raised her from a day old kid on a bottle. Consequently, she never really developed into a strong doe; she has always been kind of frail. She was more of a pet than a profit center anyways and I didn't think it would be right to sell her. So when we sold the other goats, the pet went with them on loan. We had arranged to bring her back once the weather broke.

My wife and I asked our daughter what she wanted to do recently one Saturday. Without hesitation, she said, "Let's get Hershey!" Hershey is the name she gave to the orphan. So, we went that day and fetched Hershey.

Now that the grass is starting to grow and the temperatures are moderating, it was an easy decision. We made the short drive to the farm where she was and loaded her and her new doe kid on the truck.

We got them back to our place and released them after the short drive. Immediately, I remembered what I enjoyed so much about having livestock.

I used to walk down to the pasture just so I could watch them graze.

I know; I need to get out more. But there is something therapeutic about watching them, up close, grazing.

I would consider how the goats could convert the solar energy that was stored in the grass into meat. I would marvel at how, as ruminants, they could digest the grass that is indigestible to people. I would reflect on the Bible passage where Jesus reminds His disciples that they shouldn't worry about what they should eat or wear. (Matthew 6:25) But mainly, I would just watch.

Hershey began to graze vigorously about a second and a half after she exited the back of the truck. Goats tend to make their voices heard when they want something, like feed, and this doe is no exception. I used to mess with her from my back door by yelling "Goat goat!" She would let out a raspy "Baaaa!" to let me know she wanted something. We got back into that routine about 15 minutes later.

So why do farmers do it? It must be because, at least some of the time, it brings them happiness. My daughter remarked to me as we were watching the goats graze the virgin pasture that Hershey looked as happy as the camel on hump day.

Yep, and so was I.

CHAPTER 8
Memorable cases

Photo by Michelle Sechler

I am not an overly sentimental person. Perhaps that's one reason why I chose to work on cows and not pets. In addition to not being sentimental, I am not very good with names. In any event, even though farm animals tend to remain rather anonymous, some occasionally leave a lasting impression.

While I might remember the medical specifics of memorable cases, I don't always remember an animal's name. And, if the patient is only known as a number, I have no chance to recall it. But some are so memorable that a name becomes seared into my brain, impossible to forget. If the food animal patients that appear as the subject of an article were known by a name, I've included the name in the title of the article.

Many farmers opt to give a cow a name instead of a number. I recall a study several years ago that compared milk production between dairy farms of cows with names against those known only by a number. The study received a little bit of popular attention because it's conclusion was that cows with names make more milk than cows with numbers. Now, the numbers don't lie for the farms enrolled in the study, but we shouldn't read too much into the conclusion. It's possible, or even likely that the cows with names originated from registered herds with superior breeding or management tendencies and the cows with only a number were not. That's speculation on my part, but just as valid as concluding that assigning a name to an animal magically makes her a better milk cow.

Nonetheless, there are valid reasons why a farmer may choose to name a cow. He may be better with names than I am, but that's not saying much. His cows may be registered with a breed association, like Holstein USA or the American Jersey Cattle Association which require a name for pedigree continuity. But even in the case of a breed registry, the name assigned to the registered animal may simply be its number assigned at birth.

Incidentally, it's tradition in dairy breeds to assign a name to an animal that begins with the first letter of the dam's (mother) name. This might be a tradition that's hard to uphold sometimes. I've known cows named ad Q-tip and X-Ray. I wonder what those pedigrees look like?

Most farmers aren't overly sentimental either. But they do have their favorite cows. Some can even get very attached to them. I suspect that this attachment is but one of the motivations for them to endure the long hours necessary for farming. More than one farmer upon retirement has broken down and wept as the gavel fell for the last time at the dispersal sale. His girls would no longer be around, and that reality sets in like a two-by-four across the chops.

Anyhow, when a cow has a name as opposed to a number, they are just a little more memorable. And when a special cow has a name whom I've treated, it makes them even easier to remember. The following are some of my most memorable patients.

Galaxy
2-7-17

There are firsts and lasts for everything. For a new veterinary graduate, there are a lot of firsts. First attempts at a new surgery, first time encountering a particular disease and the first time treating a new patient are among the them. As for the animals, we strive to ensure our efforts aren't the last for the patient. But inevitably, sometimes it would be.

I recall a memorable dairy cow from a decade or more ago. She is memorable for more than one reason. She was very big; bigger than 95 percent of any of the dairy cows I had ever seen. She was also considered an excellent cow by the Holstein breed association. But perhaps the most memorable thing about her was a specific bad habit she had.

Whenever she stood at the feed bunk, she would take a mouthful of feed to eat. She would give a cursory chew and swallow. Hastily, she would grab another mouthful and sling the contents of her muzzle over her back. Satisfied that she had irritated her neighbors and the farmer, she would take another bite to eat. She was always easy to find at the bunk. One simply had to look down the row and watch for the silage shower as gravity returned it to the scrape alley behind her.

When I began offering embryo transfer in cattle, she was one of the first cows from which I had collected embryos. She was a prolific embryo producer, satisfying both the farmer and the vet with her efforts.

Her farmer called me to look at her one day nearly 10 years ago since she hadn't eaten for a couple of days. It is always abnormal for a cow to not eat, although not uncommon. Sometimes they get some indigestion, a bellyache or even a metabolic disorder that takes away their appetite. Often a cow will self-cure after a day.

But after two days of no appetite for this cow, something was seriously wrong with her. When I examined her, I could tell that she wouldn't cure herself. She had a belly full of feed, her belly was distended and she wasn't passing any manure. It is always abnormal for a cow to not pass manure and it usually means there is an obstruction somewhere in her GI tract.

During my examination, I decided that she was a candidate for an exploratory surgery. I had performed my first of many abdominal surgeries some years earlier, but most of them had been for the common twisted stomach. This girl was not suffering from a twisted stomach; that much was obvious.

What wasn't obvious was the exact cause of her obstruction. We secured her standing to a head gate and prepared her for surgery. Once she was clipped and scrubbed, I made my incision and reached into her abdomen. Everything was in its proper place, but there was no feed in the last half of her small intestine. I pulled a bit of her intestine out through the incision and started working my way forward toward her stomach.

Recognize that cows have more than 100 feet of small intestine and this girl must have been pushing double that. So, it took a few minutes, but I eventually stumbled upon a section of intestine that suddenly got full with feed. The question was why wasn't the feed progressing past that point? There was only one way to find out.

This was a first for me. I had never been presented with this dilemma before and the only way to know for sure was to cut into the intestine. This procedure, called an enterotomy, is fraught with danger for the patient. Inside the intestine is fluid laden with trillions of bacteria that once outside of the protected intestine can cause a raging infection. Before proceeding, I clamped her incision closed temporarily to return to my truck for some additional supplies like smaller suture and some rinse.

Once I had everything, I gathered the offending portion of the intestine and made an incision in it. I began milking out the stinky contents onto the barn floor and at the very end of the mess fell a baby tooth. This unfortunate cow had swallowed a tooth and it had caused a traffic jam in her intestine. I repaired the hole in her intestine, gave everything a good rinse and closed her up. This was the first time I had done intestinal surgery on a cow, but not the last. And it was the first time I pulled a tooth on a cow. That was, however, the last time I've performed a dental procedure.

She survived the surgery and had a productive career as a dairy cow and an embryo producer. Whenever doing reproductive checks in her farmer's barn, I would always look for the silage rain to discover where she stood. I wanted to be prepared for the feed shower when I got behind her.

I was back to his barn the other day to check some cows and I saw no flying feed. At the end of the row, I turned to the farmer and asked about her. She wasn't there. She was a cow of many firsts for both of us, but finally after a career that spanned nearly 14 years, she too had seen her last day.

Millie
8-9-14

This is a true story about Millie. Millie is a yearling beef heifer at a farm not too far from here. As I was pregnancy checking the herd to which she belongs the other day, Millie entered the chute for her exam. Millie was an orphaned calf. Well, she's not technically an orphan but she was abandoned by her mother at birth because she was a twin. Only about 2 or 3 percent of beef cows have twins and when both are born alive, it's common for the cow to only accept one calf.

But no farmer wants to give up on a healthy calf, even if it means bottle feeding the orphan. Now I suspect that beef farmers are beef farmers because the cows take care of raising their own calves. Believe me, beef farmers don't relish the idea of hand rearing a calf. But they do it when necessary.

Or, even better, the farmer might have his daughter bottle feed the calf. That was Millie's fate. Women generally do a much better job of raising calves than men. Maybe it's because women are better nurturers or maybe they have more patience, I don't know. But it is undeniable.

So last spring when Millie was born, the farmer's daughter took the calf to her house, housed her in the back yard and raised her. His daughter and her husband conveniently live in their own house on the farm. I'm going to make another generalization. Whenever a woman hand rears a beef calf in her back yard, she tends to become quite attached to the calf. In fact, they often end up as pets.

Cattle don't make the best pets. They eat a lot and are impossible to house train. Nonetheless, the farmer's daughter became quite fond of Millie. But Millie has a bit challenge. Her twin sibling was a bull calf.

Cattle are not supposed to have twins. But occasionally they do and if the calves are a bull and a heifer (boy and a girl), the heifer will usually be sterile, unable to reproduce. From the moment of conception, the calf's fate of being either a bull or heifer is determined by its chromosomes. Early on in gestation, we think around 30 days or so, the chromosomes direct the development of either the male or female parts.

When there are two calves sharing the womb, some of the hormonal signals get mixed up and the female's development gets confused. The developing female will receive some of the male's signal and her reproductive parts won't form correctly. Consequently, she will be sterile. The bull, on the other hand, will usually develop normal. Studies have shown that about 90 percent of these heifer calves twin to a bull are sterile. Those are not very good odds. But without a blood test, you can't tell definitively if the female calf was affected negatively.

Millie was never blood tested. I remember pregnancy checking at this farm last year and the farmer's daughter was telling me about her calf that she was raising. The calf would follow her around the yard like a dog. And she relayed to me how she was probably going to bawl when the calf had to leave.

A heifer calf that can't get pregnant is a drain on the resources of the farm. In fact, feeder calves in today's market are fetching more than $1,000 each. Cattle make lousy pets but they do make great steaks. If Millie was sterile, her fate would be the latter. But if Millie could have the farmer a calf, that would be even better.

So Millie entered the chute. The farmer's daughter was recording the cows' identification and how many days pregnant they were as I told her. She was around the corner, however, and couldn't see who entered the chute. Her father would let her know the cow's identity once caught.

When Millie entered the chute, I heard the daughter ask who it was. The farmer got a smile on his face and said, "Uh oh! It's Millie!"

I heard his daughter in the corner of the barn, "Oh, please! Oh, please!"

The farmer told me, "Tell me if she has all of her parts." I then remembered Millie's story, even though it was the first time I had seen her. I reminded the daughter about the 90 percent odds, preparing her for the bad news.

I reached my ultrasound probe up inside the heifer looking for the evidence of a small, undeveloped uterus. And there was a single developing embryo, and only one, with a nice normal heartbeat. I told the daughter and her dad, "She must be one of the 10 percent. She's pregnant."

You'd have thought that I just handed the daughter keys to a new pick-up truck. "Yaaaaaaaayyyyyyyyyyyyyy! Millie, you get to stay!" Millie had beaten the odds.

Nut
9-7-13

So many people in this day and age think that cattle farmers and dairy farmers in particular, don't know their cows but as nameless cogs in a machine identified only by a number on an ear tag. While that may be the case on some of the very largest of commercial farms, by and large many of the farmers that I know recognize their cows by just looking at them.

I often marvel at this skill when doing pregnancy checks on the farm. As we walk around the barn in search of a particular cow, some farmers know just where certain cows like to hang out. I was pregnancy checking a herd for a farmer one day in the free stall barn. Cows run loose in a free stall barn and to find the ones we needed, each cow had to be observed to see if she was on the list. I was about to ask him to provide me with a list of ear tag numbers to help out, but I noticed that none of the cows in this 200 cow herd had ear tags. When I asked him how he knew one cow from another, he replied, "I just know them."

Sure, cows can run together and to keep them straight, there are computer programs that record production data like pounds of milk and component percentages of individual cows. Most cows are indeed identified by a number, but many of these have names too. And, every once in a while, a special cow comes along that needs no number.

What constitutes a special cow? Maybe on some farms it's a cow that is exceptional in the show ring or has champion blood lines. On others, it may be a high producer.

On one local dairy farm, there is a truly special cow. I've seen literally tens of thousands of dairy cows in my career and this one is, by far, the most special. She is not the highest milk producer on the farm, nor does she have champion bloodlines or blue ribbons. She will certainly never win a beauty contest, but everyone she meets loves her. Her name is "Nut."

Most cows have an instinctual fear of humans. This fear prevents people from approaching the cow in a pasture or barn and touching her - she will normally leave before a person gets too close. Few cows lack this fear and when they do, well, they almost become like pets.

Nut has no fear.

It doesn't matter who you are when you enter this barn; Nut will be the first cow to greet you. She will approach slowly but deliberately, cock her head to one side and stare at you with her crossed eyes. After leaning in for a good sniff, she'll not leave until getting a scratch on the head.

My brother, who doesn't have much experience with cows, met her once about two years ago. He was visiting for the day to get in some bow-hunting and tagged along with me on a herd check. As we looked for cows to check in the barn, Nut followed him around as she sniffed the back of his neck. He still asks about her. I send him a text message with her picture once in a while.

An employee at this farm remarked to me recently that the day this cow dies is going to be a very sad day at this farm. Instead of being sold for meat like most cows, Nut will be retired. In fact, when she does die a natural death, she just might be stuffed instead of buried.

I had mentioned to the farm hand that I'd like to write her obituary when she dies. But instead, I think it would be better to give her some recognition before that unfortunate day arrives. Nut is slowing down a quite a bit, but she still gives it her best... and brings a certain measure of joy to everyone who frequents this farm. And she does have an ear tag in her ear, but I'm not sure if anybody knows what number is on it.

Bloat
10-16-12 to 10-23-12

Some days you're the windshield and some days you're the bug. I get to see a lot of cattle suffering from a variety of maladies. Some get better; some do not. Whenever I work on a tough case, either medical or surgical and everything works out the way it's supposed to, I'll tell my wife, teasingly, that I snatched another one from the jaws of death. She always gives me the same, "Yeah, OK, whatever. There's that God complex again." She likes to keep me humble.

So, it's with all humility that I tell this story about a calf that I worked on recently. When it comes to dealing with gravely ill cattle, the defeats far outnumber the victories. I am under no illusion otherwise.

Having said that, a client called us about a calf that was bloated recently one afternoon. He impressed upon our secretary that this calf was in a tough spot and we should waste no time getting there. She promptly relayed the message and I was on my way hastily.

Bloat in cattle is caused by gas accumulation in the rumen, the largest chamber of the ruminant's four chambered stomach. The gas can accumulate by a variety of mechanisms; either nerve damage, physical obstruction that prevents burping or frothy bubble accumulation in the rumen itself. Regardless of the mechanism, bloat always has the potential to be deadly.

Bloat will quickly kill a bovine if severe enough. Just like a constrictor snake squeezes the life out of its prey from the outside, a bloated rumen does the same thing, only from within. As the rumen increases in size, the pressure builds up and causes the circulatory system to shut down and breathing becomes nearly impossible. To treat bloat, one has to remove the accumulated gas from the rumen one way or another. One way to relieve bloat is to run a stomach tube down the animal's throat.

When I arrived at the farm, the farmer was placing a halter on the sick calf's head. You can't treat a case of bloat unless the animal is properly restrained. I've witnessed firsthand cattle die from bloat. It usually happens during treatment. Since the animal's respiratory and circulatory systems are so severely compromised from the pressure, any struggle will hasten death by inducing respiratory distress.

Recognizing the possibility of killing the calf during treatment, I asked the farmer if the calf was turning blue yet as I gathered up my stomach tube. As he tied the halter to the gate, that farmer told me that, yes, the calf was indeed turning blue.

The calf was fighting the halter as I was making my way in the barn to pass the tube. The excitement started when the calf dropped lifeless to the floor of the barn. I heard the farmer yell, "You'd better hurry up – She doesn't look good!"

The calf was dying before our eyes. To make matters worse, I've not yet been able to resuscitate a dying bovine in more than 15 years of practice. Sure, we've revived some calves after a tough delivery, but nothing beyond that. So, I was pretty concerned about this calf. Well, concerned doesn't adequately describe what I felt- I was worried. I dropped the stomach tube and returned to my truck.

Another way to relieve bloat is with a trocar. A trocar is like a very, very large needle that we can stick directly into the rumen through the skin to quickly relieve bloat in an emergency. Since this calf was no longer breathing, it met the threshold for an emergency. I fetched a trocar from my truck and hurried back to try to quickly deflate the calf.

When I got back to the calf, the farmer and I rolled her over so that the rumen was facing up. I punched the trocar into the rumen, screwed it into place and removed the stylet. She deflated with a loud PSSSSSHHHHHHhhhhh like somebody had just let the air out of a balloon.

The calf was now deflated, but so was the farmer because the calf was completely unresponsive. Fortunately, the calf still had a faint pulse, so I returned to my truck again, this time for some epinephrine. My needle found the jugular vein and I pushed the plunger on the syringe, injecting the epinephrine to jump start her heart.

I hope you recognize that it's pretty impractical to do mouth to mouth resuscitation on a 400-pound calf. So, we did the next best thing and set her upright and rapidly compressed her thorax. We could hear the air moving in and out of her mouth every time we pushed on her ribs, so I thought she might be getting some oxygen. By this time, the epinephrine had kicked in because her pulse was noticeably stronger.

After a minute or so, she took an agonal breath. The farmer looked at me with great hope and I immediately cautioned him that an agonal breath was actually bad news. Agonal breaths, more like a last gasp, are never good. They mean death is imminent.

Nevertheless, we continued to work on her and the agonal breaths became more frequent. Eventually, they were so frequent that I no longer tried to compress her chest. She was still unresponsive, but she was moving air and, by now, even I was encouraged. I stuck my hand in her mouth and suspended her head allowing her bottom jaw to hang open to reduce any impedance of airflow to the lungs.

After about five minutes, she started to chew and grind her teeth and I thought that, maybe, just maybe, we could get her over this.

After a little while longer, she was able to hold her head up, so there was no reason for me to kneel beside her to hold her head. I stood up and the farmer and I both finally offered a smile. She wasn't out of the woods by any means, but she was a lot closer than she was 15 minutes ago.

We decided to let her lay until she was good and ready to get up on her own. The farmer asked me if when she was able to stand, it would be a good idea to move her into her own pen so the pen mates don't take advantage of the situation to abuse her. I affirmed his good idea.

Just then, the calf gave a feeble attempt to stand. Almost immediately she gave a second, wholehearted attempt to stand but only this time, she was successful. Since she had the indwelling trocar in her rumen, I prescribed some penicillin for five days so the wound didn't get infected. I walked out of the barn hardly able to believe what had just happened.

I thanked the farmer for the adrenaline rush and he thanked me as well. We both agreed that we'd rather not do this again anytime soon. I left the dairy that afternoon feeling a great sense of accomplishment and when I recounted the story to my wife, she looked at me like, "There you go with that god-complex again." She's always trying to keep me humble.

After a little reflection, however, I concluded that if it weren't for the inborn adaptations, or compensatory mechanisms for survival of the bovine, resuscitation would have been impossible.

For example, when the calf went limp, it slowed her need for oxygen and prevented irreversible brain damage. The ability of the heart to respond to epinephrine in an emergency allowed for improved circulation after treatment with epinephrine. And finally, whatever the mechanism, the calf did start to breathe again by herself. All we really did was get her over the hump. When I spoke with the farmer last week, the calf is still doing well. We now expect a full recovery.

Author's note:

When this article appeared in my column in 2012, it appeared as a series of two articles and the fate of the calf was not known to the readers until the second half was published. I heard from many readers that cliffhangers were not a good idea. Everyone wanted to know the fate of this calf before the conclusion was published and I held my ground for the most part. As I recall, it was a popular article.

I ran into the same farmer a couple of months after this article was published. He thanked me for writing the article and let me know that he enjoyed reading it. But in a cruel twist of irony, the calf hadn't been so lucky.

The trocar we use to temporarily relieve bloat is left to remain in the rumen for an average of about 3 weeks. As the hole in her side heals, it eventually pushes the trocar back out. By then, whatever was the original cause of the bloat passes.

And for this calf, the trocar did fall out in time and the wound in her side healed. The bloat, however, returned a second time and she succumbed before anyone knew she was in trouble. Irony has a cruel streak to it.

Rocky
2-25-14

Many of you are no doubt familiar with the common breed of cow known as Holstein. They are the black and white dairy cow that populates most of the barns in Somerset County. They are also recognizable from such television commercials as the happy cows from California and the Chick-Fil-A cows that encourage viewers to "EAT MOR CHIKIN."

Holstein cows make up the vast majority of dairy cows with some estimating that 90 percent or so of all dairy cows in the United States are Holstein. Many of these cows are registered with the breed registry, Holstein Association USA. But many more of them, while truly Holsteins, are never registered.

In 2012, there were about 360,000 new cattle registered with the Holstein Association. Besides maintaining pedigree information, one of the functions of the breed registry is to improve the breed. In order to improve the breed, superior cows and bulls must be identified.

The best animals might be the ones with the highest milk production. Or, maybe they might be winners of the many dairy shows that occur both locally and nationally. Finally, some of the best animals are identified through a scoring system.

Dairy breeds have a fairly objective system of scoring animals based on body type. The ideal cow should be one that is a high producer and lives for a long time. This scoring system is used to predict which cows may fit that bill.

Cows are given a score or a "grade" on a scale of 0 to 100 points. Cows that score more than 90 points are considered excellent and are uncommon. Cows that achieve a score of 95 are very rare. Just for reference, there were only 20 cows in the entire country in 2013 that achieved the score of 95 for the first time. Remember that more than 360,000 new Holstein cattle were registered a year earlier.

Typically, a single classifier from the breed association will travel to a farm and score the cows that the farmer wishes to have scored. Obviously, only the best cows are picked to be scored. In the case of a cow that the classifier feels may be 95 points, a committee of three classifiers must be assembled. If the committee agrees with the classifier's initial assessment, the cow is awarded the coveted 95 points.

Somerset County is no stranger to the 95 point cow. Several years ago, we got two of them in one day. One of those cows, Pennwood Leader Rocklyn, also known as "Rocky," was one of them. She is certainly one of the best of the Holstein breed. In addition to scoring the rare 95 points, she has been a prolific milk producer and perennial show winner.

Rocky has lived in Somerset County longer than I have, so she's been around for a while. I've come to know Rocky pretty well over the years. I remember the day several winters ago that she was suffering with a bad case of pneumonia. It was on that day I came to the realization that, eventually, every farmer's prized cow would meet her end. Rocky survived that ordeal and continued to excel.

She had a bit of a scare a year or so after her bout with pneumonia. A lump appeared in front of her shoulder that looked as though it might be cancer. The biopsy, fortunately, came back as benign.

Most dairy cows at the end of their productive life are sold for beef. But nobody at the farm would ever consider selling Rocky. Special cows are destined to retire when their productive life is over.

Rocky, however, could not escape the inevitable. This winter, another lump appeared on her that looked suspicious and this time, the biopsy came back as malignant. In fact, the pathologist felt that this one was sure to spread quickly. The family who owns her and all of the employees of the farm knew that the end was near.

I don't get the opportunity to end the suffering of very many cows. But the farmer called me one afternoon to give me the news that he felt Rocky was beginning to suffer. The family didn't want that; we knew what had to be done. The next morning, she drifted off to sleep peacefully after I gave the injection.

Rocky has left quite a legacy. Her memory will live on with the multitude of her daughters produced through the process of embryo transfer. I suspect that a wall is dedicated to the ribbons she has won as well. She was the pride of her farm and I am proud to have known her.

C-Section
11-21-17

I get to do a lot of cool things in the practice of my profession. The cool things are intermingled with the uncool things. And where the cool and uncool intersect, I occasionally find myself.

Possibly the coolest of the things I get to do is deliver calves. Cows instinctually deliver most calves on their own. When they get into a little trouble, the farmer usually knows how to help her out. But when the cow is in serious trouble, the vet gets called. I rarely get to see the easy ones but getting a live calf out of a struggling cow is always cool.

On the other hand, euthanasia of suffering animals is a necessary service. Humans employ, for lack of a better word, domestic animals and owe them diligence when it comes to ending their suffering. Cows, especially, are prone to disease and accidents that sometimes render them unfit to slaughter for human consumption.

When euthanasia is necessary, farmers and ranchers usually take this task upon themselves also. It is quick and painless with a well-placed bullet. Nevertheless, I can't say that the task is anything that we undertake with joyful anticipation. Some might even call it uncool.

A dairy farmer called me recently to ask for help with a difficult delivery. It was determined by the farmer that the patient had a twisted uterus. This condition is common, especially in dairy cows, because of their deep body conformation.

A uterus twists when the calf inside rotates upside down, or even more, and wraps the uterus (womb) up along with it like a blanket. There are many ways to fix it. But in her case, none were necessary because the calf was positioned correctly when I checked her. Cows do this from time to time; it happens.

But as we were preparing to deliver the calf without incident, the farmer asked me to look at another cow for him after we were done. "By the way, Doc, there's another cow outside that's supposed to have a calf today that I wouldn't mind your help with."

This is rarely good. Just when you think you're going to escape with an easy calving, some farmers play the "By the way…" card.

We delivered a live calf from the first patient. That was pretty cool. I then asked him to describe the problem on the second cow. He told me that the cow, who was about 8 months pregnant, (normal gestation is 9 months and 9 days) injured herself a couple of weeks ago and was unable to stand. He gave an injection two days ago to induce labor and wanted me to check the progress.

I believe a couple of words about inducing labor in cows is in order. When the calf is done cooking, it sends a chemical signal to mom. The delivery process can be artificially initiated by tricking the cow into thinking the calf has given the signal that it's ready to be born. That signal is the hormone cortisol, but we use a synthetic analog called dexamethasone. A side benefit of dexamethasone is that it causes the calf's lungs to rapidly mature to prepare it to breathe, which is important in an immature calf.

So, the calf was prepared to be born, now we just had to deliver it. Here is where the cool and uncool intersect. The cow was unable to ever stand again because of her injuries, so she had to be put down. That's uncool. But we could still deliver a live calf from her. That's cool.

It seems counterintuitive to euthanize the patient before delivering the calf, but that's what we did. A well-placed bullet ended her suffering swiftly so she didn't have to endure the surgery. Did I mention that we would deliver the calf by Cesarean section?

I have only delivered one live heifer calf in 20 years of practice this way, and she wasn't very vigorous. Believe me, I've been keeping track. I was due for a success. After dispatching the cow, I made a quick incision and located the calf in her belly. We have a couple of minutes before the calf gets into trouble, but we still needed to work quickly. As I retracted the calf's legs out through the incision, my feet got tangled up on the feed bucket and I landed flat on by back. It was embarrassing, but at least I didn't have to worry about remaining sterile at that point. Sorry, that attempt at humor was a little dark.

I brushed myself off and went back to work. I relocated the calf's legs and made an incision in the uterus and removed a live heifer calf from my now deceased patient. Not only was it alive, but it was alive and vigorous. That was very cool.

Against All Odds
5-10-16 to 5-17-16

The clinical practice of veterinary medicine involves decision making. We make decisions about what medicines to use, what test to run or even if surgery is indicated. Those decisions are the easy ones.

Our practice works only on livestock animals, so the decision to euthanize a family's beloved pet or not doesn't manifest very often. But the decision to treat or not to treat an ailing cow does present regularly.

This decision is rarely an emotional one. It is either a matter of economics or, if slaughter for salvaging the meat isn't an option, it is a matter of doing right by the animal. Sometimes it is better to slaughter an animal for meat than incur the cost of treatment. Or, if she is unfit for slaughter, euthanasia becomes the best option.

I didn't make the rules, but they are the rules we have to live by. It makes long and complicated treatment regimens for serious medical conditions cost prohibitive except in the most valuable of food animals. Every once in a while, we get to try something new and complicated. But there are never any guarantees that it will work.

I ran into a farmer the other day and he told me about a cow with whom I am well acquainted. It seems that she just had another set of twins. The fact that she had ever made it to deliver a calf at all was a surprise for all of us.

About 10 years ago, this farmer called us about a sick calf. I was the first to look at her and she had what we sometimes call an "ambiguopathy." That means the cause of her disease is rather ambiguous. She was just dull and acted like she had a belly ache.

When I examined her, I couldn't find anything specific wrong with her. She didn't really look like she had a surgical condition, so I treated her symptoms and gave her a magnet in case she had hardware disease.

Hardware disease happens when cattle swallow a metal wire or nail. They are not very discriminate eaters, so this happens more than you might think. If it does, we can force her to swallow a magnet which will stick to the offending metal, assuming it is ferrous, and render it harmless.

The next day, she wasn't any better. My partner, Dr. Dave took the call this time and she did look like a surgical case to him. At this point, the first of several decisions had to be made that would determine her fate. She is a 6-month old beef calf with uncertain potential. Despite the uncertainty, the farmer elected for exploratory surgery.

When Dr. Dave opened her up, he discovered the unexpected. She had a rather uncommon condition called intussusception. This is when the intestine attempts to swallow itself. Imagine the intestine as being like the sleeve of your sweatshirt. You reach all the way into the sleeve and start to turn it inside out by pulling the cuff. But after getting half way, you change your mind. Then reach in from the other end of the sleeve and grab the cuff again to pull it back out. When you are half way out and your sleeve is three layers thick, it is an intussusception.

If this happens in the intestine, the blood supply becomes compromised, the tissue swells, food can no longer pass through the swollen lumen and the intestine starts to die. This is exactly what Dr. Dave discovered in this calf's belly.

The farmer was faced with a second decision. Does he stop there and euthanize the animal or proceed with an attempt to repair the damage? Surgical correction is a risky proposition in the best of circumstances. Surgery, without help, in a barn, with the wrong equipment is very, very difficult. She wasn't a top show animal, nor was she a proven producer. She was a 6-month old calf with an uncertain future. Assuming she survives the surgery, she could turn out to be a good cow, or a dud.

Often, the cost of the treatment, either surgical or medical, exceeds the value of the farm animal. Many farmers opt to sell the animal for meat if it is fit for slaughter or euthanize the animal if it is not.

Farmers are obliged to concern themselves with matters such as these. Farms are truly small businesses, often the sole income for an entire family. If a farm fails to turn a profit, it will cease to exist. It is better to salvage an animal for meat than jeopardize the entire farm. The farmer elected to have Dr. Dave proceed instead of euthanizing the calf.

Unfortunately, the damage was already too severe and he had to cut the diseased section out and reconnect the two ends of the intestine. This surgery is technically one of the most difficult we do and fraught with danger for the patient. If there is even the slightest leak, the patient will suffer from a fatal infection in her abdomen. Dr. Dave removed the diseased intestine and reattached the two ends together again. He told the farmer the chances for survival weren't very good and to call and update us on the condition of the calf in a couple of days.

Two or three days went by and the farmer called to say that the calf had initially improved and eaten some, but had taken a turn for the worse. She had quit making manure again and was bloated.

The farmer now had yet another decision to make. There were obviously complications with the surgery and this is never good for the patient. Does he pay us to come up and examine this calf yet again despite its very poor prognosis, or does he quit and euthanize her?

The farmer elected to stay the course and try again, even though his vet bills had already surpassed the value of the calf. I had advised him against it.

Dr. Dave and I both were back up that afternoon. This time there were two of us and surgical equipment appropriate for what we were about to get into. We knew we had to go back in, but we didn't know what we would find. To complicate the picture even more, she was now bloated, leaving us very little room to work in her belly.

After delivering a heavy dose of sedation, we went back in through the original incision. We found the site in the intestine that had been removed and reattached and the reattachment had held. But there was a lot of swelling and it was preventing the passage of feed; that's why she was bloated. We had to cut out the swollen tissue and reconnect the ends again.

About 2 and a half hours later, we had finished stuffing her dilated intestines back in her belly and got her closed up. We didn't know what to expect, but the calf had made it this far. Maybe she had nine lives like a cat?

A couple of days later, she started passing manure again. She soon regained her appetite and her strength. She had made it again. The calf, against almost all odds, had survived. The farmer never gave up on her and was rewarded for it.

I checked the calf again about nine months later to see if she was pregnant. I knew it was her by the scar on her side and she was indeed pregnant. It was her first installment to the farmer for not giving up on her.

The next year she got pregnant again and gave the farmer twins.

She has delivered a calf each year since the surgery. I saw the farmer the other day and he said she had calved once again. It was her third set of twins.

These results are not typical. This type of surgical correction rarely is successful in the field. Beef cows don't often deliver three sets of twins in a lifetime. Farmers usually don't elect to have us do surgery when the prognosis is very poor. But this girl defied the odds and paid the farmer back in full, and then some, for his investment in her.

Nadine
4-17-12

I've been practicing veterinary medicine on cattle for nearly 15 years. One would think I've seen it all but in reality, almost every day presents a new challenge. Such is the case when I was recently asked to examine a cow that wouldn't eat.

It's common for a food animal vet to be presented with a cow that won't eat, but there was nothing routine about this case. This Holstein cow was a special one. You see, she was 14 years old and due to have a calf any day. Fourteen years old might not seem that old, but it really is when you consider the average lifespan of a dairy cow is about 5 years.

To make matters worse, the most critical time for a dairy cow to quit eating is just before she delivers her calf. In her last couple of weeks before calving, the dairy cow undergoes tremendous metabolic changes as she prepares for the grueling task of producing milk. Any disruption in feed intake can complicate the situation greatly.

When I examined her, it was quickly evident that this cow had a twisted stomach. The twisted stomach is indeed a common condition in dairy cows, but it usually happens several weeks after she delivers her calf, not before. Fortunately, it doesn't happen often in the late pregnant cow.

Abdominal surgery to replace the displaced stomach is the method of choice for a cure. In the late pregnant cow, however, the presence of the very large developing calf in her belly makes maneuvering inside the abdomen during the surgery quite difficult. In fact, it can be so difficult that often we elect to induce labor and deliver the calf before surgical correction is considered. But this cow was special.

Not only was she 14 years old, but she was the farmer's show calf when he was lust a lad. I was well acquainted with this cow, whose name I won't divulge because of confidentiality reasons. Last year, I unsuccessfully tried to repair her badly lacerated and fractured tail after another cow had stepped on it. Eventually, we had to amputate the tail behind the laceration. Suffice it to say that I know her by name. (There are less than a dozen cows in the county that I know by name.)

She was also found by sonogram seven months ago to be carrying a heifer calf. Heifer calves are much more desirable for the dairy farmer than are bull calves as the heifer calves are kept and raised up to eventually become milk cows.

If that wasn't already enough, the farmer is engaged to be married this spring and the cow is to be featured prominently in the wedding photographs. In 15 years of practice, I had yet to operate on a 14 year old cow with a twisted stomach. Neither had I operated on a cow scheduled to be featured in a wedding photo shoot. No pressure.

I considered inducing labor because of the difficult nature of the surgery, but in the end, we decided to go ahead and operate immediately. The surgery itself went well with no complications, but I knew that just because we corrected the displaced stomach she wasn't out of the proverbial woods yet. She still had to start eating again. She still had to deliver her heifer calf. And she still had to grow her fur back at the surgery site to look good in the photographs.

Some would try to convince us that farmers couldn't care less about their animals' well-being and they are only a means by which to make a profit. It is true that without profit a farm is unsustainable, but most farmers I know recognize well that they are stewards of both the land and their livestock. Most cattle are indeed known only by a number, but they are taken care of as if they were known by name. Without this attention to their welfare, the animals would be unproductive and thus unprofitable.

Occasionally, we run across a truly special cow and consideration has to be given to the bond the farmer may have with the animal. Neither the farmer nor I would ever consider them as a member of the family or even as a pet, but they are special nonetheless.

I heard from the farmer recently about this cow. He let me know that she delivered a live heifer calf and was eating everything she could get her mouth around. Now we just need to find a way to hide the scar on her flank for the photo shoot.

CHAPTER 9
Wholesome Food

Photo by Rick Cramer

I've devoted a lot of time trying to dispel the myth that food marketed and labeled as "certified organic" is in some way better for us than food without such designation. I am passionate about this subject. My passion stems from the misinformation about conventional farming practices offered as fact by those with a platform.

It's a topic that gets the hackles up of those who work in agriculture; the criticism levied by some that, somehow, food isn't wholesome unless it is certified organic, non-GMO, all natural or whatever sustainable, yuppie friendly name one can attach to it. It is a scam perpetrated on the American public like none other.

I don't begrudge farmers for taking advantage of new markets that promise a higher price for their products. Most farmers are simply trying to eek out a living under whatever management or production system fits them best. Many of them find out the hard way that, after increased expenses and decreased yields, the profits don't materialize as they had been promised. The problem I see, however, is the assertion that somehow, food and livestock grown outside of these niche labels are inferior and unhealthy. Technology is often made to be the villain.

But technologies like GMO, pesticides and even some antibiotics play a crucial role without compromising the wholesomeness of the final product. The main role they play is increasing yields, both of crops and animal products. These are not shortcuts for good management and husbandry, they are accents to it. While technologies contribute nothing to the wholesomeness of the final product, they do allow more food to be raised with less resources. That means more land available for wild animals, less fuel used in the harvest of the crops and less toil for the farmer.

On the other hand, farmers who grow food under niche production systems can't (and usually don't) claim there is any difference to conventionally raised crops and animal products either. They are substantially the same. The production method is different; the end-product is not.

Contrary to what the niche marketers would like us to believe, our food is as safe and plentiful as it has ever been. People who drank milk in the 1940s were at risk of developing a disease called undulant fever. It is caused by the bacterium, Brucella abortus which was shed by cows in their milk. Today, because of an aggressive eradication effort undertaken by farmers and their veterinarians, the disease has been eliminated from dairy cows. And even before it was eliminated, the process of pasteurization killed the bacteria, rendering it harmless to consumers of milk.

Prior to the 1970s it was common for antibiotics to be present in milk. Some antibiotics were even added to food as preservatives as late as the 1960s. That is unheard of today and, frankly, it was a bad practice.

New standards for slaughterhouses have made foodborne illness from meat a rarity. Quality assurance programs for livestock farmers result in less trim of diseased tissue at slaughterhouses. But that notion hasn't permeated the culture, yet.

My main aversion to these niche marketing gimmicks, though, is that is a step backwards. Raw milk, another niche food, is that which is not pasteurized. There are those who believe it has some special, almost magical properties. But even though Brucella abortus was eliminated from dairy herds, listeriosis and salmonellosis have not. Skipping the process of pasteurization in the pursuit of eating a food that is raw is just dangerous.

Another step backwards is the loss in yield caused by the avoidance of pesticides and synthetic fertilizers. We are a planet with a growing population. The land mass, however, isn't getting any bigger. So, we, as a society, have to decide if we accept the use of pesticides, synthetic fertilizers and other technologies like GMO that can help farmers provide enough food for a hungry planet or if we become hungry purists. Today we have the luxury of buying niche foods as they are also plentiful. But the day will come when technologies will be absolutely necessary to prevent mass food shortages and not those caused simply by geopolitical turmoil.

At the turn of the 19th century, about half of the population in this country had a direct involvement on agriculture. Today, estimates range from 1-2 percent. More and more people have no idea how their food is produced and are susceptible to scare tactics by a vocal few. I have made it my mission to allay these fears, albeit in a platform much smaller than my competition. We have a lot more work to do.

We are so incredibly fortunate to live in this country in this age. Yes, cultural mores are drifting and political rancor is on display 24 hours a day. But our food has never been as safe, diverse, affordable, wholesome and plentiful as it is today. The hard work of the farmer is the primary reason for this reality.

Scandal of Confusion
9-15-15

Throughout human history, we have been governed by fear of the unknown. The ancients were afraid of what was beyond the horizon and dared not travel or risk falling off the edge of the world. Several centuries ago, people lived in fear of witches, going so far as to execute anyone who might be accused of dabbling in the occult. Today, too many of us fear our food.

Well-meaning and unscrupulous people alike capitalize on this fear to forward their agenda, whether it be animal rights, anti GMO, or a niche agriculture markets such as "all natural" or "organic." They seek to darken the clouds of ignorance when it comes to farmers and the methods they employ.

And it truly is a source of frustration to me to see the people with whom I work on a daily basis be accused of harming their livestock or scamming the food consuming public solely in pursuit of profit. That has been the primary motivation for this weekly column. But recently I came across a headline that was truly disturbing. It read, "All ground beef in the U.S. contaminated with fecal matter, according to Consumer Reports." Truly, that is a disgusting thought. If we have learned anything over the ages, we have learned that disease can be transmitted through poop. But what of the sensational headline?

Consumer Reports sampled several hundred packages of ground beef bought in retail stores and cultured them for the presence bacteria. The ground beef they sampled ranged from conventional, to grass fed to organic. Not surprisingly, they found that every sample grew bacteria. And most of the samples grew either a bacteria called Enterococcus or E. coli, common in the feces of mammals; hence the headline.

This created an opportunity almost too good to be true for anyone with a platform to capitalize on the story. But how safe is ground beef, headlines aside? According to the same article, in the 10-year span ending in 2012, there were 80 outbreaks of E. coli from tainted beef sickening 1,144 people and even killing five of them. I don't wish to minimize this, yet it should be put into perspective.

Americans bought about 4.6 billion pounds of beef last year, of which half was ground meat. That's enough ground beef for about 9.2 billion hamburgers in a year's time. The odds are about 1 in 80 million that a hamburger will make a person sick. And one can effectively reduce the risk to zero by doing something very simple; cook the burger.

Now look, thinking about poop in your burger is not a pleasant thought, which is why the headline disturbs me. There is not poop in our hamburger. Sterility, however, is a standard which is not possible unless we irradiate the stuff. If you want to kick another hornet's nest, start discussing irradiated food. There's a discussion for another day.

I have been infected many times with gastrointestinal maladies, I'm sure as a direct result of my proximity to the rear end of the cow. I shudder to consider just how much cow poop I inadvertently consume in a year's time. (That was not an endorsement of eating cow poop.) But it is a fact of life for those that work with cows. And it is also a fact of life that eating raw hamburger could make you sick. Since burger is made by grinding up the trimmings during processing, contamination can come from anywhere. Cook your burger, please.

And for those of you with infant children, I came across another study. It showed that infants who had a pet's fecal bacteria colonizing their own gastrointestinal tract had boosted immune systems and protection from allergies. The authors stopped short, thankfully, of endorsing anything that would be considered drastic.

This is not the first time those in the media have chosen to grab the attention of many by sensationalizing a story and it won't be the last. And many will continue to capitalize on the fear of the unknown. But neither will I and others be deterred from pointing out the folly of these headlines. Because ignorance and fear are accomplices in the scandal of confusion.

Good News
3-11-14

I'd like to take this opportunity to do something a little different. I'd like to report some good news.

You may be hard pressed to find good news, especially when it comes to the food we consume, but I've found some. The annual report of the National Milk Drug Residue Database compiled the results from milk and milk product testing nationally. This is a credible report put together by individuals under contract by the Food and Drug Administration. If you want to read it for yourself, it can be found here: http://www.kandc-sbcc.com/nmdrd/fy-13.pdf

There is strength in numbers and this report is strong. Of all milk products tested that were pasteurized and ready for human consumption, more than 40,000 samples in all, there were a whopping zero that tested positive for the presence of antibiotics. That is a lot of samples and zero is a very small number.

If you search the internet for stories on antibiotics and milk, you'd probably think that there is milk in our antibiotics. Let me say without equivocation; it a big, fat lie. Yeah, I know that is a strong assertion, but zero positive samples is a very strong number.

Out of morbid curiosity, I Googled "milk" and "antibiotics." I'd like to share a little of what I found. On the first page I found an article on the Huffington Post (from 2011) that cited a study in the Journal of Agriculture and Food Chemistry. That study found 20 different drugs in milk through new, sensitive sampling procedures. The headline read, "Painkillers, Antibiotics, Growth Hormones Among The 20 Chemicals Found In Typical Glass Of Milk."

What was buried in the article was that the source of the "typical" glass of milk tested was from Spain and Morocco. As far as I am concerned, the headline qualifies as a big, fat lie. The rest of the search results I found were the typical array of "buy organic" articles and animal rights stuff.

The milk that was tested and reported was conventional milk and dairy products. By conventional, I mean that it was not labeled as certified organic. That's right, organic milk contains exactly the same antibiotics as conventional milk does, none.

The reason for this good grade is that there are layers of safeguards in place that are meant to prevent adulterated and unsafe dairy products from reaching the market. At present, it is still permissible to use antibiotics and some other medicines to treat a sick dairy cow.

The first layer of protection occurs on the farm. If a cow has to be treated with an antibiotic, the farmer is obligated to keep her milk from being sold until the milk is free of antibiotic. If the amount of time for the antibiotic to clear is not known, her milk can be tested. If it is clean, her milk can be sold. If it is not, the milk must not be sold until the test is negative.

A second layer of protection occurs at the milk processor. All loads of milk are tested for the presence of antibiotics. In the same paper, it was reported that there were almost 3.2 million samples of milk reported from milk trucks. Drug residues were found in 445 of these samples. Those positive samples represented 0.014 percent of all samples and almost 20 million pounds of milk. That milk was disposed of and never entered the market.

This discussion about antibiotics in milk has been going on for at least 50 years. My Google search also uncovered a scientific paper published in 1964 discussing the presence of antibiotics in milk. I found one particular quote interesting. "Elimination of the risk of the presence of antibiotic residues in milk would require the banning of antibiotics…" Well, I think zero positive samples gets us pretty close to having eliminated the risk, and without banning antibiotics.

Fortunately for farmers, their cows and consumers, that prohibition never happened. Without the ability to use antibiotics to treat cows that have infections, the cows would suffer and the quality of their milk would suffer as well. That does neither the cows nor the consumers any good at all.

The same paper also discussed the use of tetracycline antibiotics as a preservative that were added to poultry and seafood to extend its shelf life. Wow, antibiotics were added to meat 50 years ago to prevent it from spoiling? We've come a long way.

In case you're wondering, dairy farmers do not feed antibiotics to their cows en masse to increase production, keep them healthy or for any other reason. Doing so would be a one way ticket out of the dairy business.

By the way, my Google search didn't turn up any mention of the report that all 40,000 samples of milk destined for domestic consumption in the United States tested negative for residues. I guess good news is no news.

Genomics
1-16-18 to 1-30-18

Several decades ago, scientists backed by the United States government made a commitment to map the human genome. It was a monumental project and would take years and many millions of dollars to complete. I wondered what on earth anyone could want to do with that information.

While they were at it, they decided to decipher the genome of other creatures, like the cow. Now I know why.

Farmers have been in pursuit of breeding the perfect livestock for millennia. If you cross the best cow with the best bull, you produce a superior offspring. At least that's the intent. Through trial and error, the genetic merit of domesticated animals improved over the years through selective breeding. But nobody ever really knew why it worked.

There was a logistical problem, though, before the modern age. The best mate to a cow may have been a bull that lived several hundred miles away. It was hard enough to travel several miles a hundred years ago, so a farmer's options were limited.

Fast forward to the 1950s. Animal scientists developed a method to collect and store bull semen to artificially inseminate cows. That innovation overcame some of the logistical challenges of breeding to a bull that lived hundreds of miles away.

This technology was revolutionary. Think about the impact that it had. Even if you have never even seen a cow in person, I think you would appreciate the opportunities that this created. A farmer could pick a bull from anywhere in the country, even the world, and breed him to his own cow. It allowed much quicker improvement in cattle genetics and their phenotypic traits. (Phenotypic traits are the physical manifestation of genes in an organism.) Artificial insemination had profound impacts, especially on the dairy farm.

But scientists and farmers still didn't really know the genetic mechanism that produced superior offspring. That is, until scientists started to crack the genetic code. When Deoxyribonucleic Acid (DNA) was discovered as the "language" for the genome in the middle part of the last century, the picture began to develop.

Fast forward again to the development that opened this article, the mapping of the genome. Knowledge grew about genes and chromosomes and the image became even clearer. Detailed information about individual genes, their locations on individual chromosomes and even individual nucleic acid sequences were discovered. The map became incredibly detailed.

What could scientists do with this map? I can look at a detailed map of Katmandu, but if I have no intention of ever going there it is simply trivial.

So far, there have been game-changing effects. Consider first the ability to modify the genome of an organism. Through sophisticated molecular tools, genes can be inserted or deleted from an organism. Once the genes were discovered, phenotypic traits could be modified by inserting or deleting a gene. This has been met with incredible antagonism from some people.

The most well-known of these genetic modifications is one that confers resistance to an herbicide on crops. This allows farmers to spray a field to eliminate weeds without killing the crop itself. This saves countless hours and billions of gallons of diesel fuel that would be needed to reduce weeds through cultivation.

This new genetic modification is delivered with intention and specificity. One desired trait can be controlled with one genetic modification. It is possible to select for herbicide resistance by selective breeding over time, however, the resulting organism wouldn't be the same. Herbicide resistance can be developed by exposing generations of plants to an herbicide and the few already resistant plants will survive. Breed the resistant plants for the next generations and, over time, the resistance becomes stronger. Finally, after many generations, you're left with a plant strongly resistant to a specific herbicide.

But the other traits of interest, like grain yield or resistance to drought, for example, may suffer. Unintended genes that may be linked to herbicide resistance are inadvertently selected. They are brought along for the ride, if you will. But with direct genetic modification in the lab, the desired change is made with both intention and specificity.

Now, this is important, so remember this. Presently, there is no commercially available means to genetically modify a cow like is done to a plant. When farmers breed cattle to improve their traits, however, it is no less of a genetic modification than inserting a gene into a plant. The problem with modification through selective breeding is that while it is done with intention, it cannot be done with specificity. Selecting for a single trait may involve thousands of genes and other unintended traits often come along for the ride.

With the genetic modification that can occur in a lab, unintended genes aren't brought along as they are with selective breeding. The result is a modification that happens exactly as intended. Unintended consequences can happen when breeding with intention but not specificity.

Take, for example, milk production in dairy cattle. With the introduction of artificial insemination decades ago, farmers bred their cows to bulls born only to high producing milk cows. But the true genetic merit of these bulls was still unknown even as they were being used. A bull may have been a winner in the genetic lottery and a superstar, but he may also have been a big loser and dry as the Sahara Desert. To find out if a bull was a winner or a loser, a system of testing was developed on dairy farms that was crucial to determine the bull's genetic merit.

It started with farmers weighing the milk from individual cows. The data from all those milk weights were stored through an organization called Dairy Herd Improvement Association. Recognize that there were literally tens of millions of dairy cows in the U.S and milk weights were taken monthly. Not all cows were enrolled, but enough of them were to generate a lot of records for analysis.

The milk records from individual cows were analyzed to see if the bull who fathered them threw productive offspring or not. But this was neither easy nor quick. Consider a bull that is used to breed a cow today. In roughly 9 months, his calf is born. In another two years, she produces her first drop of milk. After another year, she has a complete lactation record. It took nearly four years to evaluate a bull's ability to produce a high producing cow. And at least 100 of these offspring had to be evaluated to consider a bull proven.

And for every bull above his parents' average, there was another below the average. These below average bulls produced a lot of offspring in four years before it was determined that they weren't up to snuff. So, while genetic merit of the average cow was improving faster than it had before artificial insemination became available, it was still pretty slow.

And there were unintended consequences with this type of traditional genetic modification, otherwise known as selective breeding. The trait that was of most interest to dairy farmers was milk production. Milk production per cow increased by roughly a percent or two every year in the United States. Granted, some of the improvement could be attributed to environmental factors like improved feed and comfort of the cows, but much of it was still the result of genetics.

Genetic improvement in milk production came through metabolic improvement of the cow. But this was imprecise. This metabolic improvement allows the cow to be able to mobilize a tremendous amount of nutrients from her bodily stores to support the rigorous demands of milk production. Some cows could handle the process without problem, while others got terribly sick.

All of these mobilized nutrients must be processed by the cow which can lead to some nasty diseases around the time that she has her calf. Diseases like milk fever, ketosis and twisted stomach have been like a long-term plague on dairy cows. Nobody could foretell the unintended consequences of this imprecise method of genetic selection.

So, there are two major unintended consequences of imprecise genetic modification – the long time to prove a bull and the metabolic stress on the cow. The genetic modification had to happen to improve the dairy breeds, but in hindsight, it didn't exactly go as planned.

Then the genome was mapped. This map is still under development today as scientists continue to assemble the jigsaw puzzle of genes and their functions. But the landscape is starting to become visible.

Remember the development of artificial insemination in cattle. Semen of bulls has been collected, frozen and stored in liquid nitrogen for about six decades now. And information from cows tested for milk production has also been collected, analyzed and stored for the same amount of time. The genetic material from many of these bulls is still in storage yet today.

Scientists have been able to roughly match up the genetic information from these long dead bulls with past cow milk weight data records through pedigree information and algorithms. As they analyzed genetic markers in their chromosomes, they could decipher which markers were associated with certain traits. Progressively more markers were analyzed, and a formula was developed to evaluate the genetic merit of an individual animal.

Remember also how a bull was evaluated before this technology. After four years, his offspring were tested for milk production and he was determined to be good, bad or somewhere in between. Today, a genomic sample can tell if he is good, bad or somewhere in between. This can be done, however, when he is just a baby calf. What used to take four years now takes about three weeks.

Milk production isn't the only trait being analyzed for either. Other important traits like body type, immune system function, fertility and other traits that aren't physically apparent on the cow can be predicted through genomics. Genetic progress is moving at light speed now compared to a generation ago.

This technology is also available on the females who are destined one day to become cows. Farmers can submit a skin sample and see if a baby calf will be a genetic superstar, a dud or somewhere in between. This technology isn't perfect and some surprises do happen, but it is still roughly two and a half times as accurate as the average of their parents' genetic merit.

This technology already exists today and is widely utilized by farmers to make decisions about breeding. It doesn't modify the genome, but there is another even more powerful genetic technology that is not yet commercially available. This technology can improve the genetics of cattle, and other species, with laser-like precision. It involves directly altering the genetic code of an animal.

This is scary to many people, and probably rightly so. We can imagine a scientist in a lab underground somewhere messing with nature and playing God. Some may think scientists want to create a master clone of an animal that can take over the world. Or some might imagine an unscrupulous person that will corner the market of animal breeding and enrich himself beyond any comprehension.

Motivations aside, this technology exists and has already been used on cattle. But it is not available commercially to farmers yet and will not be any time soon because of regulatory hurdles. But here's how the technology works.

Let's use the horn trait in cattle as an example. Most cattle naturally are horned. It is a defense mechanism against predators. But since cattle have been domesticated, they have little reason to fend off lions and other predator animals. Horns are detrimental to the farmer since it opens the possibility of harm to the farmer or other cattle from a boss cow with horns.

The conventional way of dealing with this problem is to surgically dehorn cattle. Usually this is done to the calves, sometimes as young as a couple of days old. It is an expense for the farmer and a source of pain for the calf.

Now, scientists have found a way to eliminate horns in cattle by altering one of the genes that codes for horns. Some breeds of cattle, like the Aberdeen Angus, (a.k.a. Black Angus) have a naturally mutated copy of a gene that codes for horns. Consequently, they are born polled, or without horns. That same mutated gene can be spliced into animals of other breeds resulting in calves being born polled. This has been done to a Holstein calf in a research setting and the calf was born totally normal, except it lacked horns.

There are other possibilities as well. Imagine the impact if resistance to Hoof and Mouth Disease can be introduced to cattle by this method in countries where this disease exists. Hoof and Mouth

Disease causes blistering of the mouth and hooves in cloven-hooved animals. It causes terrible pain and results in severe loss of body weight in affected animals. The disease is endemic in the developing world. These are not the only examples. Resistance to other diseases conceivably could be introduced to cattle by this very method. Production traits like feed efficiency, milk production and muscling could improve the ease by which cattle produce meat and milk. As the human population expands, technologies like this someday may be critically necessary to feed a hungry world.

All this is possible because scientists embarked on the ambitious project of mapping the genome. The Human Genome Project began in 1990 and it has changed everything.

I'm not necessarily advocating wholesale adoption of this technology, at least not yet. But the technology is here and ready when we need it. And because of regulatory hurdles, this technology is still unavailable to farmers today. The old way of selective breeding is still the only way farmers can improve their livestock. Farmers simply cannot splice a gene into a cow to get the perfect trait in their offspring.

Nonetheless, the genomic revolution is here and it is truly revolutionary in every sense of the word. So much so that I predict that historians will remember it along with other world-changing events like the industrial revolution and digital revolution. The genomic revolution is a game changer with lasting implications, I believe, for the better.

Be Not Afraid
11-9-10

"Therefore I tell you, do not worry about your life, what you will eat (or drink), or about your body, what you will wear. Is not life more than food and the body more than clothing?" (Matthew 6:26, New American Bible) I am neither a preacher nor a psychologist and I didn't stay at a Holiday Inn Express last night. I hesitate a little opening a column about agriculture with a Bible verse, but hear me out.

Relative to our recent ancestors, we live in a time of abundance. Despite the "Great Recession," we are much better off than a century ago. I have long maintained that one of the primary reasons for our prosperity in the United States is the productivity of our farmers.

With only 1 or 2 percent of our population engaged in agriculture, the rest of the population is free to engage other productive endeavors, like teaching, medical research or engineering. We don't have to worry about where our food comes from.

But, lately, there seems to be a lot of worry about our food. It isn't so much worry about starvation, but worry about the type of food or even the method by which it was grown. Many have been led to believe that if food isn't certified "organic," it isn't worth eating.

Even the mass media seems to be an advocate for organic food. A search of "organic food" on Time Magazine's website yields 66 hits in the last 12 months. Yep, that's 66 hits if you think that was a typo. It's no wonder we are worried.

Some are so worried, in fact, that a new eating disorder has been discovered. It's called "orthorexia nervosa" and is defined as extreme fixation on eating proper food that becomes pathological.

Oh, the irony; a fixation on health food that can make you sick.

To be honest, orthorexia is not just trying to eat healthy. We could probably all benefit from eating a serving or two more of veggies in our diet. It becomes disordered when the person believes that consumption of anything other than the proper food will cause sickness. What food is proper varies from person to person.

And the proper diets do vary. There is the vegetarian diet, which abstains from meat. There is the vegan diet, which is vegetarian without dairy or eggs. There is the organic diet that allows only food grown under production methods free from pesticides and chemicals. There is the raw food diet that shuns anything cooked or pasteurized.

I find the raw food diet especially troubling. Pasteurization of dairy products is essential in preventing food borne diseases, including salmonellosis and listeriosis among others. Raw milk does have the potential to cause sickness, pasteurized milk does not.

And the list goes on. The "paleo" (AKA caveman) diet eats only that which can be hunted or gathered. The caveman gorges on meat and nuts followed by a period of fasting. I hope nobody tries to combine the raw food and caveman diets. The "Genesis 1:29" diet claims it is a sin to eat meat and we should eat only what Adam and Eve had available to them.

I guess since we have the luxury of not worrying about the quantity of food we can worry about the type of food we eat. Well, maybe it would be best not to worry. "Can any of you by worrying add a single moment to your life-span?" (Matthew 6:27, New American Bible)

Miracles
9-8-15

Al Michaels, the esteemed sports broadcaster during his call of the 1980 Olympic ice hockey game between the USSR and United States asked his audience as the game was ending, "Do you believe in miracles?" It did seem miraculous at the time that the United States could beat the mighty Soviets. But what about the question? Do you believe in miracles?

Most of us hear talk of miracles, yet we don't necessarily experience them firsthand. We might pray for a sick loved one who receives healing, but not really grasp that it is miraculous. We might hear of a miraculous event in a distant land, but we have no attachment to, or investment in it. I have never been the beneficiary of an instantaneous miraculous event, which I know of, but I wholeheartedly believe in miracles. The evidence is just too strong.

And the miracles repeat themselves year after year, as if once weren't enough. They are easy to see when we live in the country because all we have to do is pay attention. Drive around the country roads and have a good look at the crops. The farmer starts with tiny seeds and buries them in the dirt. After several months, the tiny seeds, after soaking up water and sunlight, become bushels upon bushels of food for people and livestock.

OK, I can tell that not everyone is impressed yet that this is really a miracle. Well, consider the weather we experienced this year. It went from dry, to monsoon to dry again. It wasn't exactly perfect weather for growing crops. But look in the fields and observe the bounty. It won't be record yields here this time, but the crops are there, ready to be harvested. I recall hearing more than once during the flooding rains earlier, "If the crops make it at all it will be a miracle." Indeed, it will be.

But even more miraculous than the challenging years are the good years. Our neighbors in the county east of us may actually experience record yields this year. For our neighbors, the rains came at just the right time, the temperatures hit just the right point and the sunlight was abundant. Yes, it almost seems Providential.

The naysayers, however, have been telling us for years that there are too many people on this planet and we would not be able to feed everybody. So, what was the result? Farmers just increase yields every year. And I don't mean that they plant more acres every year. On the contrary, total acres in production have actually decreased over time yet crops produced increase. It has resemblance to a story I read once about some loaves and fishes.

But still many are not convinced, I'm sure, as science has contributed greatly to the advancements we have seen in agriculture. Take the much maligned technology of genetically modified organisms (GMO). Scientists have found a way to splice a gene from one organism into another that codes for a specific trait. The result are crops that have amazing ability to resist pestilence or tolerate the herbicides that kill weeds. Technology such as this contributes greatly to the increased yields that farmers, and the rest of us, benefit.

But what is science but the reverse engineering of creation? The fact that we even have this ability to splice genes must be a gift. It is a gift that keeps on giving.

A good chunk of my time anymore is spent on the process of embryo transfer in cattle. The process puts 7 day old embryos of one cow into the womb of another recipient cow. To do this, one has to observe the tiny embryo, invisible to the naked eye, through a microscope. These embryos have characteristics that change, literally, by the hour as the embryo ages. We can observe an embryo as it develops from a morula to a blastocyst (sorry for the jargon) in a bubble of fluid through the microscope. These tiny embryos are truly a miracle in and of themselves.

But that embryo will be born, grow and turn into a cow someday. That dairy cow will perform miraculous feats like make 9 gallons or more of milk in a day. That beef cow might give birth to a calf that will become almost 400 pounds of beef for a hungry family. Cows do this by eating fibrous forages that are completely indigestible to people. They even consume byproducts like citrus pulp or soybean hulls that are otherwise trash from other commodity products. They seem to have the ability to make something out of nothing. If that isn't a miracle, then I don't know what is.

GMO
3-20-12

Over the last few years, there has been a lot of negative hype over genetically modified organisms (GMO.) GMOs are plants, bacteria, or even animals that have had their genetic code modified in a laboratory. Many of these organisms are marketed commercially for agricultural production. Environmentalists have voiced concern that these modified genes may inadvertently make their way from the intended population to a wild species and cause unintended consequences. Some even claim that eating these GMO foods could be harmful. I'd like to try to ease some fears about this process.

In the interest of full disclosure, I own no stock in biotech companies, nor do I have a financial interest in this technology. I do have an interest, however, in putting to rest unfounded hysteria. So, I'd like to take the unpopular position of defending GMO technology.

Let's start with what it is. In a nutshell, if a desirable gene is identified, like one for disease resistance in a plant, it can be deliberately inserted into a plant's genome. This new plant with a new genetic code will have resistance to the specific disease. The gene that codes for the resistance is precisely spliced into its new genome.

A similar, albeit low tech, process has been used by plant breeders for thousands of years. Disease resistance in plants was acquired by selecting, generation after generation, for the plants that exhibited the desirable trait. The process was imprecise and often carried with it unknown or even undesirable genes.

In fact, such is the case with all genetic selection. Allow me to use our family dog as an example. We have a Golden Retriever named ZEEEK. (That's not a typo, we really spell it like that.) ZEEEK, being a purebred Golden Retriever, has had his genetic code selected for over hundreds of years. His genome has been modified by the process of genetic selection through breeding over many generations. He is essentially a genetically modified organism. (That's probably why he is so goofy.) Only the modification didn't take place in a lab; it happened over hundreds of years of breeding.

And that's the major limitation with traditional selection through breeding. It takes hundreds of generations to achieve the desired result. Hundreds of generations of selection have given us some pretty amazing critters, don't get me wrong. Today's dairy cow is a metabolic freak, in the most positive sense of the term. She is able to produce milk in quantities that were unimaginable a hundred years ago.

GMO crops allow for increased yield while reducing the need for fertilizers and chemical pesticides. But as the world population continues to increase, the land available for farming does not. Increased yield allows for less land to be put into production, allowing for more land to remain as habitat for wildlife.

As for the safety of this technology, here's something to think about. There are millions of diabetic people in this country. Many of these people with diabetes require at least daily insulin injections. Today, essentially all insulin is produced from genetically modified bacteria. The bacterium was engineered to contain the gene that produces the protein we know as insulin. And diabetics inject it into their bodies every day and it keeps them healthy.

As with any new technology, we should be cautious about unintended consequences. But GMO technology has been around for several decades now and has been proven safe and effective. So, when the fear mongers rant against this essential technology, remember, your dog too, is a genetically modified organism.

Crabs Produce Firewood
7-15-14

"Crabs produce firewood."

That was our family's new catch phrase for vacation this year. Previous catch phrases included "You stepped in what?" and "I love asparagus." I would explain the latter, but it might take another article.

The new catch phrase produces any number of mental images. We had a lot of fun with our kids. "Dad, how do crabs produce firewood?" Maybe with great swarms, they use their pincers to cut up logs that the campers can use in their campfires. Maybe they eat branches and the necessary byproduct can be turned into firewood? You can use your own imagination.

I'm not a wordsmith, but I appreciate a phrase that makes one take pause. With the right combination of words, the reader will conjure an image of just what the writer wants him or her to see.

So it is with rhetoric used to put a group in a bad light. Politicians, activists and special interest groups are all adept in this regard.

So, if I may, I'd like to pick apart one of my favorite catch phrases used by activists to paint agriculture in a bad light, "factory farms."

Activists claim that all dairy cows are raised and housed on these factory farms. It effectively causes the reader to imagine a farm with machines, smoke stacks and cows who are just cogs in a machine.

Nobody really knows what actually constitutes a "factory farm," but its effect on the mental picture of the reader is undeniable. Maybe a factory farm is one with more than 50 cows. Or maybe a factory farm has machines on it. There must be a lot of employees that are just there for a paycheck and the owner must be a nameless and faceless corporation.

Today's dairy farms are not what they were 50 years ago. They are bigger and there are fewer of them. From 1970 to 2006, the average herd size rose from 20 cows to around 120 cows. In Pennsylvania, the average herd size is still only around 75 cows according to USDA statistics. But 75 cows is still a lot more than 20 cows.

So, what really is a factory farm?

If it means that a dairy farm milks cows two or three times a day on a regular schedule without ever taking a day off, then all of the farms I work for are factory farms. If factory farms have more than 20 cows, then, I guess that all of the farms I work for are guilty of that as well.

Today's dairy farms certainly have machines. Machines like tractors, skid loaders, silos and their impressive unloaders and vacuum pumps for milking cows are present on nearly all farms. But these machines were also there in 1970. Maybe factory farms have been around for longer than we knew?

If hired labor is a criterion for a farm to be a factory, then many of our clients, with very few exceptions, would be guilty of this as well. Jobs are a good thing, both on farm and off. Hired labor on family farms allow the farmer to take a day off now and then, even though many of them still don't.

And despite what the activists want us all to think, the vast majority of dairy farms, about 99 percent of them, are owned by families and not nameless corporations. So, I guess factory farms are family owned.

So, our latest catch phrase, "crabs produce firewood" came from a sign displayed along the highway just before we reached the shore. At first, I thought the proprietor was exclaiming some profound discovery like "cows produce milk." Then we realized it was a list of items they had for sale – crabs, produce and firewood.

They could have listed it as produce, firewood and crabs. Or maybe even firewood, crabs and produce. But I think he may enjoy the irony of words as much as I do. I'm sure that everybody figured it out eventually, just like they will figure out the other phrase, "factory farms."

Slaughter
8-22-17

I love a good steak. In fact, I'm a fan of meat in general. Steaks, burgers, roast and jerky are delicious. I'm not alone. Americans consume a lot of meat. According to the United States Department of Agriculture, last year there were well over 30 million cattle and calves slaughtered in the US. That's just cattle. There were also 118 million hogs and more than 2 million sheep slaughtered. I'm not even gonna try to count the poultry. We like meat.

Even though we love meat, we don't really like to think about the hard part of meat production. If we eat meat, we have to accept the fact than an animal was slaughtered to make that meat.

I've never worked in a slaughterhouse or taken a meat science course, but I did have some exposure to the end process in veterinary school. I am acquainted with the process. Slaughterhouses are tightly regulated by the government and layers and layers of safeguards are in place to protect both the meat consuming public from bad meat and also to the animals being slaughtered from needless suffering. It is figuratively a well-oiled machine.

We recognize that making meat is a job not for the faint of heart. In fact, the dirty side of politics had been likened to the process of making sausage. In this day and age, most of us would rather watch sausage being made.

It can be a messy job. The animals get killed and systematically taken apart. Very little is wasted, though. All the meat is used. But the meat makes up only about half the animal. There is still the hide, entrails and some other. Obviously, the hide can be used for leather. The entrails can be rendered for pet food, fertilizer or other uses.

I don't really want to go into the details in this article about the slaughter process as it isn't for everybody. But recognize that once the animal is quickly stunned and unconscious, the process is over for it. It really is over once they've been stunned. If you've seen video of the slaughter process, you've seen that the animals will still move and flail after stunning. But these are involuntary central nervous system movements that happen after the stunning. The animal has already ceased to be sentient.

I write this in the context of the annual Somerset County Fair being held right now. At the fair are hundreds of market animals that were hand raised by 4-H and FFA members. Most of these animals will be sold on Saturday for meat.

Recognize that the lads and lasses selling these animals know full well their fate. They know their fate, but that doesn't necessarily mean they relish in it. In fact, there will certainly be more than one tear shed on sale day.

But they are market animals; slaughter is their purpose. It's not always easy for the kids to realize that their work will have such a definitive end. But personally, I think it's a good lesson in detachment. Being able to let go and accept change is all too hard for some people. Granted the check they receive after that sale lessens the sting significantly. But I'm sure there are some second thoughts.

As for the rest of us not raising livestock, we don't give it much thought. Out of sight, out of mind as the saying goes.

We love meat, but we don't like the saying goodbye or the slaughter part. So, instead, farmers do it for us. It's just another in the long list of things we should appreciate from the American farmer.

And if you want a really tasty beef, hog, lamb or goat, there's a bunch on them for sale on Saturday. Shipping will even be provided. And don't worry, you won't have to do the slaughtering yourself.

Food for a Superhero
7-23-13

My wife and I took the kids on a short holiday to the beach this past weekend. I'm not much for vacations; I guess because I'm wound a little tight and unwinding takes too much effort. At any rate, I bit the bullet, packed up the stuff and left early Thursday morning, beach bound.

Once on the beach with the kids playing in the water, I became rather hypnotized by the pounding surf. It's a funny thing for a guy who lives in the mountains to sit at the edge of land, look out into the sea and see nothing at the end of the horizon. It's no wonder our ancestors thought the world was flat.

Peering at the edge of the world from the surface doesn't give any perspective and it's that lack of perspective makes the world appear flat. Under the waves live countless sea creatures, from the tiny sand crabs to the porpoises and half-ton sharks that find their way up and down the shore on occasion. The only way to see them is to dive under the water or dig in the sand. Perspective is important.

As I stood in the surf with my daughter looking for seashells under the water, waves would crash near us making it impossible to see the bottom. Just at the time the disturbed sand would settle from the previous wave, another one would pick up where it left off. We could never get more than a split second opportunity to see the bottom.

It seemed analogous to the work we all do to survive. I don't suppose it really matters what line of work you are in, be it health care, selling cars or farming. As soon as we seem to get caught up and see the bottom, another wave brings more work. Farmers finally get the corn in the ground and the first crop of hay is ready. As soon as the first crop is in, the corn needs sprayed. As soon as the corn gets sprayed, well, you get the picture.

As enjoyable as it was to watch the surf, it was just as enjoyable to observe the hundreds of other families gathered with us at the edge of the world. I found myself wondering where they were all from and what their stories were.

Were they from the city, suburbs or maybe some were country folk like us? It was obviously a diverse group of people, many speaking languages that I didn't understand. What different perspectives did they bring along with them?

We were trying to find a place for lunch one afternoon on the boardwalk. There was no shortage of choices but seafood was the most plentiful. One little café caught my attention. They announced that they served locally grown organic raw vegan food. Wow, the people that eat there must be super heroes; bullet proof and able to leap a tall building in a single bound.

We didn't eat there. I have no desire to spend eternity on this earth anyways. I had to wonder about the perspective of the folks that would seek out the type of food served there. I've always wondered about that.

We have so many choices for food in this country that people can even eat superhero food if they desire. But for mere mortals such as me and my family, conventionally grown food that contains at least one serving of meat grown somewhere else and cooked before consuming is sufficient.

Perspective is important. I try not to question the motives of people who partake only of food that conforms to whatever lifestyle diet. To each his own; I'll never understand that perspective. Admittedly, my perspective probably becomes clouded like the pounding surf sometimes because I just can't see what's underneath.

But the waves never do end and trying to get ahead of them is indeed pointless. As soon as one passes, another one is right behind it. It's best to just play in them as they arrive.

A Persistent Myth
8-5-14

When I was an undergrad some…, well, more than 10 years ago, the field of epidemiology was beginning to take shape. One of the purposes of epidemiology is to accurately predict risk factors for certain diseases. For example, in dairy cattle, we know that a cow who has a calf while she is too fat is at risk for developing a twisted stomach. It doesn't mean that every fat cow will get a twisted stomach, but her chances will be better than a cow that isn't fat.

I remember one of my college professors say during a lecture that epidemiologists were able to accurately predict what would eventually lead to my demise based on risk factors such as lifestyle habits and family history. I figured I was destined for a heart attack because of my personality type, diet, lack of exercise, family history and I was, at the time, a smoker.

Wow, I reflected, they can tell me what's going to kill me. That's a nice thought. I had a great uncle once that was convinced he was going to live to be 99 years old then be killed by a jealous husband. But that really didn't work out for him; he died of a stroke before his 99th birthday.

So, the epidemiologists have been hard at work for the last 50 years trying to tell us what's going to kill us. Jealous husbands aside, much of the research has been focused on diet and components of our diet. Red meat and dairy products have been public enemy number one. The conventional wisdom has been that the saturated fats in meat and dairy cause heart attacks and strokes.

The consumption of polyunsaturated fats like vegetable oil and margarine was touted as "heart healthy." Supposedly this plant fat was better for us than animal fat. As a person whose livelihood depends on people eating dairy products and red meat, that's never been news that I cared to accept. Conventional wisdom can be rather unconventional sometimes.

Epidemiologists make their case for risk factors through studies. Studies usually start small and if a risk is suspected, increasingly larger studies are done. Eventually, the risk factor becomes part of the conventional wisdom with time and lots of studies.

People who have high cholesterol are at an increased risk for heart attacks; we all accept that. The theory was that since these polyunsaturated fats had been shown to reduce cholesterol in people who eat them, they must be better for us. Many people made the jump to "eating polyunsaturated fats reduces the risk for heart attacks" without really examining the evidence. That's a problem. In fact, the evidence was lacking.

Recently, a very large review study actually examined the role of consuming saturated (animal) fats as a risk factor for heart disease. (Association of dietary, circulating, and supplement fatty acids with coronary risk: a systematic review and meta-analysis. Ann Intern Med., 2014 Mar 18). Review studies look at the body of the scientific studies on a topic and combine all of the data to draw a very strong conclusion.

So you might imagine my lack of surprise when the researchers found no evidence to support the conventional wisdom that cutting back on red meat and dairy reduces the risk of heart disease. The authors have come to the conclusion that, "Current evidence does not clearly support cardiovascular guidelines that encourage high consumption of polyunsaturated fatty acids and low consumption of total saturated fats." Who knew?

Now, I'm not conspiratorial by nature and I'm not going to draw any conclusions as to why it had been gospel for 30 years now that meat and dairy is bad for us. Things happen; people once thought the world was flat. I'm willing to move on and continue to eat red meat and dairy without fear. Something's going to kill us all eventually one day but it's not likely to be red meat or dairy foods. And it had better not be a jealous husband.

CHAPTER 10
The Cow, For Her Own Sake

Photo by Justine Petenbrink

Since the time cattle were first domesticated, they have been a blessing to mankind. Their overriding purpose has been to provide food, fiber and draft for humans. They have peculiarities that can only be recognized after spending much time around them. I am in the presence of cattle for a good portion of my waking hours and I appreciate them more every day. I've devoted a lot of print to the cow, for her own sake.

Why do I love cows? I guess it's hard to explain, but I'll try. In addition to their overriding purpose, they provide income for farmers and those who support them. There are a lot of cattle in this country and the stakes can get quite high. There can be as many as 80 million or even more cattle in this country alone at times. If one considers them just a basic asset, their value would exceed $100 billion. But they are more than a basic asset. They are a self-replicating asset.

Financial matters aren't the basis for my love of cows. Yes, without them I'd have to find another way to make a living but working with them is enjoyable in and of itself. The work can be challenging, tedious and dirty at times, yet I couldn't envision an alternative that would be as good.

I get to enjoy both beef and dairy cows during the practice of my profession and they each have their peculiarities. Dairy cows are slow, habitual and usually relatively docile. Beef cows, on the other hand, are a little high strung, lumbering and sometimes a bit hard to handle. Their different personalities can be explained by the way each is raised.

Dairy cattle, with few exceptions, are hand raised from a baby calf by the farmer. The purpose of this practice isn't necessarily oriented towards making the animal calm, but it's a side benefit. I've seen some dairy calves raised from birth on a beef cow and, in the end, they take on the temperament of a beef cow. Beef calves, on the other hand, are raised by mama, a beef cow. But if a beef calf is orphaned as a baby calf and hand raised by a farmer, she takes on the temperament reminiscent of a dairy calf, or even a pet.

I consider the mere existence of cattle to be Providential, even miraculous. Consider what the cow does. She eats grass or other fibrous feed indigestible to people and converts it to meat, milk, leather or even energy for draft.

But if cows were left to their own devices, humans wouldn't benefit. That's where the farmer and rancher comes in. They manage the cattle to optimize their efficiency and ensure the propagation of their herds. Farmers and ranchers feed cattle properly to produce a product acceptable for human consumption and market that end-product once it's ready. Without farmers and ranchers, cows might as well be in a zoo.

Yes, I enjoy cattle and even feel affection for them sometimes. But they can be difficult to like sometimes. We ask them to do things that they don't want to do, like go in the chute and take her medicine. When it's time for her to deliver a calf and she's having problems, we ask her to stand still while we lend a hand. Cattle don't like to stand still when there's a vet's arm up her rear end. When we want her to move to another pasture or pen, she sometimes goes where she wants. And when she goes where she wants, she gets into trouble.

It took me several years to figure out that getting mad at cows is pointless. They are instinctual critters and have no concept of free will. Hence, if we as humans don't understand what their instincts are telling them, we get stymied. I still get frustrated with them, or myself when I send the wrong signal, but it's wasted emotion to get mad at them.

Cows are incredible creatures. Working with them is rewarding, challenging and sometimes even fun. And the farmers that make this all possible have my respect and gratitude.

Cow Tipping
10-18-11

A friend and colleague sent me an article recently debunking the urban legend known as "cow tipping." Cow tipping, I believe, ranks right up there with other myths like snipe hunting and organic foods are healthier.

As the legend goes, since cows sleep standing up, a stealthy person can sneak up on an unsuspecting snoozing cow and push her over. By the time the tipped cow regains her wits, Jack the tipper can make his escape. In reality, trying to tip a cow would be about as smart as running a 10K race the morning after judging a chili cook off.

Until I read this article that my friend had forwarded me, I had never seen a report testifying to the fact that cow tipping is a myth. Indeed, cow tipping sounds quite plausible. That is unless you have ever tried to make a vertical bovine horizontal.

Even if a cow is restrained, it is extremely difficult to get her off her feet. She weighs more than a half a ton and will lock her legs so that her center of gravity is low. I doubt that even a nose tackle could budge a standing cow. It can be hard just to get her to simply take a half step to her side let alone fall to the ground. It is possible to put her on the ground, but there's much more involved than just "tipping" her.

But the implausibility of cow tipping becomes even stronger when you consider that it is impossible to sneak up on a cow. If you don't believe me, try it – just be careful of the electric fence and maybe the bull. Cows are prey animals and feel seriously threatened by anything they perceive might eat them. If you have hamburger on your breath, you won't get to within 100 feet of a cow.

But the myth states that the cows are asleep when the stealthy tipper makes his move, you say? Well, that's what the myth claims, but again, it isn't based in reality. Cows don't sleep standing up. Horses may nap in the upright position, but cows surely don't. Cows do sleep; I've seen it. She will curl herself up in a ball, put her head in her flank and saw logs. Cows don't sleep much, maybe less than an hour a day, but they can snooze pretty soundly. They sleep so soundly that they can be difficult to arouse. But since they are already lying down, tipping is out of the question.

The sleeping cow is truly a sight to behold and I'm always in awe when I see one sound asleep. The first time I saw a cow sleep, I literally thought she was dead. But she eventually started to twitch involuntarily, presumably because she was dreaming. I wonder if she was dreaming that a crazy cow tipper was chasing her through the meadow? We'll never know.

Yes, there are times when we want to force a mature cow down to the ground to perform certain procedures. A skilled operator in possession of a 30-foot rope can cause even the most obstinate cow to lie down by "casting" her. There is more than one way to cast a cow, but my favorite is the half hitch method.

First, a rope is placed around the cow's neck and secured with a bowline knot. We like a bowline knot since its loop won't tighten. The cow won't strangle herself with a bowline knot and lose consciousness-that would be cheating.

Once the rope is in place around her neck, two half hitches are placed around the cow's trunk with the long rope. One is immediately behind the elbows and the other immediately in front of the udder. The rope is continued beyond the rear of the cow where a single person, by pulling on the rope and causing it to tighten, forces the cow to lie down. I don't know why it works, but I have yet to see it fail. The cow will usually fall to whatever side the half hitches are placed. With practice, a person can pick a spot and drop the cow.

If you want to put a cow on the ground, she must be cast, not tipped. And don't even think of sneaking up on her. But if you ever want to tip a cow, tell her to avoid the guy with the 30-foot rope and hamburger on his breath.

Virtual Reality
7-30-13

I came across a news report about a study done by a group of Stanford University scientists. It seems that they used federal grant money to study whether virtual reality could cause people to eat less meat.

I'm paraphrasing, but essentially the study's participants put on virtual reality goggles, got down on all fours and experienced what it is like to be a cow. The virtual "reality" show portrays the hapless bovine being prodded as it is led to the slaughterhouse.

I won't discuss the implications about the federal government funding stuff like this, except to say that if that's what my tax dollars are being used for, I'd respectfully like to request a refund. Funding sources aside, I would like to take a stab at the whole virtual reality thing, if you'll indulge me.

I should suggest that the techie who designed the virtual "reality" show come and spend a day or two with a person who spends about half of his waking hours around cows. We'll design a true virtual reality together, not a virtual misinterpretation.

To spend a day in the hooves of a dairy cow would go something like this. Wake up at about 5 a.m. to get milked. She probably was already awake since a cow only sleeps only about an hour or so a day. But she was most likely lounging peacefully in her bed, sheltered in the barn from the elements outside.

After milking time, she visits the feed bunk for some fresh feed. The farmer knows that unless she has access to copious amounts of fresh, high quality feed, she won't produce much milk. The farmer depends on that milk to make a living, so it behooves him to keep her happy.

After a large snack, she wanders about a little and visits her buddies on the east end of the barn. She tries to avoid those cows from the other side of the barn since they don't really get along very well. Cows are very social critters and, like people, they are friendly with some, and not so with others. I guess it's somewhat like I am with the animal right's activists.

After her visit, she goes and lies down in her bedded stall and enjoys a vigorous session of cud chewing. Cows will regurgitate and chew their cud, on average, for about 8 hours a day. If the techies can virtually replicate that for the participants in the study, I'd truly be impressed.

Then, at about 5 p.m., the whole thing starts over again. It's pretty mundane, as long as the cow is lactating. But at the end of her lactation cycle, she gets a two-month vacation before she delivers her next calf. And, yes, a cow has to deliver a calf in order to produce milk. I'm certain the regular readers of this column already knew that; I'm less certain about the folks involved in the study.

To be fair, most dairy cows will indeed end up as beef at the end of her career. It's a reality that's necessary for the cycle of life to continue. But, humans just can't comprehend the "reality" of being a cow as she is going to her demise. Humans can anticipate with fear and anxiety a negative event that is in the future. Other animals simply don't anticipate death the way people do, much less with fear and anxiety.

To attribute human qualities to animals speaks either to the scientist's gross lack of understanding about animals, or to their agenda. The vegetarian activists continuously seek to impose their will, regardless of the facts. Besides their constant accusations of abuse towards farmers, the activist vegetarian agenda of imposition is probably what disturbs those of us the most who make a living working with livestock, even more disturbing than the thought of chewing on a virtual cud.

Stampede
4-4-17

We've all seen the old movies with the cowboys gathering the herd from the wilderness. All of a sudden, the cows are spooked.

Somebody shouts, "Stampede!" and behind the cloud of dust are the several hundred frightened cows running for their lives leaving nothing standing in their wake.

It's enough to give the impression that cows are prone to stampede. I've never seen a stampede. I've been working cattle for going on a quarter century now and I'm inclined to think that this whole stampede thing is the stuff of which legends are made. Cattle spook, yes, but they aren't really made for distance running.

In fact, domesticated cows tend to be curious by nature. When treating a sick cow in a pasture among the herd, the rest of the cows invariably arrive to investigate. We have to spook them to get some peace whenever that happens and I've never caused a stampede whenever I've yelled "Git!"

Less domesticated cattle, like the Brahma influenced breeds of the deep south are not predisposed to stampede either. While I don't have a lot of experience with them, I did spend three weeks on the back of a horse among them in the late 1990s.

These Braford, Simbrah and Brangus cows, not to mention the Brahmas themselves, are unusually spooky. And they're aggressive. But they don't stampede. They may run away from you individually, or even charge you individually, but they don't really stampede.

Maybe western cows are different, but I suspect not.

Even whenever a loud noise like a gunshot might spook cows, I haven't seen a stampede. A popular and effective method of euthanasia in cattle is a well-placed gunshot to the head of a suffering cow. In fact, it's a method endorsed by the American Veterinary Medical Association and it's my preferred method for a number of reasons. Since many of the cows that require euthanasia are unable to stand and be moved, we elect to perform the euthanasia in the field among the rest of the herd. I use a gun that has a pretty loud bark to it and I rarely see an onlooking cow flinch, let alone begin a stampede. Even on the rare occasion when I may have to shoot a cow in a barn, the other cows don't become anything more than curious.

I've even worked cattle in a thunderstorm. Cows don't mind either lightning or thunder nearly as much as the veterinarian or the farmer does when standing on a water soaked concrete floor inside of a metal barn. Cows have been known to huddle under a tree instead of running during a thunderstorm. This is evidenced by discovering several dead cows under a splintered tree in the hours following the storm. If cows could reason, they still wouldn't stampede during a thunderstorm. They would walk slowly but deliberately away from the tall tree that acts like a lightning rod.

Cows just don't seem to mind loud noises as much as they hate sudden movements.

Granted, I've never worked cattle in an earthquake. That may be a different story. Nah, probably not.

I was performing some embryo transfer procedures in a heifer barn one day on the Eastern Shore of Maryland. While in the barn, I kept hearing what I thought was thunder. The barn was a long and sided with corrugated steel. Every minute or so, while I was checking the heifers, I heard a loud, rumbling noise. I kept looking at the sky thinking there were thunderclouds, but it was a clear day.

I considered that the wind may have been buckling a poorly attached piece of steel siding, but the barn was less than 2-months-old and I found that to be an unlikely scenario. After we had finished, I asked the farmer about it.

"What was that noise in the barn? Was it thunder? Was it the wind?" I asked.

He looked at me like I was weird, "What noise?"

I said, "It sounded like thunder or maybe a piece if corrugated steel buckling in the wind. Is there a rock quarry nearby blasting?"

He paused for a moment and his eyebrows went up. "Oh, that was probably just Aberdeen. I don't even hear it anymore."

His farm is about five miles from Aberdeen Proving Grounds. They were blowing stuff up that day.

I stopped for a second and listened. In the distance, I heard a boom. "There it goes again," I said.

"Nope, I didn't hear anything," was his reply.

And out of nowhere, the ground shook and a long, rumbling boom became clearly audible. It felt like an earthquake.

A smile took shape on his face, "I heard that one!" Meanwhile, the heifers were eating with contentment oblivious to the nearby explosive ordinance exercises. Stampede was the furthest thing from their minds.

Cow Society
1-26-16

Cows are social creatures; they exist in herds. When a cow is by herself and separated from the herd, we can be certain that there is something ailing the solitary cow. As such, we recognize that cows observe certain social norms.

Now when I say that they observe social norms, I don't mean that they have any sense of morality or law. They simply have instinctual behaviors that they adhere to when it comes to behavior within the group. Cows are far from unique in this respect. All pack or herd species are governed by instinctual behaviors that allows for group cohesion.

But since cows are the most interesting species… ever, they have the most interesting behavior patterns. At least that's my opinion. I am far from a bovine sociologist, but here are some observations I've made over the years while watching the cud chewing beasts.

First of all, cows have a hierarchy, or pecking order. There is always a boss cow; and she is the boss. The subordinate cows know not to get in the way of the boss when it comes to the feed bunk, milking parlor or even the most comfortable stall. She has a weapon and knows how to use it.

What is the weapon? Is it her hooves or maybe her teeth? No, her weapon is her head. And I don't mean that she tries to outsmart her adversary. She has a head that's enormous and the energy released from her fast moving head striking another cow is enough to cause serious injury. Broken ribs, bruises and hematomas are just some of the injuries that can be caused by a cow employing her favorite weapon.

So cows have a definite hierarchy, but the hierarchy can change at a moment's notice. The herd may be getting along fine one day. The boss cow knows she is the boss and leaves the other cows alone. The subordinate cows know their place as well. But once a new cow is introduced into the group, the whole social order is sent into chaos.

It's at this point that the entire hierarchy has to be reestablished. This phenomenon is well known by dairy farmers. In fact, farmers know that if group dynamics are in a constant state of change and turmoil, the cows will be stressed and more likely to get sick. It takes about two days for a group of cows to sort out their differences.

Cows are also very much creatures of habit. You may have noticed herds of dairy cows waiting to be let back in the barn late in the afternoon in anticipation of milking time. But who makes the decision first to go back to the barn from the pasture? Is it the boss cow? Is it the cow that is in the biggest hurry to be milked? Is it all of them? I honestly don't know. Only the cows know.

But like teenagers in high school, cows also form cliques. They hang out together and generally stay in the same areas of the barn together. They tend to not co-mingle with other cliques. That is, until, a cow comes into heat. When in heat, her drive to reproduce sends her in search of a mate, even if she winds up in another clique's territory.

Cows can be enigmatic. To watch them when the social order is at ease, they appear docile, even gentle. But they are far from gentle. Cows, even dairy cows, have been known to attack and even kill a farmer if she has recently had a calf. They will attack and try to injure another cow to establish dominance.

I once heard them described as gentle creatures. They really aren't gentle by nature. Their nature is to be violent. Farmers have selected them however, over time, to be manageable.

Moody Cows
8-23-16

People can be moody. Occasionally, I meet a farmer having a bad day. And veterinarians, well, we get grumpy once in a while. But cows have bad days too. And there are definitely things that will set them off.

Cows don't come right out and tell you they are mad. One has to be able to interpret their body language. Sometimes it's easy to interpret, like when she puts her head down and tries to mash you into the wall. Other times it's subtle; they just give you that look.

Cows can really get set off around the time they deliver their calves. Maybe it's hormonal. No, it's definitely hormonal but since cows can't read, I don't guess I'll make any of them mad with that comment. They are actually hard wired to be irritable when they have a baby calf at their side. It is meant to give them motivation to protect their vulnerable bundle of joy from predators. Just ask any farmer that has to put an ear tag in a beef calf to identify it from the other calves. She can be downright nasty.

But once the calf is grown and it's time for it to move on, there is some more drama. Beef farmers typically wean the calves from the cows at around 7-months of age. When that happens, get ready for a good shouting match. The cows are in one pasture and the calves are in another and both are bawling. The cows are mad because somebody took their baby away. And the calves are mad because mama doesn't love them anymore. But after a couple of days of the noise, they will all eventually forgive and forget.

Dairy cows, believe it or not, can have fits of ill-temper too. But what puts a cow in a bad mood? There are a lot of things. Cows are creatures of habit and when they get out of their routine, they can get a bit peeved. Just ask any dairy farmer when he is 30-minutes late to the milking parlor. The cows will be at the door waiting for him and mooing as if to admonish him for being late.

But all habits have to start somewhere and when a cow has to be milked for the first time, she will definitely let you know that she's unhappy. Consider that a cow's teat is meant to have a calf's mouth attached to it. For the new dairy cow, the first trip to the milking parlor can be a weird, and irritating experience.

Dairy cows are quite management intensive and they have to be handled quite a bit. Besides milking time, they actually prefer to be left alone. But once she has had her calf and enters the milking string, she gets a lot of attention. And often, it makes her angry.

Dairy cows will get vaccinated periodically to prevent specific infections. And they can resent the attention. Farmers will make a list of cows to vaccinate and go to the barn looking for the right ones. Once the cows have all gotten their shots, the will farmer end up on the cows' list – and I don't mean their Christmas list.

You know, when I think about it, dairy cows are actually pretty hard to please. When you try to wake one up, she gets irritated. When you ask one to get out of bed, she just looks at you with contempt. If you make a sudden movement, she'll scram. Slippery floors will her draw her ire. Approach her head and be prepared for consequences. Sneak up on her and experience her fury. And by all means, when I go to check her for pregnancy, well, then I get the look that cuts right through you.

But if you really want to make a cow mad, let her see you accuse her farmer of doing wrong. Start stirring up hysteria over the evils of eating meat and dairy and I think you'll find a cross bovine. Without meat and dairy products, there simply could be no cows. The thought of there being no cows is maddening.

But despite all of these things that agitate a cow, they still do their job every day. And most of the time they are pleasant. But if you do something to her that she doesn't like, she just may end up in a bad mooood.

<h3 style="text-align:center">5-23-17
Duality of Cows</h3>

You've heard of Dr. Jekyll and Mr. Hyde? Well meet Miss Gentle and Mrs. Rawhide. She is a tale of two critters.

OK, that's enough of the classical literary references. But these are not fictional characters. They are real, not persons, but cows. Cows, especially beef cows, sometimes suffer from multiple personality syndrome.

Take a look at the cows grazing the pastures this time of year. You will see a serene, peaceful group of animals munching contentedly on some green grass. You are looking at Miss Gentle.

Along comes a dog to investigate. And then, like a spell has been placed on her, she transforms into a raging beast. She aims to not chase the intruder off, but to kill it without mercy. You are looking at Mrs. Rawhide.

Once she runs the predator off, or at least what she perceives as a predator, the spell is broken and she resumes her role as nurturing mother. She strolls up to her calf bedded down in the tall grass and gives it a gentle nudge. The calf, unaware of her mother's curse, ignores her. Mom, undeterred, desires the attention of her offspring.

Softly, she licks at the muzzle of her baby calf. Grooming relaxes her. She is at peace.

Eventually, the calf responds to her prompting and it stands. Miss Gentle continues to lick and love on the calf. Since it's been at least an hour or so since the calf's last meal, it ultimately finds its way to the other end of the cow for some milk.

The calf, however, is far from gentle. It latches on to a teat and pulls and tugs for faster service. Still unsatisfied, it bucks the udder relentlessly to get more.

Miss Gentle, on the other hand, chews her cud contentedly as the calf nurses.

But then, a stock trailer backs up ominously to the gate and out comes four new heifers from another pasture. Miss Gentle transforms instantaneously into something that would scare a comic book villain. Filled with a different type of determination, she approaches the trespassers.

The new additions have caused instability in the social hierarchy and Mrs. Rawhide is charged with resetting the pecking order. She takes after the heifers and they scatter. One decides to confront her and is met with a blow from Mrs. Rawhide's tree trunk sized head to her ribs. That's all it took. All of the heifers decide it's best to be subordinate, for now.

And, once again, like somebody flipped a switch, Miss Gentle is back and returns to her calf.

Some time passes and the farmer stops to check on the herd. Leaning on the gate, he takes in the picture from a safe distance. The herd soon notices and they get up to investigate.

Miss Gentle is the first to greet him from the other side of the gate. She approaches with calf by her side and sniffs his hand. Her curiosity not satisfied, she sticks out her tongue for some more answers. She is as pleasant as a summer breeze.

The farmer notices that one of the new heifers has a limp, though. Not wanting to take chances, he calls the vet for an exam. And since the vet is already there, it seems like a good time to vaccinate the whole herd.

The farmer gathers the cows in the holding pen so they can be run through the chute; new heifers, Miss Gentle and all. As Miss Gentle enters the chute, she disappears and Mrs. Rawhide returns. She snorts and bellows and thrashes around since her calf is away from her sight. She kicks the vet and charges after the farmer.

Farmers select for this trait to a degree. A good mama cow isn't afraid to take on a predator if she thinks it is a threat. And she knows how to raise and care for a calf. A good mama cow also isn't a threat from a distance, but she has enough spunk to stay alive.

One person might see the cow as a gentle giant. Another may perceive her as a threat capable of causing bodily harm. The truth is that they are both right. Beware of the change from Miss Gentle to Mrs. Rawhide.

Trivial
10-31-17

Cattle inspire awe in me whenever I stop and consider what amazing creatures they are. They eat grass, have a complex four-chambered stomach in which to digest the grass and they convert that feed into meat and milk. No scientific laboratory will ever be able to duplicate the miracle that cattle perform naturally.

That might not seem as interesting to you as it does to me. I know, I can be fascinated by some strange things. But there is surely something about the cow that is worthy of your respect if you only knew the entire story.

There are facts about cattle that may seem trivial to some that make me sit up and take notice. Here are a few of them.

Cattle can develop a malady called hardware disease. Since they are indiscriminate eaters, they eat first and deal with the consequences later. They rarely even take time to chew their food properly. That is, until they lie down and chew on their cuds for a while.

When a cow grazes or even eats feed at the bunk, a wire, nail or other piece of metal debris can accidentally find its way into the cow's feed. Once it winds up in her mouth, it's destined to be swallowed.

Since metal is relatively heavy, it finds its way into the lowest chamber in the cow's forestomach, the reticulum. Once there, it lays on the bottom of the chamber. But for some unfortunate cows, the sharp metal object can puncture the wall of the reticulum and cause a nasty infection. The remedy for this is sometimes a powerful magnet that can attract and bind the offending metal and render it harmless. But if the metal is not ferrous, it's bad news for the cow.

There's a new champion in the Holstein breed. A cow in Wisconsin named 3918 produced in 365 days' time a whopping 78,170 pounds of milk. To put this in perspective, the average Holstein cow produces less than one third that amount in the same amount of time.

Helping her to set the record are literally trillions and trillions of tiny bacteria, fungi and protozoa organisms living in her rumen. The rumen is the large fermentation chamber of the cow's complex stomach. Without these bugs, she would be incapable of digesting her feed and wouldn't produce even a glass of milk.

The rumen bugs begin to ferment the feed she has eaten, but never take it to completion. With the fermentation process, there is usually an endpoint that results in the death of the microorganisms.

But in the rumen, the fermentation process never reaches an endpoint. Before it can happen, the reticulum, assuming it isn't affected by hardware disease, sorts the stuff that needs to go downstream from that which needs to stay and cook a little longer. And the cow is constantly adding to the pot by eating to keep it fresh, so to speak.

You may have noticed that the record setting cow has more of a number than a name. Farmers have to identify their cows somehow, and some of them are named and some are numbered. Many of them get both. If she is registered in the Holstein breed association, she will have both a name and a number.

Several years ago, there was a study published that looked at the difference in milk production between cows that were given names and cows that were assigned numbers. Guess which ones produced more milk? If you guessed the ones with names, you know something about cows. Cows with names produced more milk than cows with numbers.

That caused a small debate among agricultural scientists about study design and the concept of cause and effect. Needless to say, the act of assigning a name to a cow doesn't give her some supernatural power. And I know nothing about the farms selected for the study. But it is plausible that farmers who have registered cows with names may have better stock than other farmers who pay little attention to cattle genetics. But somewhere in Wisconsin, there is a cow named 3918 who didn't read the study.

In the Mind of a Cow
11-3-15

I spend a lot of time amongst cows. So much time, in fact, that I often wonder what they might think when I'm around. Granted, when I'm near a cow, she might be just a bit anxious. After all, no animals like to see the vet.

I can't hardly blame them. But the cows who are most familiar with me seem to tolerate me the best. I'd like to think it's my stall side manner, or even my bovine charisma that relaxes my patients, but I recognize that my older patients have probably just mellowed with age. Much of my time is spent around the rear half of the cow doing pregnancy checks or embryo transfer. For those of you unfamiliar with the process of pregnancy checking, I feel I should explain. To determine if a cow is pregnant or not, we have to reach into her rectum. There, we can feel the uterus, or womb, to check for the presence or absence of a pregnancy. Sorry if you're reading this on your lunch break. And yes, of course, I do wear a large, shoulder length glove.

So, it's common for a farmer to have a group of cows for us to check at one stop. The cows are sometimes in stalls, restrained at the feed bunk or even in special chutes designed for this purpose. As I work my way down the line, I can see the cows in front of me giving the evil eye.

The heifers are always the most anxious and like to dance. By dance, I don't mean that they waltz. No, instead they swing their rear end from side to side as to throw a mountain lion from their back. If I could read her mind, I think I might hear, "Hey! Your hand's cold!" Or maybe even, "You're gonna stick that, where?"

I could imagine the grizzled old cow standing next to the nervous heifer and handing out a dash of hazing, especially around Halloween. "Little Bessie, you know what he's gonna do with that arm of his? He's gonna reach up inside of you and pull out your eyeballs!" as she snickers. It's no wonder the heifers are so squirrelly.

But if only they could understand what it means when I call out to the farmer, "PREGNANT!"

Bessie's eyes would get wide and she would let out an audible "Moooooo!" That's cow for "Yes! I get to stay for another year!" You didn't know I speak cow, did you?

There are situations when the farmer and I might walk among the cows in the pasture or in the barn. Cows are curious by nature and there is always a pet in the bunch. Invariably, a group will come close to investigate and leading that group is the pet. The pet is amusing for about 30 seconds or so, but she will persist in her quest for affection until she has annoyed everyone present.

"Hello! Here I am! Scratch my 150-pound head!" she'd say if

I could hear her. As I get back to work after a quick scratch, she continues. "Hey, where are you going? My head still needs scratched… Come back here!"

Perhaps if I could get inside a cow's head in only one situation, it would be during surgery. In the field, we do almost all surgeries on cows while they are totally awake. And these are no minor surgeries I'm talking about. I mean complete abdominal surgery including cesarean surgery, twisted stomach surgery and even sometimes intestinal surgery.

We do these surgeries under a very generous local anesthesia so the cow rarely feels anything, yet she can still look back and observe what I'm doing. It seems that every time I do one of these surgeries, the thought enters my mind about what the cow might be considering at the moment I pull out the scalpel blade.

The cow looks back at me and might say, "Excuse me! That's my stomach you're playing with there!" Or in the case of the cesarean section, she would say, "How did that get in there?" Like she doesn't know…

But in reality, I'm quite certain that the cow doesn't really wonder these things. If they could consider thoughtfully what I'm really up to, I doubt I could get within the length of a fast moving hoof of her. Domestication has caused the cow to become tolerant of humans and the things we ask of them. They have no anxiety about pain because they can't usually anticipate it.

It's fun to ponder the thoughts of the cow, but I suspect I already know what they are really thinking at any given moment and it isn't too obscure. "I'm hungry." "I'm ready to be milked." "I think I have to chew this cud that I just regurgitated." There's a glimpse into the mind of a cow and also the sometimes distorted mind of a cow vet. Unlike the cow's vet, however, the cow's mind just isn't very complicated.

Expect the Unexpected
3-28-17

There's a paradoxical idiom that says to expect the unexpected. It's also sound advice.

Farmers, more than anyone, appreciate that. Very little happens on the farm that is surprising; anything seems possible sometimes.

If the forecast calls for clear skies and the hay is mature, farmers will mow the hay. Yet, most of them expect the hay to be rained on. Is it pessimism or just preparing for a contingency? I expect it's a little of both.

The weather is one thing; we know predictions don't pan out all the time. But livestock are another story. Cattle are predictable and we expect that they always will do something unpredictable. Well, that would actually make their actions expected; it's just that we never saw it coming. I feel like I'm writing in circles.

Here's what I mean. A farmer builds a fence to keep the cows in their pasture. But he knows that they will probably figure out a way to break out of the fence. The grass is always greener on the other side, you know. And because they're cows and have a knack for causing chaos, they eventually get out. The farmer saw it coming, but it was still unexpected.

Well, OK, we really don't know what to expect with these girls. I mean, we try to plan for the unexpected, but when it happens, we are still surprised.

While working cattle, expecting the unexpected is not just a nice idiom, but an imperative. I spend most of my time at the business end of the bovine. That leaves me susceptible to a swift kick in the shin if I do something that she doesn't expect. So, I expect that every time I approach a cow's rear end, I'm going to get lit up.

The expectation of getting kicked serves a dual purpose for me. First, when I don't get kicked, it makes me happy. But since I expect it almost every time I approach a cow, I let her know I'm behind her. Cows don't like surprises.

And sometimes I forget to expect it and I get it. Ouch.

Farmers, while they do expect to be surprised from time to time, still don't really like surprises. When a cow has a calf, we expect them to have only one calf most of the time. That is, unless, we diagnose twins at pregnancy check. It's really not that uncommon for a dairy cow to deliver twins; some farms have a twinning incident rate of up to one in 10. But we try to let the farmer know ahead of time so he expects it.

And since it's hard to prove a negative (rule out that there is a twin hiding in the womb somewhere) occasionally we're surprised to find two calves with mama instead of only one. That's not that big of a surprise. Conversely, now and then we tell the farmer to expect twins on a cow only to have her deliver one. Sometimes a twin doesn't make it. We anticipate that it happens sometimes. But rarely, a farmer expects to find two calves but instead finds three. I guess we should have expected that.

When examining a sick cow, we try to get as much information from the farmer as we can since the cow can't communicate with us. We ask how long since she delivered her calf, when did she eat last, how much milk did she produce this morning and so on. This information is essential to not only make a diagnosis, but also to give a prognosis. I always try to overcome any unexpected bias that may be offered to me.

Farmers know their cows pretty well. They know how long since she's had her calf, about her appetite and her milk production. But since farmers have a lot of cows, they have to identify them by ear tag to keep them straight. And if a cow decides to slip her ID and steal the identity of another, it can cause some confusion.

I was presented with a cow recently that had a twisted stomach. In preparing to do the surgery, I wanted to gather from the farmer as much information as possible to be sure she was a good candidate for surgery. I inquired how long it was since the cow had her calf and was told that she had only delivered a calf a couple of months ago. But when I did my internal exam before surgery, she felt about 5 months pregnant.

That was unexpected. Either there was an alien growing in her or she was the wrong cow. After confirming it was a pregnancy and not a tumor (or alien), I told the farmer she must have stolen the identity of another cow. We eventually got it straightened out and did the surgery.

We expect that the old girl to be fine.

Cows are Cool
4-12-16

People love cows.

I heard a caller to a radio talk show remark about how she loves to hear the sound of cows mooing. She never heard them in person since she was from Boston, but was content to hear them on the radio.

Clever advertising campaigns utilize the bovine to impart a connection with the merchandise being sold. Take, for example, the promotion from a few years ago featuring the talking "Happy Cows" from California selling dairy products. People fell in love with them.

And there's the deeply ironic campaign by Chic Fil A featuring clever cows urging people to eat chicken. I guess the folks who came up with this idea must understand that for people to actually like chicken, they need the endorsement of cows.

There are cow prints on boxes that sell computers. There are cartoons featuring cows. Every toddler in America knows what sound a cow makes, even the ones that have never seen a cow in person.

There are cultures that believe the cow is sacred. In those places, it is even a crime to kill a cow.

There is the famous "cow parade" art exhibit featured in major cities, starting with Chicago in 1999. I happened to visit Chicago then for a veterinary conference while the cow parade was first on display.

I wondered out loud to some colleagues why anyone would make such a big deal over an artist's rendition of cows. I didn't, at the time, understand the iconic nature of the cow. To me, the cow has always been special – and accessible.

I could postulate the reasons why this phenomenon of the cow has endured for generations. But I think we all already know the answer.

Cows are cool.

What else can explain why dairy farmers do what they do? Wake at 4 a.m. (or earlier) to milk, feed and clean up after the cows. Do it all over again in the afternoon.

Some beef farmers literally live with the herd during calving season to see that, if a cow gets into trouble trying to deliver a calf, someone is there to help.

The idea of leisure to many farmers is taking some cows across the state or even the country to a show where they can exhibit their cows. At the same time, they can look at other farmer's cows.

Farmers invest small and large fortunes alike into cattle enterprises. Many of them have returns on investments that would make a rational investor instead stuff his money into a mattress. Do you know the best way to make a small fortune…?

Invest a large fortune into cattle farming.

People who know cows know that there is more to life than "return on investment."

But what is it about this big, slow, grass eating lumbering beast that makes people long to hear the sound "MOOOOOO?" Why are cows so cool?

That question eludes me. Why is the sky blue? Because it is, I guess.

How do you tie your shoes? I can't tell you how to do it, but I can show you. I can't tell you why cows are cool, but if you are wondering, stop and watch them from across the fence as they graze in the pasture. Don't touch the fence, though, or you might get more of a jolt than you bargained for.

Cows remind us that hamburger and ice cream and leather have their origin in the imagination of the Good Lord who gave us the cow. Cows remind me that life on this earth is fleeting and we would all do well to remember that. Cows remind us of a simple life, even though the life of the farmer isn't simple at all. She reminds us that, even though life can be tough, we can still smile when we hear "MOOOOOO."

Maybe that's why they're so cool.

Workaholic
11-7-17

Work, work, work. It's all some of us do anymore. Farmers work a lot; you've seen me write about that many times before. And veterinarians, well, yeah, I work a lot too. But when it comes to working, few of us can beat a cow.

When somebody is described as working a lot, he is said to work like a dog. The proper phrase should be working like a cow.

You don't see it? You think cows do nothing but eat and lay around all the time. Cows may seem lazy but only because they are so good at their job.

Let me explain from the perspective of a dairy cow. I don't mean to take anything away from the beef cow; she works hard too. But the dairy cow is a workaholic.

Her obsession is making milk. It comes naturally to her, yes, but it still is a lot of work. And I mean work in the literal sense. She converts the plants she eats into milk. Believe me, it takes a good deal of effort to accomplish this. Here's how it works.

The forages the cow eats are practically indigestible to humans, but the cow has a rumen. The rumen is the large fermentation chamber of her complex stomach. The rumen, with the help of trillions and trillions of microorganisms, can break down the fibrous plant material into simple components that can be utilized by the cow.

You still don't see it? Well, her work hasn't even started yet. A typical milk cow makes about 80 pounds of milk a day and much more when she's in peak lactation form. Milk is about 88 percent water and 12 percent solids. The solids are milk fat, milk protein, lactose and some minerals like calcium and magnesium, among others.

The milk solids don't make themselves. The cow has to build them from scratch. The complex protein, fat and lactose are all assembled from simple fatty acids, amino acids and other simple molecules. That's the cow's job and she does it well to the tune of about 10 pounds of milk solids a day.

If you think I'm giving the cow more credit than she deserves, consider this. It takes energy to build these complex components of milk. Milk has calories, doesn't it? (Don't despair, they're good calories.) Pound for pound, a dairy cow uses as much energy as a marathoner does running the 26.2 mile race to produce her 80 pound quota of milk. She does this every day.

And she does this all day, every day. When she's up eating, she's working. When she's lying and chewing her cud, she's working. When she's being milked, she's working. She's truly a workaholic.

She loves her job; that's her purpose in life. The farmer, to his credit, makes her job as easy as possible. He keeps feed out for her at all times. A hungry cow just might be tempted to go on strike. He keeps her comfortable so she can lie down and chew her cud.

Cud chewing both relaxes her and makes her job easier. As she grinds the feed into progressively finer particles, it allows fermentation to proceed more efficiently through her rumen helpers, the microorganisms. Technically, she is lying down on the job, but she's still working.

She works the hardest when she's being milked. At least twice a day and sometime three or even more times a day, she relinquishes her milk to the farmer. She does this every day without a day off. She really doesn't want time off, either. At every shift, some cows will precede the farmer to the milking parlor.

She does take the occasional sick day but only when necessary. When she gets sick, her milk production can cease completely. The farmer can tell when she's faking a sick day, which never happens.

At the end of her year-long shift, she finally gets a well-deserved break. Dairy cows take advantage of a dry period in anticipation of the delivery of her next calf. She can't make milk without delivering a calf. What would be the point in that? A full six to eight weeks before she is due, the farmer quits milking her and she dries off. That is, her milk production ceases. Consider it a lactation vacation. She fusses about it for a little bit; she loves her job after all. But she eventually settles in for a little rest and relaxation. Just long enough to prepare for her next shift.

CHAPTER 11
Animals Other Than Cows

Photo by Kelly Jay Rorhbaugh

As a veterinarian, I took an oath to use my scientific knowledge and skills to benefit society through the protection of animal health and the prevention and relief of animal suffering. While I have made a conscious decision to concentrate my efforts on farmers and the food animals they raise, I have occasion to interact with other species. Some of these are food animals, like hogs or goats, and others are companions or working animals.

I am not much of a horseman, though. I know just enough about them to be dangerous. My first job at a veterinary practice provided service to horse owners, so I know a little about them, but I rarely interact with them today. My fondest memory of horses is a three-week stint I spent at a cow-calf ranch in central Florida while a senior in veterinary school. The purpose of my trip to that ranch was to gain experience with beef cattle, but I learned more about horses than anything.

This ranch, like most beef ranches, used the quarter horse for working cattle. We would move cattle, drive cattle, herd cattle, cut cattle and anything else that could be done from the back of a horse. It was a worthwhile experience, but the Quarter Horse isn't the most comfortable horse to ride. After a four-hour trip following a herd of 200 cows to a fresh pasture and back, the horseman's bottom can take some abuse. I learned the meaning of the term "saddle sore," and the sore wasn't on the horse. To this day, I don't believe that the guy who sings the country and western song about wanting to be a cowboy has ever been on a quarter horse.

Discomfort aside, it was good. For those of you acquainted with the cutting horse, you might find this boring. But one afternoon, the cowboy to whom I was assigned was charged with separating a group of yearling heifers from the yearling steers. To separate them, the cowboy would run two or three yearlings down a lane and, from the back of a horse, I had to push them toward the heifer pen or steer pen depending on what they were.

From the belly or rear end of the yearling, it's identity is obvious. If you don't know what I mean, simply put, their plumbing is different. But from the animal's head, they all look the same. The farm had a practice of putting a notch in the ear of all bull calves when they were steered (castrated), so I had to pay close attention to the ears to tell the heifers from the steers. Once identified, I had a couple seconds to decide which ones went left or right.

Before saddling up the horses that morning, the cowboy asked me if I had ever ridden before. I was pretty green, but I didn't want to look bad in front of the cowboy, so I said, "Yeah, yeah, I've ridden a horse." It wasn't a lie; I had ridden a horse, once, 4 years earlier. After traveling 100 yards and getting bucked off, I led him back to the stable with the reigns. But I had ridden him.

I got the saddle on, with the cowboy's help, and figured out how to get my horse to follow the cowboy's horse to the yearling pen. It was more the horse than my directions, but it worked out. But once in the pen, I was on my own. Now, I had always thought that you steer a horse by pulling on the reign in the direction you want to go; so that's what I did. But there's a method called "neck reigning" that works the opposite. To get the neck reigned horse to turn, you lay the reign on the side of its neck toward the direction you want the horse to travel. The first several groups of yearlings would simply scatter once they got to me and the horse, and the cowboy was getting mad. This horse was trained to trained to steer by neck reign, and I was giving it mixed signals.

Once I figured out what the problem was, I just let the horse do what he was supposed to do; separate the steers from the heifers. It was almost like the horse knew that the ones with the ear notches went right and the others went left. I just held on and enjoyed the ride. That horse taught me more about moving cattle than any farmer or professor in veterinary school. If we missed one, the horse would turn on a dime, chase the critter down and move it to the right pen. It was something to behold.

So, even though I don't work much around horses, I have a healthy appreciation for them. I just don't have any material on horses to write about. But I have dealt with many other domesticated animals on farms, from cats to birds and from dogs to hogs.

The subject of this chapter is some of my favorite non-cow animals and I should make special mention of critters of the ovine persuasion. Sheep are food animals first, but also moonlight as a fiber animal. Sheep have a reputation for being, well, less intelligent than other livestock. This is remarkable since other livestock aren't very bright. Livestock are bred for production, not intelligence. Nonetheless, sheep are just as smart as they need to be. They are a bit flighty and do everything as a flock. If one is separated from the flock, it comes unglued. I suspect that's how they earned their reputation.

Sheep were always the subject of jokes and wise cracks in my veterinary school class. Do you know the only thing dumber than a sheep? A flock of sheep. Yes, I have made a habit of ridiculing sheep in my column. I don't do this to be mean; I really do like sheep. But they are just easy to poke fun at.

Commensalism
11-14-17

When the Good Lord created the Earth, He filled it with creatures that are too numerous to count. I like to think he did this for us, whom He created after everything else. Whether you believe in the literal, allegorical or don't believe in the creation account of the Bible at all, you can't deny the existence of a multitude of animals that are here to help man.

Animals have always fascinated me and the cow above all. But domestic and wild animals alike fill me with wondrous awe by their interactions with each other. There are commensal relationships between some wild animals to be sure. But to see a domesticated dog and domesticated cat not only coexist but play together seems to defy the natural order. That natural order was seemingly upset by domestication.

My favorite of God's creatures is the cow, obviously. But many of God's other creatures have been recruited by man to help in the husbandry of the bovine.

We all know of the horse used by cowboys to maintain the herd. That example is familiar to all of us. But the horse is more than just a mode of transportation for the cowboy. They can be invaluable when separating animals from the herd. Cutting horses, usually of the quarter horse breed, are trained to steer (pun intended) animals in whatever direction the cowboy desires. He may want to separate the cows from the calves or the steers from the heifers. But whatever the job, a good cutting horse makes it easier.

There are other more obscure examples of domesticated animals helping man with the raising of cattle. Take the donkey, for example. Donkeys are known to be excellent pack animals and are pretty stubborn at times. Some farmers take advantage of the donkey's stubbornness to deal with another stubborn animal – the show steer.

Steers that have a particular look are raised to be shown off at county fairs and even large regional and national shows. To be shown, the steer must be trained to lead on a halter. A 500-pound steer calf that doesn't want to lead can be a handful for anyone to break. But if you tie the other end of the lead rope to a donkey, in a couple days the calf will walk like a trained dog on a leash. Steers can be stubborn, but the donkey will eventually win out.

The goat is used by some for a rather unique purpose. Cattle are susceptible to a topical fungal disease known as ringworm. It has nothing really to do with worms, but it can grow in a ring pattern on the skin and make the cows itchy. By the way, ringworm is contagious to people.

But some believe the presence of a stinky mature buck goat has ringworm repellant properties. A stinky mature buck goat certainly has people repellant properties, but I remain skeptical to this day that it cures ringworm. Nevertheless, some swear by the billy goat.

The dog is a valuable companion to most cattle farmers for one reason or another. Some use them as herding animals and many breeds have excellent instincts for bringing in the herd. Some dogs are kept as companions or even to alert the farmer if a stranger is lurking on the property.

The most intriguing use for a dog I have ever known is one that alerts the farmer when a cow is in heat and ready for breeding. Many farmers breed their cows by artificial insemination. But cows are only fertile once every 21 days or so and if a bull isn't around, she may not let on that she is receptive. Some have trained dogs to alert the farmer to which cows are in heat on any given day. Heat detection is a major bottleneck for breeding programs and a trained dog has the ability to make it easier.

I could go on. There are many more examples of domesticated animal's interactions with other species that benefits man. Guinea fowl eat insects that bother cattle. Cats patrol the farm for rodents and other vermin. Guard Llamas protect lambs from predators like coyotes. Wild animals contribute as well. Raptors patrol barns in search of the nuisance starlings that rob the cows of their feed. Predatory wasps keep parasitic insects under control.

Whatever the task, the mutually beneficial interactions of animals of differing species is nothing less than providential. If only some people of differing backgrounds cold learn that lesson from the animal kingdom, we would all be better off.

Human Animal Bond
8-18-15

There is a well described phenomenon known as the human-animal bond. It defines the kinship between people and domesticated animals. The notion is somewhat abstract yet the human-animal bond is very real and arguably as strong as super glue.

This bond is one of the motivations for a farmer to drag himself out of bed at 4 a.m. and start the chores. This bond is the reason for millions of pet owners to share a home with an animal. This bond causes nursing home residents to light up with excitement when a service dog arrives. And this bond can turn hardened criminals, literally, into loving, nurturing caretakers and it can assist in their rehabilitation.

Being a veterinarian gives me a front row seat to observe the human animal bond up close from a plethora of points of view. As an animal owner myself, my family and I experience the bond in its truest sense. It is part responsibility and part relationship.

A high school teacher nearly 30 years ago gave her class a bit of advice that stuck with me for a long time. She told us that when we were to get married, one of the first assignments should be for the new couple to get a dog. I don't know why she told us that, but it does make a lot of sense. The dog might act as a distraction from the newly revealed faults of the relatively unfamiliar spouse, of which my spouse and I were both immune, of course.

Nonetheless, 20 years ago, my new bride and I went out and purchased a shiny new Golden Retriever puppy. Since then, we have always owned a Goldie or two. That is, until this summer when our third one, Zeeek, took ill (we really did spell his name that way.) I've written about Zeeek before and his genetic modifications and tendencies to lick everything. He was a good dog and the entire family felt the sting of separating that bond. We found ourselves without a dog for the first time since we became a family and it was weird.

I also get to experience the human-animal bond from other perspectives. While the animal rights activists would argue that livestock farmers are a cruel and uncaring lot; that has not been what I've seen. Granted, not all farmers have a strong emotional attachment to their stock; many do and most have at least some bond. This bond is different than the bond of a pet to a family, but more of a respect for the animal. This bond contributes to, along with the incentive for profit, the farmers desire to keep the animals healthy and comfortable. Cruel and uncaring farmers won't be farming for very long, believe me.

This bond does allow for favoritism in a herd; there is no hiding that. But this favoritism doesn't mean that there is mistreatment of the others. In the case of livestock showing, some animals in a herd will have the privilege of being primped and groomed before going in the show ring. It is true that only the favorites go to the shows. The county fair will soon be here and this form of human animal bond will be on display for everyone to see.

Many children and young adults will be displaying their livestock in search of a blue ribbon. Their bonds with the animals have been cultivated all summer and will end with the livestock sale at the conclusion of the fair. There will be some tears shed as the market animals go to their ultimate destination. The bond is very real to these kids.

Most of the farms we visit have a farm dog or two. Some are talented working dogs that assist in retrieving the cattle from pasture. Others act as doorbells in the event of a stranger snooping around the premises. One farmer's life was recently saved by his dog as a cow had him cornered and was pummeling him. The bond between that farmer and his dog got a little stronger that day while the bond between him and the cow was broken.

While the scope of my professional practice is limited to livestock, I am nonetheless asked to care for some farm dogs occasionally. Whenever a farm dog is injured beyond the expectation of recovery or is just old and tired, I am charged with putting them to sleep. It is unpleasant yet necessary and rarely is the farmer not affected.

I think the Good Lord may have given us domesticated animals to keep us honest. Maybe it was His intent that the animals should domesticate us? After all, we treat our animals better than we treat our fellow humans sometimes. As for my family, we have bonded again with another Golden Retriever puppy. It took about five minutes for the bond to set up like concrete. Life is, without question, better with animals.

Bleeding Pigs
9-1-15

There exist for most people during the daily routine of life those duties that are unpleasant. For the cashier, it might be a grumpy customer. For the teacher, it might be an unruly student. For the food animal veterinarian, it could be a number of things like retained placenta, prolapsed uterus or maybe downer cows. But for me, it is bleeding pigs.

By "bleeding pigs," I don't mean a pig that is hemorrhaging. No, "bleeding pigs" means intentionally collecting blood on, not one, but a herd of pigs. It can be quite unpleasant.

In fact, when I found out that the practice I work for did offer that service some 13 years ago, before I signed my first contract I legitimately had second thoughts about closing the deal. But fortunately, I decided to take the good with the bad.

You might be wondering why on earth would one need to collect blood on a herd of pigs and how in the world would it be done. Pigs, like all farm animals, are susceptible to a number of contagious infectious diseases. Agriculture departments in most states like to know whenever particularly destructive diseases are present in their state so they perform routine surveillance. Part of the surveillance is to monitor the blood of swine herds for the presence of certain infections.

Now the agriculture departments don't have quite enough staff to go around and do all of the blood testing necessary for proper surveillance, so they enlist the assistance of private practice veterinarians, like me. We bleed cows, pigs, and the occasional horse to test for a variety of diseases.

As for the how, there are days that I wonder if I even know how to bleed a pig at all. The process is actually quite easy… when it works. Step one is to snare the pig.

Pigs have a reputation for being smart. I, however, have to question the conventional wisdom as it concerns the degree of intelligence of a pig. Here's why.

To snare a pig, we use a tool called the Iowa Hog Snare. I'm guessing that it was invented in the hog capital of the world, Iowa. At any rate, the snare consists of a two-foot long hollow steel rod with a loop of cable extending from one end. On the other end is a handle that, when pulled, closes the loop of cable. There is also a latch that prevents the loop from opening up before the operator is ready.

The pig is allowed to bite the loop of cable and, as it gets further back in the pig's mouth, the farmer tightens the loop, snaring the pig by its snout. I question the intelligence of the pig because it's not always successful on the first attempt. But we can always trick the pig into investigating this steel cable with its mouth a second, or third or even fourth time.

Please don't misunderstand me; I have great admiration for the pig. My day is always better when it starts with bacon. Most… no, all food is made better with bacon. I once gave instructions to a butcher for preparing my freezer pig to just make the whole thing into bacon. Any critter that tastes half as good as bacon is top notch in my book. Swine, being the source of bacon, are indeed special. But they are also a major source of frustration for me before they become bacon.

I believe they make up for their lack of intelligence, however, with sheer determination. That's why the snare works so well. Once caught, they are determined to back out of the snare. So they pull back against the weight of the farmer holding the snare with everything they have. And when they are preoccupied with backing away from the snare, I stick my needle in the vein and steal a sample of blood. It's as easy as that.

So, you might be thinking that it sounds much more unpleasant for the pig than the veterinarian. I'd like to invite those who think that to accompany me on a pig bleeding excursion. The source of the sample is the pig's jugular vein, which lies buried about two inches deep in the hog's jowls. Try hitting one of those in an angry, squirming squealing tube of meat while hunched just above ground level. The only thing endearing about the whole experience is the company of the pig farmer.

There are days when, like a pitcher tossing a no hitter, I can't miss a vein. We know never to remark about it on those days, though, as the karma may vanish before the last pig is bled. And there's other days when the veins seem microscopic. It's as if somebody sprayed vein repellant all over my needles.

So how does an intelligent pig escape the clutches of the snare? The truly intelligent pig goes for a quick dip in the wallow and covers itself with fresh mud. That pig will likely be identified as one that doesn't require testing.

I've been regularly bleeding pigs every quarter on one farm in particular for about 10 years now. I've come to appreciate it as a challenge; a challenge in hitting the vein quickly and with the least stress for the pig, the farmer and, of course, me. It's one of those duties that, while unpleasant, must be done. Unpleasant, yes, but I like to think I'm doing my small part to safeguard the supply of bacon for generations to come.

Chase
4-26-16

The animal rights movement, while completely wrong, must be given credit for something. They have shifted the public perception to be sympathetic to their agenda. Roll the sad footage of the sick and infirmed companion animals behind a cage door while playing a weepy ballad. Tug at the heart strings of well-meaning folks, while at the same time imploring them to make a monthly donation to save the animals.

The implication is that all sick animals are victims of abuse. Unfortunately, whenever some people see an ailing animal, they now figure it must have gotten that way through abuse. I could take a video camera into any animal hospital and record footage that would elicit emotions strong enough to coerce a gullible animal lover to send me money. With that money, I could "save the animals." Sick animals are pathetic animals. And sick animals make great props.

Some time ago, I had stopped at a gas station in my work truck to fill my tank. We were towing our box trailer that day that acts as a mobile laboratory, complete with a roof mounted air conditioning unit.

There was a lady getting gas at an adjacent pump and she kept looking at me, at the trailer and back to me again. She must have figured that I was a veterinarian who works on livestock by the equipment on my truck. When her tank was finally full, she made her way around to the front of my truck and asked me in a concerned voice, "Excuse me, are there animals in that cage?"

Confused, I asked, "You mean my trailer?"

"No," she said, "that cage up there," as she pointed toward my air conditioner.

"No, Ma'am, that's an air conditioner." Satisfied that I wasn't abusing caged animals on top of my trailer, she walked back to her car and drove off.

I wondered why she would think such a thing. Then I remembered the commercials featuring a sad ballad by Sara McLachlan asking me to send money to the ASPCA.

But all companion animals do eventually get sick and die of something, including farm dogs.

An irate farmer related an unfortunate circumstance to me the other day. His family has a farm dog. It's a dog that just happened to show up at his farm one day. The dog adopted them.

The dog has been at this farm for as long as I can remember. He has a nice life. He has as much dog food as he wants to eat. He greets visitors to the farm and gets a little scratch from time to time. He can lay in the barn anytime he wants or travel to the house.

He chooses to lie in the grass most of the time and observe. He observes the cows or the passing cars or the many visitors to the farm. Or, if there's snow on the ground, he lies in the snow. If it's raining outside, he lies in the rain. It's his choice; I guess he likes it that way.

But he has a bum leg and he's had it for some time. The dog has arthritis in his ankle joint and it's progressive. Progressive to the point that he doesn't use the leg much. It hasn't slowed the dog down, though, as he still follows his owner from the house to the barn every day.

So when the farmer told me he got a visit from the humane police, I wish I could say I was surprised. A passerby apparently confused infirmity with abuse, again. It's not the first time it's happened, but it was the first time it happened at this farm. The goal of the animal rights agenda has been to write the story of the typical abusive farmer. This story sadly becomes confused for non-fiction by some people.

I'd wager that people are more likely to abuse other people than animals.

But all animals do suffer from pain, eventually. Pain doesn't equal abuse. I suffer from chronic back pain. This farmer has certainly had his share of pain in his life; we all do. It doesn't equal abuse. It's just a part of life. Some pain can't be fixed.

I wonder what this dog's life would have been like if the farmer hadn't taken him in. Would he have been feral? Would he have ended up an animal shelter somewhere and euthanized?

We would all be well served to not infer malice in the motivations of others. I interact with hundreds of animal owners in my professional life and I can say that none of them maintain a herd, keep some dogs or tolerate cats because they hate them and want to abuse them.

Neither should I necessarily infer that when the ASPCA implores us to send them 20 bucks a month, that they are just in it for the money.

Farm Dogs
1-25-11

Even though my scope of veterinary practice doesn't include companion animals, we still encounter plenty of barn cats and farm dogs. Both species have their purpose.

The barn cats are sometimes a nuisance, but a lot of farmers do appreciate their ability to keep birds, mice and rats away from the grain stores. You would be hard pressed to find a farmer to admit their appreciation of the feline, but most of them do provide some cat food – and a fresh pan of milk (non-salable, of course.)

The farm dogs do, occasionally, act in the capacity as vermin predator. As useful as a rodent exterminator is to the farmer, nothing compares to a dog that can hunt down a woodchuck. The woodchuck, or groundhog, is universally hated by farmers for their destruction of hayfields and pastures.

But even more important than the predator dogs are the herding dogs. Herding dogs constitute an entire breed classification, but the most common breeds I see on farms are the Australian cattle dog and the border collie. Both are herding dogs, but their similarities end there.

The Australian cattle dog, sometimes called blue heeler or simply heeler, lives to harass cattle. As the name implies, they encourage cattle to move by giving them a little bite on the heel. You might think that the heeler is pretty ambitious to latch onto the heel of an animal that outweighs them by a factor of 20. If you think so, you are correct. The heeler is the most ambitious animal I have ever seen.

Used mostly to get stubborn cattle to move, they also serve to get an animal to its feet that may otherwise not want to get up. If a sick, or simply stubborn animal must be moved, the incentive provided by a nip from a heeler is usually enough to accomplish the job.

These dogs are fearless and tougher than a pine knot. I have seen them kicked in the chops and run over by tractors. They usually just shake it off and get back to work, minus a tooth or two. My first encounter with a heeler was before I started veterinary school. I was with a veterinarian one day that kept a heeler with him in his truck, in case of emergency.

One afternoon there was a particularly ornery angus bull in a pen that we had to load in a head catch to examine. The bull apparently knew of our intentions and would have no part of it. After risking our lives for about 10 minutes in the pen, Doc brought out the secret weapon. "Danny, go get him," was all that was needed to be said. The dog went into the pen, latched on to the one-ton bull's heel and moved him into the chute like a bat out of you know where. The heeler breed immediately gained my respect.

The border collie may lack the toughness of the heeler, but they make up for it with intelligence. Some are known to respond to a couple hundred distinct commands. Popular with shepherds, they excel at keeping a herd or flock together as a group and moving them in the proper direction. They seem to know instinctively exactly how to approach an animal and steer it.

Most farms are partial to either the heeler or border collie, but I know of one farmer that has one of each. I guess he likes diversification.

Many other breeds of dogs can be found on area farms. The German shepherd deserves mention. They lack the herding ability of the heeler and collie, but their ability to act as a farm security system is second to none. They seem intimidating, but the ones I know are pretty friendly. Sorry, I probably just blew their cover.

Most farm dogs like when I show up on the farm; especially when it's time to dehorn the calves. After I numb a calf's horns, I scoop the small bud out with my hot dehorning iron. I doesn't lie on the ground long before the farm dog gobbles it up. As soon as the dog recognizes what I'm about to do, they follow me around with great anticipation. They know a warm treat (in the form of a recently removed horn bud) is soon to come their way.

A client of ours recently shared with me a story about their dog, Max. Whenever I pull in their driveway and they say "There's Doctor Bill," the dog runs to the window and barks wildly. He knows a warm horn bud is in his future. Recently, the television was on and the announcer proclaimed "Here's Doctor Phil." Without hesitation, the dog ran barking to the window. Dr. Phil may have a celebrity client list, but he doesn't have warm horn buds.

CHAPTER 12
The American Farmer

Photo by Hayley Waddell- Barns and Bows Photography

There are a lot of farmers in this country. Many estimates put the number of farmers in the United States at about 1 percent of the population. By my math, that's about 3.2 million of them. Collectively, they grow a lot of food and they do it well. But farmers are not all the same. Some farm row crops, others raise vegetables or fruit. The farmers who raise livestock for meat and milk production are the ones with whom I'm most familiar. I've provided services for farmers from no less than a dozen states and, while no two farmers are exactly alike, they have striking similarities.

Every farmer I've met is conscious that farming is a business. Make no mistake, farming without the pursuit of profit is called gardening. Without at least the opportunity for profit, why would anyone risk huge sums of capital and invest 80-hour work weeks to operate a farm? That doesn't mean that farmers are greedy, uncaring people concerned with nothing but money. On the contrary, the return on investment in farming pales in comparison to other businesses. Farmers know that. In fact, I've always had a theory that the reason corporate America has never taken over farms like Walmart has taken over small-town America is because the return on investment is too low. I've never met a farmer who made his career choice because he thought it would be the quickest way for him to get rich. The vast majority of farming enterprises in our country are still family owned, even the much maligned "factory farms." The United States Department of Agriculture estimates that a full 97 percent of farms in the United States are family owned.

The pursuit of profit, however, doesn't mean that there is a guarantee of profit. As any farmer knows, there are good times and bad. All of us involved in agriculture know this and accept it. Since we live in a free market economy, the law of supply and demand reigns supreme. And since farmers are really good at what they do, the supply of their products rarely gets low. Consequently, the price for their goods rarely gets very high. And I don't suspect that will change much anytime soon. The price for all commodities, including food, ends up averaging close to the cost of production over the long term. For every good year, there is a bad one, or two or three. As knowledge advances about the best way to grow crops or raise livestock, their efficiency improves. But this isn't just opinion, farmers have a long-term track record of doing just that.

Farmers are also advocates for animal welfare. That statement might shock you and if it does, let me distinguish between animal welfare and animal rights as they are two completely different things. Animal welfare is concerned with the humane treatment and well-being of animals. Animal welfare recognizes that animals are not equal to humans and there are legitimate uses for animals, including to be slaughtered for food; yet they deserve to be kept comfortable and free from abuse. It makes no sense for a farmer to treat his livestock inhumanely. Content, comfortable cows are profitable cows and farmers know that. Farmers really like profitable cows. They advocate for animal welfare simply by managing their livestock in the proper way.

Animal rights, conversely, believes that all animals have the same rights as humans. A cow or a cat or a bug or a person are all created equally and deserving of the same dignity. Farmers, and even the vast majority of people in this country, don't believe that. We can love animals but should not direct to them the affection due only to humans. The animal rights activists would have us believe, because a video might show an unscrupulous person abusing a cow, that all farmers abuse their cows and all cows are abused. This simply isn't the case; but if you have a big enough tree, there's sure to be a squirrel or two in it.

Farmers are risk takers. I don't mean that they jump out of airplanes, although some of them probably do; they are a diverse lot, after all. But their business is inherently risky, and they embrace that risk. Cows are expensive with common, commercial grade cows fetching at least $1,000 even in a down market. When the market is good, commercial cows, both beef and dairy, can bring upwards of $2,500 or even more. The average dairy herd in the country is at about 100 cows by recent estimates and that number has been steadily increasing for decades. The best seedstock cattle will routinely fetch 6-figures regardless if the market is up or down. So, farmers invest heavily in a portfolio that has potential for a nice return on investment some years, potential to lose a lot of money in others and could all be gone from an outbreak of a virus on any given day. If that's not risk, I don't know what is.

I could go on, but this chapter is about farmers and some of my interactions with and observations about them. It has been my privilege to work with them.

Stereotype
7-20-10

I was watching the television one night when I punched the wrong button on the remote and landed on a program I've never seen before. It was about a circle of well off housewives in New Jersey. Out of morbid curiosity, I watched a little.

After watching a little, I was sucked in, kind of like watching a train wreck – I couldn't look away. Now I realize that much of the drama can be manufactured in the editing room, but there was probably some grain of truth behind the smoke and mirrors. After a good chuckle, it got me thinking.

A recently disgraced politician used to claim that there were two

Americas. Well, there may be two Americas, but probably not the way he claimed. In general, there is urban and rural America. Both have been tagged with stereotypes, some justified but mostly not.

The characters in this "reality" show were made to look like narcissistic, spoiled children. In much the same way, people in rural America are often portrayed by the media to be backward. A wise hippie once told me to believe none of what you hear and only half of what you see. I usually dismiss anything that originates from a hippie, but this stuck with me. Over the years, it has proven to be sound advice.

I work with farmers. Farmers are as rural as you can get. Collectively, farmers are probably the wisest group of people I have ever been associated with. All too often, however, our culture defines them as toothless idiots. Following are just a few of the many valuable lessons farmers have taught me.

Problems are fixed with ingenuity and hard work, not duct tape and baler twine. While improvisation maybe necessary in the short term, farmers who have long careers understand that there is no substitute for planning and investment. Hard work alone isn't enough. I can work hard turning big rocks into little rocks all day, but at the end of the day, I have nothing more than a bunch of rocks and a sore back.

If you have livestock, you will have deadstock. Cows will die of old age sometime after they reach 20 years old. Cows rarely die of old age, though. Most become food for a hungry population of Americans, including those living in New Jersey. Some, however, do get sick and die on the farm, despite the best efforts of the veterinarian.

Food doesn't come from the grocery store; it comes from the farm. We have a pretty complicated system of food production in this country, but all food originates at a farm somewhere. (Tofu may be the only exception.) American farmers have given us affordable, wholesome food without fear of famine. Food is so affordable, in fact, that obesity is a bigger problem than hunger.

Instant gratification gratifies only for an instant. This is being driven home to me this year as my family planted our first real garden. Every evening as we go out to weed, I see the plants growing, but only the lettuce and a cucumber or two are ready to eat. We started preparing the garden three months ago and we are still waiting to eat.

I tell the plants, "grow faster," but they grow at their own pace.

The same is true on a much larger scale on farms. The corn planted in May won't be ready for harvest until September for silage or October for grain. A beef calf born today won't be ready for slaughter for at least 16 months. A dairy calf born today won't produce a drop of milk for the farmer for about 2 years. And she won't return the cost it took to raise her until she is about 3 ½ years old.

Now I know that people living in the D.C. – New York – Boston corridor aren't all spoiled and narcissistic like those portrayed on the reality shows. The quest for fame from a few threatens to stereotype an entire region. Ironically, just like rural America and farmers have been stereotyped by the urban dominated media.

Five Freedoms
10-7-14

According the American Farm Bureau Federation, about 97 percent of farms in the United States are family owned. I know some of these families well, having worked as their farm's veterinarian for years.

While some dairy farms sell direct to the consumer, they are the minority. Most family-owned dairy farms, because of a host of reasons, sell milk on the open market as a commodity. A farm will sell to the same buyer consistently, be it a cooperative, independently owned company or even a multinational corporation.

I recently came across a press release from a multinational corporation which is a major buyer of dairy products. The release was in reaction to an incident that occurred on a dairy farm in Wisconsin in 2013. An animal rights activist had misrepresented himself and taken a job as a hired hand in order to procure video of animal abuse on this dairy. The video was eventually made public and caused much embarrassment to both the dairy and the corporation to which their milk was ultimately sold.

The press release made mention of the "Internationally accepted 'Five Freedoms' as applied to animals" and the corporation's newfound commitment to them. They are, as quoted in the press release: 1. Freedom from hunger, thirst and malnutrition. 2. Freedom from fear and distress. 3. Freedom from physical and thermal discomfort 4.

Freedom from pain, injury and disease. 5. Freedom to express normal patterns of behavior.

These five freedoms are pretty lofty standards indeed. In fact, I'd be willing to bet that the majority of Americans don't enjoy these freedoms.

Here's a quick history lesson. The "five freedoms" originated in the UK in 1965 and were a little different at the time. According to the Farm Animal Welfare Council, the original five freedoms were "to stand up, lie down, turn around, groom themselves and stretch their limbs," also known as Bambrell's five freedoms. The Farm Animal Welfare Council is a government advisory group in the UK that advises the British government on matters of animal welfare. Much to the delight of animal rights groups, these standards have evolved.

The Farm Animal Welfare Council even states on their website that these five freedoms "define ideal states rather than standards for acceptable welfare." In other words, achieving these impossible standards is akin to an animal utopia.

Now I would argue that standards are important and animal abuse is unacceptable. As a veterinarian, I've taken an oath to relieve animal suffering, a duty which I take seriously. But like the proverbial frog in the pot of boiling water, animal rights groups through their activism have turned up the heat on farmers slowly over the last 50 years to where the standard is now unattainable.

So, in response, I propose that farmers should demand from busybody multinational corporations that they adhere to the five freedoms, only this time as applied to farmers.

1. Freedom from fear and distress of low milk prices. Dairy farms have traditionally been subject to a roller coaster ride of milk prices depending on the market. Currently, the environment if good for the farmers, but we all know it is bound to change.

2. Freedom to build cow friendly facilities. Perhaps if farmers received consistently fair compensation for their products, more of them would have state of the art housing for their cows.

3. Freedom from unattainable standards. The vast majority of dairy farmers recognize that they while they own their livestock, they are also stewards. They do the right thing even when it means a financial loss when necessary. But unrealistic standards leave them in an impossible position.

4. Freedom from regulatory harassment. Be it the animal rights crowd or environmental regulators, farmers are often subject to harassment.

5. Freedom to express normal behavior. Farmers are often the subject of ridicule in the popular culture and are portrayed as bumpkins and hicks. Yes, we may lack the sophistication of the big cities, but farmers are sophisticated in their own way. Tractor pulls and cow shows are more normal than most of what one might find in New York City or Chicago.

Do these seem absurd? They are no more absurd than freedom from "physical and thermal discomfort" or freedom from "fear and distress." No farmer worth his salt is an abuser of animals. But when large corporate buyers of milk products pay lip service to politically correct nonsense, the only beneficiaries are the animal rights extremists.

Farmer for President
10-2-12

Election season is in full swing and the politicians are busy positioning themselves as the one who will solve all of the world's problems. I've often pondered what life would be like if the government was run by farmers. I have a few ideas.

I'm pretty sure the national debt wouldn't be about to devour us if a farmer was in charge. No, we would probably have to learn to live within our means. That old pick-up truck, even though it has a couple hundred thousand miles on it, still is good enough to get from point A to point B. It just wouldn't be right to borrow from the grandchildren to buy a new one. No, we will just make due for a little while longer.

Government waste, I think, would end overnight. Farmers, almost universally, hate to waste anything. They've just worked too hard for what they have. I've seen these lessons in action over and over again in my time working with farmers. If you have feed left over from the milk cows, sweep it up and feed it to the young stock. If you have milk that is unfit for sale, feed it to the pigs. And if you have a cow that is injured and can't be sold, butcher her for the family. Waste nothing.

And, well you can just forget about the overpriced hammers and toilet seats that the government has been known to buy. A farmer is always looking for a good deal and is rarely known to overspend. The sealed bids for government contracts would be a thing of the past, too. Instead, there'd be a live auction, complete with an auctioneer, coffee and lots of fellowship. I'd wager that the contracts would be a better value for the taxpayer also.

The unemployment rate has been hovering more than 8 percent for nearly four years now. With that many people unemployed, you might think that there just wasn't any work that needed to be done. A farmer wouldn't think that way – there's always work to be done. No farmer worth his salt would shy away from hard work, even if it was helping a neighbor.

I'd like to think that foreign countries would have a new degree of respect for the USA if it was run by farmers. There's really not much to be said here. Except that when a predator threatens a farmer's herd, he gets rid of the predator one way or another.

The art of campaigning would probably be a little different, too. There would be less lying and more debating. And if a farmer does something really stupid, like tell his neighbor who built his own barn that somebody else actually built it, he wouldn't have to hear about it for a month. The neighbor would bust his chops for five minutes and then forget about it. Farmers don't dwell on semantics when the barn is on fire. They move the cows and try to put the fire out.

And surely, political correctness would be just a bad memory. A farmer would tell it like it is. There would be no worrying about which group got their feelings hurt because somebody told the truth. Farmers know that the truth hurts sometimes and so does tough love, but the alternative hurts even worse.

Unfortunately, this is all but a pipe dream. I came to that conclusion recently as I was having a conversation with a farmer about the state of politics. He confided in me that he wasn't impressed with either of the candidates for president. Then he wisely said to me with a sheepish grin on his face, "I'd run for president myself, but I don't have the darn oats off the field yet!"

Trust
11-15-16

"In God We Trust."
This is the motto of our republic. I would like to focus on one

word of that motto: trust.

Trust is the belief that another's intentions are the same as they are represented. In what or whom do we trust and how do we know that we do? What evidence is there that one is trusted? I think the evidence of trust is rooted in the actions people exhibit and not the words they speak. I can say that I trust a person, but unless I back it up with actions, the words are shallow.

Do we trust in the government? I'd seriously doubt that many people do. We've just concluded a long, divisive, nasty campaign to elect our federal government officials. It seemed as if it was the nastiest in history, yet it seems like that every four years.

Judging by the vote totals for president, over half of the people who voted for president don't trust the person who won. Just as many didn't trust the other candidates. High profile politicians aren't very well respected, it seems. That's probably because they haven't sufficiently earned our trust. Our votes speak volumes.

Do we trust in our God? Some of us do to a degree. But in reality, none of us trust in him completely. We are a broken people and none of us can claim to perfectly trust our Creator. It's the nature of being human.

Do we trust in the law? If we don't trust in the laws of the government, we do trust in the laws of nature. What is the punishment for disobeying the law of gravity? It is a rapid descent back to the terra firma. Well, the rapid descent is only the result of the law of gravity. The sudden stop once we reach the ground is actual punishment for disobedience.

Evidence of trust is exhibited in actions and not words. I can say that I trust the president of the United States, but without evidence of such, you could still be left guessing about my sincerity. I can say that I trust in the laws of gravity and my actions confirm that I do since I refuse to take a flying leap from a tall building.

Do we trust in our farmers? Do we trust that the food they grow is wholesome and nutritious?

We read on the internet that GMO plants are going to kill us. We hear from PETA that all farmers are responsible for torturing and mistreating their livestock. We are told that antibiotics fed to farm animals are going to make us sick.

I don't trust the people who tell us such things. I say I don't trust them, yet I've already told you that talk is cheap. The evidence is in the action. My actions, however, speak volumes. I eat the food the farmers grow.

I see first-hand how our farmers conduct themselves and raise their livestock. I always aim to help them keep their stock healthy and their goal is the same. Well fed, comfortable livestock are productive. Livestock that are mistreated or taken care of poorly will certainly be unproductive. And in this economic environment, unproductive livestock will put a farmer out of business in a hurry.

I don't trust people when they say that the antibiotics in our food will make us sick. This is precisely because I know that there aren't antibiotics in our food. Farmers are required to prevent milk or meat of treated animals from entering the food supply. Failing to do so will jeopardize their ability to sell milk or cattle for meat. I trust that our food is wholesome and free from antibiotics.

There are more than 300 million people in this country. As far as I can tell, every last one of us has to eat to stay alive. Unless a person grows all their own food or is a hunter-gatherer, he also trusts in the American farmer. Despite what you might read on the Facebook or Twitter, our actions declare that we trust the food we buy is safe. After all, who would eat food that they legitimately believed would harm them?

American farmers have been the target of misinformation, half-truths and outright slander sometimes. They have been accused of poisoning consumers with chemicals. They have been accused of abusing their livestock in the pursuit of profit. Despite all this, they still are trusted by all people who eat.

So, I wish to send a message to the farmers who read this column. Do not despair. No matter what you read in the magazines or see on the television, the people of this country have voted nearly unanimously with their checkbook. They trust in you.

The Gambler
5-6-14

When I was a child, my mother was perhaps one of country singer Kenny Roger's biggest fans. As a result, I got to listen to a lot of his music while I was growing up in the early 1980s. To this day, his song

"The Gambler" is seared into my brain like few others. Usually, I don't give much real-life credence to that which is meant to entertain us like movies and music. But the other day I was considering the profound meaning of "The Gambler."

OK, profound is a bit strong of an adjective to describe a country and western song. But, at least it has some parallels to farming.

For the one or maybe two readers who aren't familiar with the song, it recounts the tale of two men who share a conversation during a train ride. The gambler shares some of his wisdom with the other man for a drink of his whiskey and a cigarette.

Farming in general, and livestock farming in particular, is a lot like high stakes gambling. The investment is large and the outcome is never certain. You can't focus group or do market research for favorable weather, after all. Livestock will become deadstock eventually, often because of the fault of no one. Good management can mitigate some, but never all of the risk.

Sometimes the odds are in the farmer's favor, like they are now. But other times, the odds favor the house as they did last year for dairy farmers. But it is always a gamble. Maybe farmers should heed the advice that the gambler shared on the train.

"You've got to know when to hold 'em..." Farmers are holding a few aces now because of a multitude of factors. The price of meat and milk are finally allowing some room for profit. Now is a good time to hold but not overplay the hand that was dealt. We've all learned at some point that when you try to bluff, eventually you'll get called.

"...Know when to fold 'em." I seem to be involved in this decision many times a day. Whether it is evaluating a sick cow or one that is just no longer profitable, farmers need to be realistic. Many times, we see an animal that has a treatable condition but the treatment costs more than what the animal is worth. In that case, the deck is stacked against the farmer if he takes that bet.

Other times, we may see a cow that cannot become pregnant for whatever reason. She may be otherwise healthy but a cow that can't have a calf is just an expensive pet. These are frustrating because the reason for the infertility is usually not able to be diagnosed and therefore can't be fixed. But after numerous attempts, the odds of eventually winning just become too low. It's time to fold.

"Know when to walk away..." Knowing you're holding a good

hand is good feeling, but it can sometimes lead to poor decisions. The value of cows are up right now because of the relative scarcity of beef and milk. As a result, cows are fetching a pretty penny if a farmer needs to add to the herd. In certain markets, emotions run ahead of reason and I've heard that some are paying upwards of $3,000 per cow if they want to add cows to a herd. Cows were selling for around $1,000 just a few months ago.

To many farmers I have talked to, this seems like raising the pot while holding a pair of deuces. Sometimes it's just better not to bet and walk away.

"…and know when to run." There comes a time in every farmer's life when it's time to cash in the chips. Some farmers want to retire someday and others don't. Some might be forced to quit because of health or financial reasons. Some may have been dealt a bad hand and others may just not have played it right. Whatever the reason, leaving the table is never easy but sometimes it is inevitable.

"You never count your money when you're sitting at the table. There'll be time enough for counting when the dealing's done." I don't think a farmer would ever want to be caught counting his money at the table or otherwise bragging about how well they might be doing in good times. But we usually do hear about it when the chips are down. At any rate, farmers know that the game is long and it's best to wait until the end to take stock.

And somewhere in the darkness, the gambler he broke even. And in his final words I found an ace I could keep… And now that you have this song stuck in your head for the rest of the day, I apologize.

Eavesdropping
5-12-15

I don't like eavesdropping. Even the thought of it creeps me out. But I know that there are folks who do it. And I wonder what they might think if they eavesdrop on a group of farmers having a conversation.

I could imagine that the eavesdropper may end up a bit confused. Farmers have their own jargon that's like a foreign language to anyone more than a generation removed from the farm. And the topics of discussion one might encounter are sure to cause bewilderment.

Here's a good example. Dairy farmers are very concerned with reproduction, in their cows that is. They are concerned about it because if a cow doesn't get pregnant and eventually deliver a calf, she won't make milk. A milk cow that doesn't make milk (a.k.a. a "dry cow") becomes a very expensive pet.

This concern leads to a lot of discussion wherever farmers may congregate. It could be at the feed store, educational meetings or even restaurants. The eavesdropper in the restaurant may hear such phrases as "in heat" or "I bred her." Without proper context, one could get the wrong idea.

By the way, I'd like to clear up one little thing; it's sort of a pet peeve of mine. I heard a goofball on the radio one morning talking about a "bull in heat." He would have been a good one to eavesdrop on a couple of farmers in conversation because he surely lacks context. In the animal would, the males don't come into heat; only the females do. Species differences exist that determine the length of the heat cycles and expression of heat behavior, but males are never in, or out of, heat.

So, farmers brainstorming on how to improve reproductive efficiency in their cows could certainly cause confusion if the eavesdropper lacks the context to understand the conversation. When a cow or heifer (a virgin female bovine) is in heat, she displays some characteristic behaviors. Bawling, excessive friendliness and mounting or standing to be mounted are the most common. By standing to be mounted I mean another animal, usually another cow or heifer, will "ride" the animal in heat. If the cow is in heat, she will "stand." If she is not in heat, she will not "stand."

So, play along with me, when you hear a farmer utter the words, "My cow was trying to ride everything but nothing would stand" or even, "I'm having trouble finding the cows that want to either stand or ride," the farmer isn't talking about the cows procuring transportation. He's talking about trying to get them pregnant. Since most dairies utilize artificial insemination exclusively, heat detection is an important topic since there are no bulls around to do the job. A cow must be bred when in heat if she is to get pregnant.

Heat detection is so important that innovative farmers have devised many devices to help them find more cows in heat. There are activity monitors that can tell when a cow is more active, i.e., riding or standing or walking around in search of a partner. Algorithms flag a cow based on her usual level of activity if she is in heat and a computer will alert the farmer so he can breed her.

There used to be a nifty little radio transmitter that was fitted to the top of a cow's rump with glue. When triggered by pressure, like when a cow stood to be mounted, it would alert the farmer that his cow is in heat. There are also less expensive versions of this gizmo. There are patches that contain dye-filled capsules which farmers can glue onto the cow's rump. When the capsule is broken by another cow mounting the recipient, the patch turns red. One of the more popular devices today resemble a scratch off ticket.

These stickers get glued to the cow's rump and when she is mounted by another cow, the gray film gets scratched off revealing a blaze orange color. It's like winning the lottery, or at least like playing it. I once heard a farmer tell about a certain person who wished to purchase only a single heat detection patch. It seems that she only had one cow. I laughed until I cried. I wasn't eavesdropping; I swear.

Since bulls are not used on most farms, a lot of them get turned into steers (castrated bulls.) The removed testicles, I hear, make a tasty treat to those brave enough to sample the deep-fried product of castration. A little pancake batter and boiling oil will make a person bring along a clean bowl whenever there are a group of calves to castrate, so I'm told.

I was explaining this to my daughter recently when she asked me what mountain oysters were. I responded that they are bull testes thinly sliced, battered and deep fried.

She got a disgusted look on her face and said, "People eat those things?" I assured her that they do. Then she said, "They're nuts!" An eavesdropper lacking proper context may have gotten the wrong idea and possibly taken offense.

But I reassured her, "Yes, they are." And after a brief pause, I said "And the people that eat those things are crazy too."

The Look of a Farmer
5-24-11

If you were to meet a farmer, how would know? Would the John Deere hat he's wearing give it away? Maybe the mud on his pick-up truck would be the definitive clue.

Maybe it's the missing finger on his hand that gives him away; or maybe even his missing arm. Farming is a dangerous job as evidenced by the missing digits and limbs of so many farmers.

I remember as a boy helping my dad and my uncle on the farm. Your head needed to be on a swivel sometimes to avoid being caught or squished by the equipment. The PTO shaft is probably the worst. My dad made it a point to remind me over and over again to stay away from the PTO shaft.

The PTO, or power take off, is a mechanism that allows power to be transferred from the tractor to an implement by way of a drive shaft. It's what allows a tractor to run a hay baler, a mower, or even an electric generator. The shaft runs at a high RPM and if it happens to snag a piece of loose clothing, or even long hair, the resulting injury can render a person maimed for life, or even worse.

Many injuries have been caused by the PTO shaft, but it's obviously not the only hazard. All mechanized equipment, no matter how small, can be dangerous. I know too many farmers who are missing digits and even limbs.

Maybe you would recognize a farmer by the concerned look on his face because it's too wet to get into the fields. We've had a wet spring and everybody is talking about how behind the crop farming is compared to normal.

Nothing causes stress to a farmer like being behind during planting season. There is never a perfect growing season; every year brings different challenges like being either too wet or too dry. Each new planting season brings a new round of worry about the crops. But in the end, a crop failure is the exception to the rule. Farmers find a way to get it done.

Maybe you can tell a farmer by his sheer exhaustion. He was up at 3:30 this morning to milk the cows, but he didn't get to bed until after midnight to assist one of his cows to deliver her calf. Or maybe the weather provided just a small window of opportunity to get a field ready for planting and if he didn't take advantage of it, the chance would be lost. He will gladly sacrifice sleep.

So, if you see a person with a muddy truck at the gas station wearing a John Deere hat that is missing a finger or two and looks worried and exhausted, it could be a farmer. But then again, what does a farmer really look like?

A farmer usually doesn't look any different than anyone else. He, or she, might drive a muddy truck, or maybe even a clean one. He, or she, may have a John Deere hat on, or maybe it's a Case IH hat. Or maybe even no hat at all. Yes, many farmers are missing digits and limbs, but most aren't. And most farmers are pretty good at hiding the looks of worry and exhaustion they feel.

But the one thing they all have in common is a healthy feeling of pride in they work they do. To know their pride, one would have to engage the farmer in conversation; his or her outward appearance alone won't reveal it. I don't know how you can really tell a farmer just by looking. Maybe stereotypes are just that.

A Farmer's Wedding
6-24-14

The love of cows tends to make otherwise rational people do some strange things. That might explain why dairy farmers accept the challenges that they face and plow on with their daily duties.

I don't mean to take anything away from beef farmers, believe me. Their job can be quite difficult as well. But the dairy farmer, with his long hours, sacrifices and financial risk must have some other incentive than just a paycheck. Dairy cows tend to do that to people.

Cows are a commodity in the most basic sense. But they are a commodity that directly interacts with those invested in them – the farmer. Corn won't do that, neither will soybeans. Pigs could not care less about people and sheep are, well, just too stupid to know any better. Beef cows make an effort sometimes, but the dairy cow genuinely has personality. Some have more personality than others, but they all have some.

All dairy farmers recognize that their cows ultimately end up as beef cows one day. (I mean that they become a roast beef sandwich or the like.) But that doesn't prevent some farmers from having genuine affection for their stock.

As a case in point, my family and I recently attended a rather unique wedding. The bride and groom both grew up on dairy farms, so they were both well acquainted with cows. That may be a bit of an understatement.

Both are accomplished fitters. Fitters make the cow look pretty. You might not think this is important to a farmer, but many times it is. There are a lot of farmers that merchandise cattle and if you want the cow to fetch a nice price, she has to look her best.

Cows that go to shows and consignment sales also have to look their best. A fitter makes this possible. I've never tried to make a cow look nice, but a fitter will wash the cow clean, clip the fur to the right length and tease the fur on her tail to make it poofy. Finally, the hair on her topline will be trimmed to make it appear perfectly straight. That may be a vast oversimplification, but I hope now you can picture a pretty dairy cow in your mind.

Fitters have a unique appreciation for attractive dairy cows like no other. As such, this couple enjoys cows and it was evident during the wedding.

The nuptials were taken outside in a hayfield on the bride's home farm. We knew that this wedding would be unique when the bridal party joined the groomsmen after arriving to the ceremony in a stock trailer, recently cleaned, of course.

There were even two cows with prominent parts in the wedding ceremony. They were technically not bride's maids but more like milk maids (sorry, couldn't resist…) Their duty was to look pretty and chew their cud, which both performed flawlessly. I don't know if the bride, the groom or both took care of fitting the cows, but the cows were certainly looking their best.

Boots and new blue jeans were the attire for the groom and his men. The bridal party donned boots as well under their dresses, including the bride. Now lest you think this was some bootleg, redneck wedding, it wasn't. No detail was missed during either the ceremony or the reception which was held in the upstairs of the barn on the property.

Even the heifers in the pasture cooperated by gazing over the fence at the ceremony and retreating to the barn once the congregation had been dismissed. Never have I seen a group of heifers cooperate like that before- they are known to be contrary. It was as if they knew to be on their best behavior.

Yes, people in love do some interesting things. But I'd wager that the love of cows makes for just as interesting a time.

Help Wanted
7-2-13

HELP WANTED. An immediate position is available for a self-motivated individual or individuals in the raw materials food industry. Interested parties must possess the following qualifications.

Interested applicants must be willing to work long hours. Double shifts are the rule, not the exception. Typical shifts last about 12-16 hours a day. On a good day, you might get an hour for supper. No lunch break will be provided; plan on eating on the job.

Days off will not be part of the job, except under certain conditions. If the applicant can find his or her replacement, then a day off may be acceptable. Plan on reporting for work every day 365 days a year and 366 on a leap year.

The applicant must be willing to tolerate extremes of temperatures both in summer and winter without compromising productivity. Summer temperatures can easily reach 120 degrees in the hay mow when there is hay to unload. Temperatures in the winter can reach 30 below zero on some mornings. There will be no days off in the event of inclement weather.

The applicant will be required to be proficient in agronomy, animal science, personnel management, veterinary science, meteorology, diesel engine repair, equipment maintenance, and accounting. Continuing education for pesticide license will be the responsibility of the applicant.

Applicants should be physically fit to meet the rigors of the job. Although discrimination against the disabled is forbidden, if an applicant cannot handle the physical aspects of the job, he or she should not bother applying.

Interested applicants should demonstrate proficiency in animal handling. A basic understanding of ruminant nutrition is a must; an advanced knowledge of ruminant nutrition is a plus.

All applicants must be familiar with and be willing to follow regulations set forth by the Department of Agriculture, Food and

Drug Administration, Environmental Protection Agency, Department of Labor, Department of Transportation, Fish and Wildlife Service and Internal Revenue Service. In addition, the applicant must follow all redundant applicable state regulations. Legal fees will be the responsibility of the applicant.

Willing applicants must have adequate collateral, and or capital before consideration for the position will be given.

The successful applicant will be compensated based on a complex formula taking into account both input costs and productivity. Some paychecks will be enough to cover expenses, but some will not.

Benefits include knowing that you are growing safe, wholesome food for an ever expanding, hungry population. If you possess these qualifications, you might want to consider buying a farm.

OK, that may be a little melodramatic, but it really isn't that far from reality. Every day, early in the morning, countless farmers go to work and their job description is pretty close to what I just described. There must be something special about this job that continues to motivate farmers to get up before dawn, go work and risk everything every day.

I don't know why they do it, but I'm pretty grateful that they do.

Mothers
10-4-16

Livestock farmers are a different lot. They see and experience things that would turn the stomach of city folk not acquainted with such things. These things could be chicken manure, surgery, routine and non-routine birthing of young livestock or even accidental lacerations and other injuries.

All of these life experiences can mold and shape the way a person views the world. Life is a series of organic events. Sometimes these events are unpleasant, like the death or ghastly injury of a cow. But sometimes these events are joyful, like when a cow delivers a healthy heifer calf destined to be a valuable herd replacement.

Farmers experience these things almost on a daily basis. They experience a little miracle of new life with every baby calf that their cows give them. And while the small miracle of a new calf doesn't compare to the big miracle of a new baby person, it sometimes draws comparisons. This can have unintended consequences.

In jest and without malice, some farmers may gently tease their pregnant wives. I have been privy to many conversations and I'd like to offer some advice to any expectant father who might consider drawing comparisons such as this or give a little gentle ribbing. It could land you in some hot water.

When a cow delivers a calf, especially a dairy cow, it is a good sign for her to immediately get up and go to the feed bunk. The farmer, after tending to the calf, will often walk up to the cow still laying on the ground and give a gentle knee to her ribs to make her stand up. Guys, never walk up to the new mom and encourage her to get up and "go to the feed bunk." It probably wouldn't be smart either to congratulate her for "eating like a cow" after delivering a baby. I don't think she will see the same humor in that as you or I might.

When my wife was pregnant with our first child, we lived in the snow belt of the great lakes at the time. And, of course, our first child was due to arrive during the height of the lake effect snow season. We had a good 45-minute drive to the nearest hospital and were always contemplating the "what if?"

One day we were discussing the possibility that our first child might decide to arrive during a snowstorm and what we might do about that. In jest, I reassured my wife that it would be OK. My calving chains were always close by in my truck and she shouldn't worry about such problems.

She gave me a look that I had never seen before. It was one of those looks like she didn't see the humor in my comment and without hesitation she said, "You will not come anywhere near me with those calving chains!" Guys, never offer to "get the calving chains." I don't think she will get the joke.

Cows that make a lot of milk are very valuable to dairy farmers. The milk they produce is income to pay the bills and provide for the family. A good wife is also loved by the farmer, even more so than a high producing cow. But guys, never compare your wife's lactation to your favorite milk cow. I suspect she will fail to see the compliment in that, even if you meant it to be complimentary.

When a farmer chooses a bull to breed to his cows, there are a lot of traits to consider. The most valuable bulls sire daughters that are hearty, have a sound body structure and make a lot of milk. But one of the most important traits is something called "calving ease."

A calving ease bull will throw calves with below average birth weights. And obviously, a light calf will be easier for the cow to deliver than a heavy calf.

The same is true with women. One of the first things known about a new mother's bundle of joy is the birthweight. If a new baby entered this world with a birth weight of, say, a whopping 9 pounds, 2 ounces, one might offer an empathetic, "ouch!" But if, on the other hand, the new baby checks in at a mere 7 pounds, one might feel relief for the mom. But guys, please don't take credit for being "calving ease." She probably won't understand.

In considering the value of any dairy cow, farmers will study a series of performance indicators like milk production, fat and protein percentage of her milk and calving interval. Calving interval describes the amount of time that has elapsed from one calving to the next. This is important to the farmer since the cow can't make milk unless she produces a calf and the more often she has a calf, the more milk she will produce.

So, I'd like to offer one last bit of advice to any new fathers out there. After your new baby is born, you probably don't want to make any remarks about trying to "keep your wife's calving interval low." I'm quite certain that comment will instead cause her "calving interval" to increase.

Picking Rocks
4-25-17

Some jobs are hard and others are easy. I like to think that I have a hard job, but my love for working with farmers and their livestock makes it easy. Slamming cases in a warehouse is a hard job; I've done that. Teaching is a difficult job; I've never done that. Being a cop must be very hard, especially in today's environment. I could go on.

But perhaps the hardest job in the world is picking rocks.

After the spring thaw, fields across the country have a novel population of rocks. Rocks are quite hard on farm equipment and rob the farmer of yield on their crops. Hence, the rocks have to go.

There is no easy way to do this, especially in our rocky soil. One by one, the rocks, stones and even some boulders have to be removed.

I remember in my youth being charged with this task. One spring on my uncle's farm, I picked the rocks out of a field. At the time it seemed like this was a 100-acre field, although it was probably closer to two. That's two acres, not 200. But for weeks, after school and on Saturdays, I would chuck rocks into a wagon hitched to a small tractor. It wasn't complicated. Chuck rocks. Move tractor. Repeat.

But once I thought I had them all removed from a row, I would look behind me to admire my diligence and see, that's right, more rocks. It was like someone was unloading them from the wagon as fast as I could put them in. It was an exercise in futility.

Eventually, my uncle was satisfied, or at least that's what I thought. It was probably just long enough into the season that he needed to get the corn in before it was too late.

So, imagine my confusion when the next year he wanted me to pick the same field. What? I didn't remove them all last year? I thought if he could grow corn as well as he grew rocks he'd be a millionaire. How could there possibly be more? But, alas, there were more rocks.

So, I went about the task of chucking rocks, moving the tractor and repeat.

Somebody once told me that the winter frost causes the ground to heave and bring up more rocks. That's a plausible explanation. But I think instead that there was an evil rock fairy somewhere that put them back to spite me.

I take some consolation in the fact that I was not alone in my frustration. Driving around the country roads reveals piles and piles of rocks. These rocks were picked out of a field by somebody at some point, probably by somebody that hated picking rocks nearly as much as I did. I doubt the evil rock fairy put them in piles.

I was recently involved in a project in South Dakota. The area through which I was traveling was sort of a geographical enigma. There were miles and miles of flat prairie as far as the eye could see until, suddenly, there appeared a landscape of rolling hills. It was like something very large dumped huge mounds of dirt and rocks in the middle of this beautiful farm ground.

According to the locals, glaciers during the last ice age advanced south bringing with them the rocks and dirt like a big snow plow. I feel a certain amount of empathy for anyone farming this ground. I just hope some farmer didn't buy land there sight unseen. Imagine the surprise upon arriving at the would-be prairie ground and realizing that he had to pick rocks.

And these were no ordinary rocks. They were like rocks on steroids. Maybe they were asteroids? Who knows. But I've driven cars that were smaller than the rocks I witnessed in some of the fields.

Nonetheless, somebody had to pick the rocks from the cornfields. My heart goes out to whomever that was.

If nothing else, picking rocks surely builds character. It certainly teaches a lesson in humility. You pick rocks all day and the only thing you have to show for it is a wagon full of rocks. And a field still full of rocks. I think if I should ever have to teach my kids a lesson, I would find a field that needs rocks picked from it. That shouldn't be hard. I'm sure the farmer would be glad to cooperate with me in administering justice.

On the other hand, that would be cruel and unusual punishment.